the art of purposeful being

I dedicate this work to God;

to the memory of my parents,
Paul and Anne Winkelmans;

to my family;

and to my lifelong friend,
Gerry Monkhouse.

The Art of Purposeful Being

Your Destiny Project

Philip A. Winkelmans, MA

Self-Directional Services
Lantzville, BC

The Language of Science Plenum and Publishing Corporation has given permission to use material quoted on pp. 61-62.
Excerpts from: *Journal of Near Death Studies,* 10.1 (1991).

Canadian Cataloguing in Publication Data

Winklemans, Philip A., 1931-
  The art of purposeful being

  Includes bibliographical references and index.
  ISBN 1-55056-659-8

  1. Self-actualization (Psychology) 2. Self-realization. I. Title.
BF637.S4W56 1999   158.1   C99-910286-9

Published by

    Self-Directional Services
    P.O. Box 496
    Lantzville, BC V0R 2H0
    Canada

    Phone: (250) 390-4696
    E-mail: phil@purposefulbeing.com
    Web site: www.purposefulbeing.com

Typesetting by Jean Robinson
Cover design by O'Neil Warner
Printed and bound in Canada by Friesens

Published in Tokyo, Japan, by Cosmo Ten Inc. 1999

CONTENTS

CHAPTER OUTLINE

PROLOGUE

The *Art of Purposeful Being* is firstly and most importantly about adventuring into an awareness of who you are *being* in the *doing* of your life. The second challenge is met by *purposefully doing* only those things that you enjoy and feel are in harmony with who you have chosen to be. Unfortunately, many of us have spent a large part of our lives more concerned about what we are doing than about who we are.

For it to be an adventure, there has to be some risk involved. For some, the risk is to be willing to believe, even for a moment, some of the information that may at first appear challenging to accept. While for others, it may confirm some previously held beliefs, which may help them integrate these beliefs more fully.

Even though my conclusions are backed up by scientific research, personal life-history, myths, stories, case histories and common sense, the acceptance and integration of this material will depend on a willingness to entertain ideas that may seem different than your own.

The Art of Purposeful Being may be likened to an intellectual and somewhat experiential vision quest. While such a quest would be worthwhile in and of itself, it is my experience that a vision alone is not enough. My concern is not just to create a vision and purpose for peoples' lives, but to provide a practical and realistic 'way' for living their lives to the full, moment to moment. Many seekers and practitioners in the areas of psychotherapy and spirituality have difficulty living meaningful lives—this book is meant to bridge that gap.

As you go through this book, you will see beliefs and principles that are common to all religions. *The Art of Purposeful Being* allows you to integrate the highest values of any previously held religious or humanitarian belief in a way that makes the living out of these principles easier and more effective.

I have attempted to include all religions in some of the psychospiritual theories that are presented in this work, however, I must admit to my own limitations in this area. While having made an effort to study various religions, I am still more familiar with my own Judeo-Christian background. I beg your forgiveness if your religious viewpoint is not adequately expressed herein. You are invited to include your own comparative viewpoints wherever possible.

How to Get the Most Out of This Book

Often, I ask clients what books they have read. What surprises me is that nearly everyone I talk to has read many of the leading 'how to books' on personal growth, yet many exhibit little real psychological advancement. I often ask them what are some of the elements that they have used from these books to help improve their lives. The most common answer is "I understand myself more." If understanding alone were all that was needed, counselors and healers would not be necessary. All anyone would have to do is read books.

Therefore, understanding oneself is only a small part of it. Once this is understood, the big question is, "What are you going to do with it?" This means learning and practising the skills and methods enclosed within and incorporating them into a *self-designed way* for living. This *'way'* takes you beyond doing things, because they feel good in the moment, yet produce conflict, stress and pain as time goes on. Many people let events and circumstances make their choices for them, which results in a roller-coaster way of living. This means that they do not have an overall plan, purpose or pre-selected 'way' for living their lives. Instead, they let the environment make their decisions.

Now would be a good time to choose how you wish to go through this book.

1. You can decide to read the book and enjoy its new in-sights, understandings and stories.
2. You can also practise the exercises, questions and as-signments, which will enable you to develop your own pre-designed way for living your life.
3. You can enjoy reading the book and quickly go over the questions and then go back and work with the material, chapter by chapter. The choice is yours.

I recommend that you obtain a journal, or a good three-ring binder with lined pages. Writing is a way of taking random fragmented thoughts, experiences and learning, then putting them into an objective rationale and understandable format. It becomes a mirror by which you can compare future thoughts and beliefs, thereby keeping better track of your progress.

The questions that are inserted both throughout and at the end of each chapter are designed to identify and objectify your opinions and beliefs. Many of the questions are open-ended. They are there for self-exploration. There is no answer sheet at the back of the book, because you are your own teacher. Once you progress through the book by going over the questions again, you will see how differently you will answer the questions the second time around. This will show you how much your thinking and beliefs have changed through what you have learned.

The reason why many of the other personal growth methods do not have the lasting effect that one would hope for is because they do not address the whole person. This book is not about fixing or solving a problem in your life. Instead, it is about helping you go beyond your reactions, your need for therapy and, yes, even physical healing to successfully live a fulfilling life. Consider this a road map designed to take you to your ultimate awareness of what it means to be you, without your former struggles, problems and fears.

Each chapter is designed to open you to a deeper understanding of yourself and your potential for living a more fulfilling life. Therefore, each chapter builds on the previous chapter. Jumping around in the book will cause you to miss some fundamental points, which are important. Consider the book like a recipe and that each chapter is a necessary ingredient for the final outcome.

Doing this work will help you gain a new perception of what it means to be you, the wondrous, majestic, magical, powerful, gifted being you truly are. It will also help you discover your most desired purpose and destiny. This means that you will always *be* the person you want to *be,* and *do* only that which you want to *do,* the practice of which, over time, elevates your feelings of joy, happiness and ecstasy to heights never imagined.

The following is a list of changes that participants are experiencing in their lives and the *Art of Purposeful Being*. It is my hope that you, too, will share similar benefits and insights.

Reported Benefits of The Art of Purposeful Being

- Participants are aware of being, doing and having what they want.
- Because they know who they are, they are more confident and self-assured. Generally, they feel good within themselves.
- They are in touch with their core, are more creative, intuitive and open to new ideas and higher flows of consciousness.
- Having found a purpose experienced in all phases of their lives, they are always true to their highest good.
- Mastery of their feelings and emotions means they no longer have unsatisfying feelings, mood swings, outbursts, and stress; they enjoy more freedom, excitement and energy.
- Knowing who they are, and experiencing the lives they want, they enjoy predictably happier lives then ever before.
- By knowing they are the sum of all their choices, they accept their empowerment to make decisions as an integral part of *Purposeful Being.*
- Due to their being constantly in harmony with themselves, they experience less stress, and are, therefore, more physically fit. As they progress in *Purposeful Being,* many old illnesses and health problems disappear.
- Through understanding and experiencing their true spiritual and psychological identity, they enjoy an enhanced sense of their spiritual nature in all areas of their lives. Experiencing joy and ecstasy becomes more of a normal daily experience.
- Love relationships usually become stronger as neediness, dependency and the blaming of others diminish.

ACKNOWLEDGEMENTS

The process of writing this book has been one of learning, discovery and appreciation. Writing for me has not been a totally isolated event; rather it has been a team project. This work has been made possible by the input, support and friendship of many people. I now, more than ever, realize the tremendous value others have had in my life and how much those values have made this work possible. Not only do I appreciate the input of all those who are mentioned on this page, but also those authors, teachers and spiritual giants from present and past generations who have inspired me.

Firstly, I would like to give special thanks to those who have contributed directly to this work. I would like to thank God for the experience, understanding and knowledge that has made this book a reality. Next, my mother, Anne Winkelmans, a 'tough act to follow,' who has supported me in so many ways. Gerry Monkhouse, a lifelong friend, advisor and sponsor. I could not have done it without him. Roger Cotting and Dr. Diane Mistler, whose wisdom, support and encouragement provided the motivation for this work.

To my editors, Dennis Winkelmans and Michiko Asari, who spent so many hours editing the content; and to Michiko for translating it into Japanese. Dorothy Young and Lynn Welburn who did the editing of my first draft. Linda Martin for her grammatical editing, technical writing of the endnotes, bibliography and index—and for her overall effort on this project. Michael Gregson for his professional critique. Dr. Michael Greenwood who has been so helpful and a great guide. Ursula Vaira for her encouragement and efforts at helping this work get published. Jean Robinson for typesetting and layout design, and her husband Earl Schmidt, agent for Friesen Printers. David and Janice Tattam. Richard Alexander, my computer expert, who was so patient and understanding and gave so unselfishly of his time. David Patterson who has never stopped believing in me. Marie-Claire Arseneault for her editing contribution. Rick Conroy, friend and artistic advisor. My son Luke Winkelmans for the graphics; and his wife Tracy for her support. Phil Babcock, a true friend and early believer in this project. My uncle, Tom Mabelson, and his wife Muriel for their many acts of kindness.

My deep appreciation to Mark and Janet Winkelmans and the rest of my children who have put up with my many idiosyncrasies. They are: Timothy, Lorraine, Pamela and Gloria. Also, my brother Bert, his wife Mary and their family.

To Abbott David Geraets, O.S.B., and his Benedictines who took me in when I was lost and started me on my spiritual journey. Robert Frager, PhD., my favorite professor. Duane and Maureen Ingram, my second family. Pat Pritchard, and Pat and Mark Dugent for their confidence. Leia D'Anlier and Terry Fisher, open-hearted friends. Dave Cochrane for his technical input. David Young for his friendship. Patrick Jamieson and Marnie Butler for their continuing encouragement and support. Ken Fenner. Jim and Darlene Robertson whose support of my journey has meant so much. Alphonse Eiber for his confidence in me. Susan Kirby for her many kindnesses. Joe and Georgina Dodd for their friendship and persistence. Garth Mellville Danbrook, a great inspiration. David Hargrave, a fellow traveler. Pat Leahy, a true saint. Marla and Geoffory Bickerton, always an inspiration and willing to help. Michael Justice, a consistent supporter. Dr. Stephen Faulkner. Fr. Jack Sproule, a good mentor and spiritual director. Ron Kerr and David Coverdale, two great buddies. Ray Woolam. Eileen Garcia and Dan Mulligan, good friends. Cheryl Fenner. My friend, Rev. Paulette Smith. Beverly Readman. Dr. Murray Wood. David and Angie Sutherland. Dennis Murphy, another pathfinder. Don and Leanne Smith. Douglas Mellish and the Mellish clan. Rev. Dale Perkins. Errol Dugan. Pat and Caron Hrushowy. Eileen McEntee. Margaret McRae and family. Judy Ravai. Stephen Godly. Eric Jenkins. Rick Levasseur. Dr. Rick Potter Cogan. Roy Linder. Lawrence Galant. Bob Baker and Wendy Byron. Michael and Kelly Craig, for keeping it together. Ted McPherson. Rev. Matthew Fox. Ed Vanderweerd. Cindy Fox. Inez and Peter Chakowski. Charlotte Delosky. Brian Danliw. Laurain Taylor. Lu Cash. Christine Lapadat. Leona Galant. Charlie Malabon. Allan Buckley. Jim Robertshaw. Paul Burke.

To all those I may have forgotten to mention—yet have impacted my life.

Finally, to all my clients and friends whose life stories have taught me so much. I thank you all.

INTRODUCTION

The Journey

L ittle did I realize what powerful changes I was facing while flying to Hawaii in December 1992. It had been a depressing fall.
As a professional counselor in private practice, I had recently han-
dled some heavy cases that I had found quite stressful. This and a
personal problem added to my being in a fairly depressed mood.

I had spent Christmas with my family in Vancouver, which had
given me an opportunity to spend time with my mother who was in
her late eighties. She was a very wise lady and had always been
quite supportive. Therefore, during one of our times together, for the
five-hundredth time, I asked her something about my childhood. I
was hoping to find the elusive answer to my lifelong problem of
bouts of depression.

She responded by asking: "Phil, how long are you going to keep
digging in the past? When will you get a life?"

My initial reaction was one of shock. Did she not know to whom
she was talking? As a professional counselor, I prided myself on
taking clients into their painful memories. I was an expert at helping
people go back into their past trauma, drama and pain. Like a lot of
others in my profession, I thought we were making them better by
digging up all their past hurts. How wrong I was.

On the plane, it hit me that for up to thirty years I had been
involved in personal growth, first for my own health, later as a
professional. Yet, after all this input, there were still these times
when I would experience depression. My mother was right, I did not
have a life. I was looking for answers in the swamp of past hurts,
traumas and emotions.

Over the years, I had tried every form of personal growth and
therapy imaginable, including spiritual pursuits. Once, I was a leader
of a faith-healing charismatic prayer group. Through my counseling
profession, I developed skills in breath and bodywork, art therapy,
group therapy, dreams, regressions, hypno-therapy and others. My
degrees were in spiritual psychology. I did not just learn these
subjects, I experienced and taught them. Yet here I was flying to

Hawaii and still depressed. I was being the doctor who could not heal himself.

I found myself wondering why it was that our profession has the highest suicide rate. Perhaps it was because we take on a lot of our client's problems. Maybe it was because we often feel like a failure when we cannot help all who come to us. Or was it because we are trying to heal everyone else at the expense of trying to heal ourselves? Or all of the above?

My most recent cause for being stressed and burned out was due mainly to two clients, one who I got to know quite well and felt very in tune with. When I heard that he had died, it came as quite a shock. No one had heard from him for a month or more. Then we received news that he had drowned on a boat trip in Israel. Due to his mental state and the conditions around the boat mishap, all of us who knew him suspected it was suicide. Prior to his running off, he was seeing both a psychiatrist and myself. Yet together we were unable to prevent his death.

The other client was a person who was then labeled as having a multiple personality disorder. Beyond a doubt, this was the heaviest and most draining case I had yet encountered. Until Christmas of that year, there had been little headway.

My personal problems were due to my recovery from a recently dissolved relationship. Needless to say, I was not a happy camper. On impulse, I decided on a three-week holiday in Kona, Hawaii.

On the flight over the Pacific, I had plenty of time to think. I realized that I had no idea of what I would do, or where I would stay when I got there. This added a level of excitement and adventure to the trip.

I arrived in Kona on New Year's Eve, stayed in a hotel for a couple of days and then rented an apartment for the next three weeks. Now I was ready for action, so that the next thing was to find out if there were any retreats or special workshops going on. There was nothing. Evidently Hawaiians go to the mainland for Christmas and New Year's celebrations, and everything else slows down.

You might wonder why I would look for a place of healing on a holiday in Hawaii. Why would I not just hang out and let loose? For close to thirty years I had become obsessed with healing, and nothing else had held my attention as deeply as this subject had, and has still.

One day as I was walking downtown in Kona, I came across a little bookstore. Inside and at the back was a bulletin board that advertised up-and-coming workshops and seminars as well as practitioners for various types of alternative healing. My gaze fell on a brochure about a person who claimed to have the gift of reading one's inner mind. Being in the frame of mind that wanted to try something different, I decided to give him a call.

Over the phone, he said he liked to interview his clients before taking them on, so we arranged to meet for coffee. The next thing I knew was that I was talking face to face with a rather likeable chap, Roger Cotting, and his partner, Dr. Diane Mistler.

Roger was sixty-two years old and a retired architect. He had been studying various forms of spiritual psychology for some twenty years or more, and one day he began receiving words that he knew were not about him, but about those around him. He has worked with this ability ever since.

Roger's motivation was due to some family problems he had had some years before. This led him to study psychology and see if he could make sense of what was happening. As with a lot of keen analytical minds, he was able to spot a lot of weaknesses in many of the standard psychological approaches being practised at that time. He further enhanced his knowledge by delving deeply into metaphysics and spirituality.

We seemed to hit it off and I made an appointment. The next day, I found myself sitting in his den, feeling slightly apprehensive about what might happen next. Roger set up a tape machine so that I could have a copy to refer to later. Then, when we were both comfortable, he just closed his eyes and began talking. Later, he said that he is always conscious while this is taking place, and is aware of everything that is happening. Over the next couple of hours, he revealed things about me that even I did not know, or had long since forgotten. He described my struggles, hopes and dreams, my disappointments and failures, along with my strengths and weaknesses—the many things I had kept hidden from others and myself. He also mentioned how, in recent years, I had turned away from my former spiritual pursuits and understandings and had kept that knowledge secret. He mentioned a vision that I experienced some years before when I was told that I had the gift of healing, yet had denied ever since. Instead, I relied too heavily on the psychological aspect of my career, at the expense of my spiritual insights and abilities.

I was in total awe. Never had so much been revealed so clearly. At last I could begin to see myself as I really was. He talked about the way that we generally practise therapy and how traditional therapies do not go far enough. Not that they do not work, but often they do not help people truly understand who they are or where they are going with their lives. Without this understanding, people are floundering around looking for an identity in the things they do.

Furthermore, Roger felt that it was unfortunate that in most counseling situations, little is said about the meaning of spirituality and the great potential it offers for living a fulfilling life.

Over the next three weeks and the years that followed, we continued to meet. The following year, I visited them again. Over a period of three years, Roger and I communicated by phone, letters and tapes. Together we worked on ways people could incorporate some of these ideas into their lives through workshops and in my private practice. For the first time, my clients began to experience exciting new differences in themselves, their relationships and their lives. As time went on, I began putting together workshops and seminars under the title of *The Art of Purposeful Being: Your Destiny Project,* which continue to meet with outstanding acceptance and success.

Because of my professional and religious beliefs, many of the ideas that Roger presented met with a lot of resistance. It was a constant inward battle to give myself permission to try these new ideas without comparing them to old ways of thinking and doing things. Yet, right from the beginning, I was experiencing more freedom and inner strength than ever before. It was these experiences of seeing myself and others become more alive and energized that kept me with the process.

Roger has never claimed to be a therapist or counselor. My take on it would be that he is more a philosopher of spiritual psychology than anything else. As for myself, my interest was to put these ideas into a practical experiential form to which my clients could relate. I am more the teacher, facilitator and counseling therapist.

Ultimately, it was this difference in our personal visions that motivated me to strike off on my own and continue developing a way that suited my personality, professional training, talents and abilities.

The following is the result of many seminars, workshops, and professional training sessions, as well as my own and my clients' experiences. I am sure you will find it rewarding.

CHAPTER 1

The Identity Crisis

. . . seeing the self as the most elementary and distinctive parts of our being—in other words its core. This core is of an entirely different nature from all the elements (physical sensations, feelings, thoughts and so on) that make up our personality. As a consequence, it can act as a unifying centre, directing those elements and bring them into unity of an organic wholeness.

—Ferrucci[1]

Identity Produces Destiny

While studying and working with this material, it gradually dawned on me that most problems and stresses that we experience in life are due to a lack of self-knowledge about who we are. This was certainly the case in my situation. As I worked with clients and seminar participants, it became even more obvious. It seemed to me that most people operate as if they were a dual personality: the person they think they are and the hidden self they have denied.

The person we think we are is often acting in a way that is either in separation from, or in conflict with, the person we have hidden. Our expressions, attitudes, beliefs and actions are usually related to the person who we think we are. Therefore, we have stress and conflict as constant companions. We all struggle to some degree or another with an identity problem. In chapter 2, I will explain the damaging effects this had on my own personal life.

In the last several years, I have spent a lot of time considering how we arrived at this stage. Some of it was due to our conforming to the 'expectations' of others. When we were born, our parents had expectations of how we should behave and express ourselves. We went along with their expectations because we desired to please. Later in school, we learned about 'cultural' and 'social' expectations. If we did not do well in school, the message we got was that we were a failure, or even worse, that there might be something fundamentally wrong with us. If we did do well in school, we may have believed that the only way to feel worthwhile was through high achievement. This may have motivated us to take on a 'nice girl,' or 'nice boy,' self-image. On the other hand, there were also those of us who reacted to these tribal and social restrictions by becoming rebels, feeling those in authority were against us and that we were their victims.

Therefore, when many of us were young and wanting the love, approval and attention of those around us, we gave up large parts of ourselves in an attempt to survive and make others happy, but often at our expense. I like to call this 'social and tribal programming.' However, even though we were too young and not mature enough to make a better choice, ultimately, it was still our decision.

By the time most of us become adults, we have lost awareness of who we truly are and live from an image that is in denial of its greater self. Feeling this separation from who we truly are is the reason many of us spend the rest of our lives seeking, searching or trying to justify ourselves through the way we relate to others and the environment. Around mid-life, if the identity issue has not been satisfactorily resolved, it takes on the form of a mid-life crisis.

The Two Selves

In my private practice, I have met many males who, at around thirty-five years of age, have a successful career but are still unhappy. Often they say, "I did everything that was supposed to make me happy and it hasn't. What's wrong?" Other than being career persons or family men, they do not know who they are.

For many women today, a mid-life crisis often comes when the children are adult and old enough to be on their own. So much of their lives was devoted to a motherhood identity that they have lost their sense of self (the empty nest syndrome). At this point, they re-enter the workforce to acquire a career, searching for a new identity which, they feel, comes through what they do, without still knowing who they are.

In an article in *Prevention* magazine, Dr. D. Goldstein states:

> Typically people ask themselves, 'Where am I going with my life? What should I do?' But midlife is not just about what you do; it is primarily who you are. If we wish to embrace the second half of life with renewed vitality and vigor, we must devote some quality time at midlife reassessing who we've come to be and who we'd like still to become. (57)

I'd like to add that the important thing is not *to become* something else, which would only keep us searching in separation, but to have a realization of who we truly are.

In our society with its focus on materialism, fame and fortune, it is little wonder that we get the impression that our identity, self-image and self-worth comes from what we do, from what we acquire, and what we achieve. There has been little focus or time spent on knowing who we are. However, this is beginning to change. In recent years more and more people have given up on society's concept of happiness, in favour of one more fulfilling. Many are making it a priority to first become aware of who they are, and then determine what it is they want to do. Today, it is becoming more common to hear of people who claim to have an awareness of their true identity.

The hidden *self* is not shaped by society or by others' expectations. It has not sold out for materialism, or other questionable values. It operates by principles, which may even conflict with those of the people around it. When understood and integrated, life changes, dreams come true, happiness is more a constant companion, all things are a possibility, and negative feelings about oneself, others and the world around one begin to disappear. First and foremost, one is content with oneself, regardless of one's circumstances, and takes this inner sense of well-being into all he or she does.

Sounds too good to be true? Not really—rather, it should be the norm for everyone. This is how life was meant to be.

For now, I would like you to look beyond your need for money, relationships, therapy and your talents and abilities. I invite you to begin a journey of self-understanding of how you are not only your greatest resource, but the most important person you will ever know.

Let us begin this journey by asking the most important question of your life which, when answered, fully accepted and understood, will change your life forever.

The First Question:
"Who am I?"

The key to fulfilling and having the life you desire is to know the answer to this question. Please take time to ponder this question and write down your answer, so that you will be able to monitor and check your progress as you continue on this journey. Writing is a way of making sense of random and fragmented thoughts. By reviewing what you have written, you are able to keep track of your own progress.

Along with your answer to "Who am I?" explain why, at this time in your life, this may be the most important question you will ever ask.

To our first question—Who am I?—most people respond with "I am a doctor . . . a mother . . . a lawyer . . . a father . . . a teacher . . . a minister . . . a nurse . . . a waitress . . . and so on." Yet, what they are describing is the self-image or role they are playing. While it may be true that they are playing a role, they are also doing much more. Each individual may be a lot of things—as a man or a woman one could have several roles. The whole is greater than the parts.

Others might say, "I believe I am really in touch with my true self." Yet their lives do not always reflect this claim. In religious, metaphysical, and New Age circles, in spite of the many advantages gained in these areas, it is surprising how many people suffer from loneliness, lack of direction, unhappy relationships, and still experience unwanted feelings and emotions. Furthermore, this is also true of many gurus, teachers and spiritual leaders. As you shall see, much of the above is due to a mistaken self-identity and the lack of a 'way' that is individually designed for his/her life path.

Was your answer to this first question (Who am I?) satisfying? Do you know without a doubt who you are, and do you have a 'way,' a pre-determined, well-designed process for how you wish to live your life to the full? Does your method keep you happy and ecstatic, while always being, doing and having what you want?

If you said "No" to any of the above, you are in a good space to experience some interesting and exciting new ways of being.

Until people start this way of being, they have little idea of the hardships they have placed upon themselves through not fully understanding the answer to the question of "Who am I?" For example, by their not realizing who they are:

1. They may be living their lives blindly. If so, this would support feelings of insecurity, stress and confusion, including feelings of being dissatisfied with their lives.
2. They may identify themselves by the roles they take on in life. If this is the case, they will, in all likelihood, judge themselves by their successes and failures according to their ability to live up to their self-made roles. Should they succeed at a particular role, they feel greatly blessed; but should they fail, they sink into depression and despair.

Does this ring a bell? Identifying yourself with what you do is like living your life on a seesaw. Your emotions are at the risk of always going up and down according to the success or failure in your chosen role, which if played often enough, becomes the you with whom you identify—your self-image. It is as if you become attached to something other than that which you really are.

Think about a time when you played a role, such as in a job, business, or even in a relationship, only to feel devastated when it ended.

This does not mean that when you know who you are, you will have to give up your achievements, success and relationships. It simply means that in spite of these, you will come to realize how you are your ultimate source of happiness, regardless of what goes on externally, or outside of yourself.

Until now, like most of us, you have probably felt that happiness comes from what you do and what you can get. Little thought has been given to discovering "Who am I?" When you understand who you truly are, you will begin to experience that you are the source of your happiness.

Gone is the belief that you need someone to make you happy, or that if you could get enough money, enough education, enough good looks, enough love, or enough of anything then you would be happy. Why? Because as you discover who you truly are, you begin experiencing all the riches, wisdom and love you carry within, which is more than you could have ever imagined.

No One Builds Without a Foundation

Not knowing your identity can be compared to building a house without a foundation. It would be next to impossible. Furthermore, the stronger the foundation, the longer the house will last. Knowing your true identity is the foundation to building a fulfilling and happy life. It is the starting point from which the rest of your life flows.

Do you think Jesus, Gandhi, or Buddha's identity and happiness were based only on external achievements and successes? These great historical figures led lives that you or I might feel would lead to the pit of despair. Yet Jesus said, "I speak this in the world so that they may share my joy completely." These words contradict the image of a suffering Christ that many Christians project upon Him. Most of us would look at His life and think of it as one of misery and hardship, yet this is not how Jesus saw Himself. Gandhi is reported to have said that the most meaningful times in his life were those he spent in prison. One of the reasons Gandhi could say this was because of the happiness he felt within, which came from his ability to love others and be at peace with himself regardless of his circumstances.[2] Buddha is often depicted as the smiling or laughing Buddha, due to the enlightenment and bliss he was said to have found.

Many people are afraid that a new identity may not suit them, even though they are unhappy with their present identity and self-image. This is natural. Any time we entertain something new and different, fear usually accompanies us for a while. Furthermore, some people may have such a low self-image that they cannot imagine being any different. Yet this illusion of feeling that they are not worthy keeps them from realizing their true identity. How many times have you heard people, even in their fifties and sixties, jokingly say, "I wonder who I am going to be when I grow up?" No matter how old, few have realized their true identity.

The Second Question:
"What do I want to do with my life?"

Several years ago, I had a client who was the funniest person I had ever known, yet he spent most of his life in shaky business ventures trying to get rich. Finally, at a very young age he had a heart attack and nearly died. I often wondered how much of his heart attack was due to his being out of touch with his true identity that might have been better served expressing itself through a career in comedy.

Many people want to do things for the wrong reasons. Some do them for money, thinking that "Maybe if I get rich enough, I will know that I'm okay, and people will love and respect me." Or, "Maybe if I could be a great doctor, or engineer, I'd then realize I'm all right and I could feel good about myself."

The trouble is, I see many millionaires, doctors, nurses, engineers in my counseling practice that are as unhappy as anyone else. Why? Because they still do not know who they are. They think they are that of the role they are playing, and become more and more dissatisfied with their false sense of self.

If you answer this question "What do I want to do?" without answering the first question "Who am I?" you would not know if what you intend to do is in harmony with who you are. Until the first question is resolved, seeking an answer to the second question would be futile.

I have arranged for you to ask these questions early in the book, so that as the book unfolds, you will find your answers to these questions will change and become more profound and insightful. I am not expecting you to get to your ultimate awareness of *self* at this time, but to explore your present beliefs by thinking about them and writing them down. Then you can make comparisons with your evolving understanding later. By the time you come to the end, you should feel quite differently about who you are and what you have chosen to do.

Next, you need to be aware of how much of your life is already under your control.

The Third Question:
"Since I was born, who created the life I have now and all I have in it?"

Again take your time and answer carefully. Also, be sure to write out your answers so that you can refer to them later.

Many people will have answers like "My parents or God created me." It is true that they played a role in your creation, but the adult that you are experiencing as yourself now is a result of every choice you ever made since birth. You are the sum of your choices. Another way of saying it is that you are your source and resource for everything you are and have in your life so far. Some people want to blame their life on things that happened in their childhood, or on some tragic event or circumstance. However, in the final analysis the way you have chosen to react to the events or circumstances of your life is the way you have shaped the person you are today.

Today, many people believe in the philosophy that argues that we are all totally responsible for the life we are having and everything in it, including our parents. Those who adhere to this theory suggest that because we have been given *free will,* it would seem improbable that this freedom to choose would only begin in this lifetime, rather than before conception. Therefore, they feel that we all agreed and worked out with our creator the kind of parents, the place of birth, and the circumstances into which we would be born to best help us advance in this lifetime. People who believe this feel it is empowering to know that we have this much freedom to choose the kind of life we wish to have.

In any case, whether or not you accept this philosophy of your choosing your parents, you are still left with the question of who created the person you are today. Since you were born, you chose the way in which you responded or reacted to the circumstances, events and situations that occurred in your life. Therefore, because of these choices, you chose the life you are having now and are responsible for all you it involves.

What is so powerful about this idea is that if you believe that you have generated what you have now, it is also possible for you to generate something else if you are not happy with your circumstances. Knowing that you created all that you have now shows that you have the power to generate whatever life you want, an idea which should be very empowering for you.

The Fourth Question:
"What is my greatest gift?"

Please take your time and think about it.

Welcome back. Well, we have already alluded to what your greatest gift might be—Is it not your *free will*? Again, this means that you have the power to choose whatever life you wish.

I now believe that my *destiny* is exactly what I choose it to be. Let us go back to the theory that we chose the circumstances that we are born into. If this were so, I have the option of choosing the highest meaning and purpose within the circumstances in which I find myself born; and this is my *destiny*.

No one would choose an accident, or any other calamity, that may cripple or minimize one's life, hence one's *destiny*. Yet, throughout this book, you will see examples of people who have had terrible things happen to them and still found true meaning and fulfillment in those circumstances. I think of Christopher Reeve's *destiny*. This man played Superman in his film career, and then became a quadriplegic after falling off his horse. Since then, his attitude, strength and willingness to persevere and find meaning in his life have inspired millions. If ever a man truly deserved the title of Superman, it is Christopher Reeve. It seems that being Superman is his *destiny*. Now, anywhere along the way, he could have chosen otherwise. In a similar condition to his, many would have given up, felt sorry for themselves and died sad and unhappy. The question, then, is, did he play the role of Superman by chance, which role, indeed, was a forerunner to the one he has since found himself playing, or was this role a choice he made prior to his birth?

I do not believe in karma, or that life is predetermined or governed by fate, the devil, our genes, or anything else. Why? Because in those instances, there is no *free will.* Accordingly, we would then be victims of powers beyond our control.

If an outside force determines my life against my free will, I might as well give up, because I have no say in the way I choose to live. If I have no control over my life, I can only be happy or fulfilled if someone, or something outside of myself wills or directs it—I would be just a pawn. On the other hand, my life is vastly different when I choose to come from the awareness of my hidden-self, versus that of my old self-image. Choosing to *Purposefully Be* my true or hidden self in all my undertakings takes me beyond all my old limitations and helps me awaken to the deep joy and serenity that lies within.

In his book, *The Doctor and the Soul,* Dr. Victor E. Frankl, a world renowned author and psychiatrist, tells of his schizophrenic patient. When asked if she were weak willed, she responded, "I am weak willed when I want to be, and when I don't want to be, I am not weak willed." Frankl goes on to say that "this psychotic patient was skillfully pointing out that people are inclined to *hide* their own *freedom of will* from themselves by alleging *weakness of will."* (86)

You may, or may not, be able to create all the circumstances and events in your life, but you can choose your responses and reactions to them. It is said that "the rain falls on the good and the bad," but the way you respond to the rain is always your choice. It is up to your free will to choose the most meaningful responses that will provide you with the wondrous life you seek.

You might now be wondering "Where is God in all of this?" It is as if God is saying, *"I give you absolute free will, which means that you are made in my image, and have the same free will that I have. Whatever you desire you can have."* Now, if you have *free will,* and with it you produced the life you have today, has God not honored your *free will* by letting you have the life you wanted? The life you have now has been chosen by your *free will* and God has respected this by supporting all of your choices.

If your life is less than satisfactory, at least now you can say, "The dissatisfaction I feel is of my own choosing. I can now make new choices." This means that you have, and always have had—the *power to choose whatever life you wanted.*

Does this encourage or disappoint you? Some want to feel that they are not responsible, hoping they can pass the blame on to others, or on to God. They want to be a victim. Others feel, "Wow, you mean I am it, and I can have whatever I want just by the way I make my choices?" They see it as a self-empowering way of life.

Another aspect of *free will* is *creativity.* This means that because you have *free will,* you are constantly *creating yourself* anew at every moment through your thoughts, attitudes, actions and expressions. You are, by your present beliefs and thoughts, *creating* the life you have now, in this instant. By always *creating* beliefs and thoughts, your life is being adjusted accordingly. Now, you can imagine how much personal power you have to create the life you desire.

There are four reasons why people have difficulty achieving the fulfilling life they want. Most people:

a. do not know who they are
b. do not know what they really want
c. do not believe they are always getting what they want
d. are afraid of commitment.

a. *"Who am I?"*
Again, the answer to this will unfold as you read further. What I can say is that you are far greater than you have ever imagined.

b. *Most people do not know what they want*
A friend of mine found a bird that was quite young and crippled. As the bird got better, it would constantly fling itself against the bars of its cage, trying to break free. Finally, she took it to the beach and lifted the cage off the bird. Guess what it did? It hunkered down,

scared to move; it had no idea what was out there or what it really wanted.

So, she said to the bird, "Shoo little birdie," and the bird flew away, made a small circle, then came back. She kept doing this, and the bird kept flying in ever-bigger circles until finally it did not return. It had at last discovered a much bigger world out there with far more options than it ever had had in the cage.

Like the bird, we all want to be free; yet, even when given the opportunity, we stay stuck in our little cages because we do not know what we want.

c. *Most people do not believe they are always getting what they want*

Let me tell you the story of four men in the trucking business. These four men belonged to the same church and one day they heard that a miracle worker who had the ability to help people manifest whatever they wanted was coming to their church. So, anxiously, they awaited her arrival. Finally, the day came when they got to meet this special person.

They approached her saying, "We understand that you have the ability to give us whatever we want. Is this true?"

She replied, saying, "Well, you might say it is, but actually it is just helping you to bring forth from your own *true self* the ability of manifesting whatever it is you desire, for did He not say, 'Ask and you shall receive'?"[3]

"Oh, yes," they answered rather impatiently, "but we would really appreciate your help, because we know that you know how to do this. Will you help us?"

"Of course," she replied, "how can I help you?"

"Well, each of us would like three trucks, if that is not too much to ask."

"No, that shouldn't be too difficult, but, perhaps it is too little. If you could have anything you desired, would you not want more than just three trucks? Would you not want more than that?" she asked politely.

"Well, perhaps we should think a little more about this. Would that be okay?"

"Of course, take all the time you like. We can talk again."

The businessmen came back a few days later and said, "We have thought it over, and while there is much more to be had, we would just like three new trucks for now, if that is not too much trouble."

"Well, three trucks you shall have. Now let us spend a moment in the benevolence and presence of God in all things and the gift of free will we enjoy that enables us to have whatever we desire."

They all agreed and very soon, within a few days of the other, the wherewithal to obtain three big brand new trucks came about for each of them.

The first man to receive his three trucks built a big and far-reaching trucking firm. He had trucks running all over the country. When he got up in the morning he talked and thought of nothing else but trucks. At night he even dreamed about trucks. In fact, he had time for little else. It was as if the trucking business now ran his life. He became a success at the trucking business, but the question is, was he a success at living his life?

The second man, very soon after receiving his three trucks, lost one due to some minor oversight of having no insurance. So, he went through life talking about his missing truck. He would say things like, "You know, if I just had that one more truck where do you think I would be today? Yes, if I had that one more truck then I could have enough money to buy a new house, or send my child to college, or even go around the world. I would have had such a big business if only I had that one more truck."

You see, he was acting like the person who says, "I don't have enough education" or "If only I had continued in school, then things would be different." Or, "If I only had more brains, or more good looks, or more money, or a better physique, then things would have worked out." His life would have been great, but he always came up against his "not enough" beliefs.

The third man lost all his trucks in a risky business venture. He went through the rest of his life saying, "Oh no, I wouldn't try that. I took a risk once and see what happened. A guy could lose everything by sticking his neck out just see what happened to me." He spent the rest of his life not risking anything because of his one-time loss.

He became like some people who are, after going through a crisis like a divorce, bankruptcy or serious illness, always on guard and who will never chance anything, seeing only disastrous outcomes for any choices involving risks. They come from fear and insecurity, and have chosen, therefore, a very small box from which they can experience life.

The **fourth man** was the most overwhelmed with the appearance of the three trucks. He could not believe how lucky he was to have such magnificent looking vehicles, so he built a huge shed to keep them in, and spent all his spare time polishing, cleaning and maintaining his great prizes. He would not risk doing anything with them for fear that they would deteriorate and lose their value, so he kept them locked up and out of service.

He was like those people who recognize their great potential, talents and gifts, and are so enamored and in love with them that they want to keep everything for themselves. Some people spend their whole life acquiring wisdom, or perfecting a skill that no one ever gets a chance to see and experience; they refuse to offer it to others.

Again, I ask you to think carefully. Who was the most successful of the four truckers? Please write down your answer before continuing.

You may feel that the first trucker was the most successful. But in fact he was no more successful than the other three. Why? Because, they all got exactly what they wanted, did they not? Therefore, they were all successful.

The first trucker was not averse to taking risks in business. Any businessman will tell you that there are always setbacks. So, the first man was able to go beyond any self limiting beliefs concerning his business and, therefore, became quite successful in the business of trucking.

The second trucker had a strong belief in "not enough," and went through life doing "not enough." He was also successful in getting what he wanted, which was "not enough."

The third trucker believed in "fear of loss" and, therefore, believed he would be safe if he never risked anything. Once he lost his trucks, he would never again take a chance. His fears and insecurity around a past loss was the center point from which he ran his life. Like the second trucker, he did "fear of loss" successfully.

The fourth trucker would not risk putting them into service, and like the man who hid his talents of silver in the Parable of the Talents, he lost any potential income he might have gained from employing his trucks. As he grew older, he lost whatever spark of ambition he had, and his gift became obsolete. He was a success in that he got what he wanted—his trucks—and that is all he got.

In the end, each of them was successful in getting exactly what they wanted. This story shows how by our thoughts, attitudes and beliefs we are always getting what we want.[4]

d. *Fear of Commitment*

Generally, people are afraid to commit, and do not want to invest time, money, and energy in themselves. They are not prepared to make themselves their number one project. Why? Because underneath, they may be afraid to know who they really are, or feel somehow that they might fail and feel worse about themselves than they do now.

The Fifth Question:
Are you willing to invest your time and energy into making yourself your number one project? Yes or no?"

Your answer to this determines whether you are willing to commit and attend to whatever it takes to *be, do* and *have* the life you choose.

Some may think that going for the life they want is selfish. So, they remain unhappy and keep everyone around them unhappy. They do not realize that if they became totally fulfilled and happy they would be far more able to help, love and support those around them. Others would begin to feel better because of their improved attitudes, actions and behaviors.

Other excuses may be, "That would not agree with my religious teaching," or "What might others think if I were to expand my beliefs or sense of self?" These people are caught up in living out other people's "shoulds" and "expectations" at the expense of knowing their own personal truth and identity.

Know yourself, and to your own self be true. Until you know who you are, you cannot be true to something you do not know.

Today, there are a great number of self-esteem and self-worth seminars, workshops, books and tapes to help people get self-confidence and self-worth. The problem is that most people have not asked the first question "Who am I?" It is difficult to love someone you do not know. Therefore, you must know who you are before you can love yourself and others. Only then will you experience the confidence, self-esteem and self-worth you are seeking.

In This Chapter We Have Explored:

1. The importance and value of knowing who you are

It is my belief that this knowledge is the foundation of all of life. A building without a strong foundation will fall. Not knowing who you are motivates you to get your identity from outside sources such as: work, relationships, activities, behaviors, achievements and goals, acquisitions and attachments. While these may be important, they are secondary to the foundation of knowing who you are.

2. Your hiding your true identity from yourself by:

- not realizing your power to choose and create your life;
- having a mistaken belief in outside forces controlling your life and deciding your life for you—such as society, karma, God, devil, fate, destiny, predetermination, preordaination and predestination;
- not really understanding the gift and power of your *free will.*

3. As master of your destiny, you need to fully understand these following points:

- Know who you are.
- Know what you want.
- Know that you are always *creating* what you want through your *free will.*

- Know that you are committing yourself.
- Make yourself your number one project.

The Art of Purposeful Being (P.B.) is designed to help you understand the way you can be master of your destiny. It is meant as a guide, helping you be aware of your own ability to teach, counsel and direct yourself.

P.B. helps you awaken to all the strength, power and resources to create your life in any way you want to live it. What you already have is what you have chosen. What you have not—you have not yet chosen. This question of choosing to awaken yourself to your true identity is the first step to fulfilling your dreams. Consider yourself as a person worth the investment of your time and energy.

I am not advocating shirking the responsibilities you have. Consider this phrase: "Always as well as, never instead of." I am saying that within your present structure make yourself your favorite hobby or project. Once you do this and begin integrating the information in the coming chapters, you will begin feeling more alive both in yourself, your relationships and all your activities.

This book is about helping you discover your *Destiny Project* through the *Art of Purposeful Being.*

If you are committed to making yourself your number one project, then I invite you to begin by answering the following questions. The benefits are many. And remember, I designed the questions for you to go beyond some of your old ways of thinking and believing. After you finish the book, looking at your answers again will show how much you have learned.

CHAPTER 1 QUESTIONS

Please answer the following questions.
Rate from one to five, five being the most extreme.
For example, Question #1—The more I am *not aware* of my present self-image the higher I would rate myself.

Self-image Questions	**1**	**2**	**3**	**4**	**5**
1. I am not aware of my hidden self.	—	—	—	—	—
2. I am always concerned with my self-image.	—	—	—	—	—
3. I have been more concerned with what I *do* than who I'm *being.*	—	—	—	—	—
4. I catch myself comparing myself to others.	—	—	—	—	—
5. I express and experience feelings of not being good enough, or having low self-worth or self-esteem.	—	—	—	—	—
6. I suffer from insecurity, anxiety and stress.	—	—	—	—	—
7. I entertain negative self-judgment or self-pity.	—	—	—	—	—
8. I suffer from depression, mood swings, despair, the blues, or the blahs.	—	—	—	—	—
9. Even when my outer life is successful I do not always feel that way inside.	—	—	—	—	—
10. I find *anger, sadness,* or *fear* a constant part of my life.	—	—	—	—	—
TOTALS	—	—	—	—	—

The closer you are to fifty, the more unhappy you are with your present self-image.

CHAPTER 2

What Single Thing Runs Your Life?

*All men should learn
before they die
what they are running from,
and to, and why.*

—*James Thurber*

The Great Secret

Just imagine the life you would have if you really understood and experienced what single thing:

- Governs your choices?
- Sabotages, or creates your chances for success?
- Makes your behaviors and outcomes predictable?
- Creates your destiny?

You are probably thinking, "Life could not be this simple; it has to be more complicated than having just one single thing running my life." However, that's the beauty of it. It is just that simple. Let me tell you how I have searched my whole life to reach this amazing discovery.

I, too, suffered under the illusion that to live the life of my dreams, it would be something I had to *get*. I thought maybe if I:

- found my right mission
- could let go of my destructive behaviors
- changed my career, location, or relationship
- did enough therapy, inner child or self-esteem work
- got spiritual enough, meditated and prayed enough
- could *get* someone to love me enough
- could *get* healed enough
- could *get* positive enough . . .

then it would all come together and I would know that I was a worthwhile person.

None of the above ever worked. Finally after years of effort, I realized why it would never work for me, and why it does not work for others.

To understand this simple concept requires a shift in thinking that takes a little time and commitment.

This is not new. Mystics and masters throughout the ages have taught it in many different ways. Yet it was never told to me in a way I could understand and accept, or put together in a simple workable fashion.

To begin understanding this powerful way of life, I want you to think of a thing you wanted, and acquired, or achieved at some time in your life. Now remember if you can, what single thing gave you the most help in acquiring it? If you said anything, which relates to *imagining* in relation to having it, then you were on the mark.

Image and Attraction

First, you had an *image* of what it was you were after. Then, you lined up your beliefs, attitudes and actions to match up with your inner *image* and *imaginations.* You then acquired your objective. Is this not correct? In fact you might say that your *image,* which was made up of beliefs, attitudes and actions, predicted the kind of choices you would make, which allowed you to realize your goal.

One time at University, I was asked to do a comedy routine for our class party. As an adult, I had never done anything like that. So, I got some crayons and drew an *image* of a clown and placed it at the foot of my bed. I did not know how, but I *imagined* that I could do it.

What amazed me were the jokes I started hearing and receiving from out of the blue. I began putting them in some kind of order and routine for the event. My performance went over so well that I was invited to do one for our graduate school's graduation, which performance was also well received.

In both your personal example and mine there was a starting point for the results to occur. That starting point was with an *image* in our *imagination* which resulted in our thoughts and beliefs about our desiring a certain thing or outcome. This is the power of *imagery* and *imagination.*

Your single thing that runs your life is an energy form, which is gathered into an image—called self-image. Self-images are made of the 'energy' produced by your imaginings, beliefs, attitudes, desires and actions. This chapter should help you identify the self-image or images that you may be allowing to control your life, after which you can decide whether you want to continue with them or not. It is my belief that all self-images, other than your *hidden-self,* are destructive and harmful to your mental and physical health. Furthermore, once there is an understanding and awareness of your real self then no other lessor self-images are necessary.

As scientists break down structures to their smallest atomic particles, they find a *single element* called 'energy,' which operates at different vibrations to form matter. Everything we see breaks down through the atomic and subatomic particles to pure energy. Furthermore, this single thing called 'energy' is the single operating principle for all things in our universe.

Think of your self-image as being the energy in a magnet at the center of your life. Then, like a magnet, you will attract and be attracted to everything that is in harmony with this self-image; and, like a magnet, you will reject everything that is not.

If you take a bunch of steel filings and place them on a glass, and beneath the glass you place a magnet, the steel filings will form a pattern. Wherever you move the magnet the same pattern will occur. As long as they are just steel filings, they consistently follow the same pattern. Should you use copper or nickel filings, nothing happens because the magnet is only identifying itself with steel-like substances. It only attracts that which relates to its single vibrating energy force.

Through self-image, you create a similar magnetic energy pattern that always produces similar results no matter where you move, or who you have in your life. Think of yourself or friends who have tried changing jobs, places and relationships, but who continue to reproduce the same patterns of behaviors and consequences.

While you can have many self-images, there is usually only one dominant one that has the most influence in your life and motivates you to make choices through which you express and experience most of your joys, sorrows, failures, successes, disappointments and pleasures.

You might compare a self-image to an engine powering a ship. As long as it runs well, the ship will stay on course and reach its destination. If the engine does not work properly, all kinds of problems may occur. In fact, having an engine failure in a storm could be a matter of life and death.

The same is true for us. We have a self-image, which runs our lives. It is different from personality in that it is our self-image that is creating our personality. Like the ship, if our self-image (engine) is faulty, then all kinds of emotional problems can happen. However, consciously being aware of the *hidden self* is like having a self-image or engine that never fails.

I AM. I have free will. I choose my imaginings, beliefs, attitudes and behaviors. These equal my self-image and make me the kind of person I am and the life I have lived.

Are self-images fixed? As I have shown, out of our compliance with tribal and social conditioning, we choose our self-image. In our Judeo-Christian world, we have been led to believe that we are flawed. In some of our churches, not only are we taught how sinful we are, but often that we were born this way. Furthermore, parents, siblings, peers, teachers and the clergy have all contributed to this by judging us through our behaviors, (i.e. what we do), rather than who we are. With this social background, it is easy to choose a self-image based on others' expectations.

Self-images are made up of our beliefs and attitudes that separate us from our *hidden self.* In other words, long after the event of being victimized, a person may continue choosing the self-image of being a victim. The key is to become aware of the *hidden self,* otherwise you identify with your self-image to such a degree that you think of it as the real you.

Because you have *free will,* you have made choices, which result in the kind and quality of life you're experiencing today. You are the product of all your previous choices. Basically you never make a choice unless it would serve you in some way. Even suicide is considered by a troubled person with a limited view of life to be the best of several, not so great, choices.

So, even though it seems foolish that we may choose destructive self-images, we chose them as a way of serving 'the self' and our perceived needs at a particular time in our life until eventually they become a habit. Usually, the denial of a self-image problem results in our seeing everyone else as having a problem but ourselves. While it is a little humbling for us to face our own weaknesses, it can also be the beginning of change and self-empowerment.

The following feelings, emotions and thoughts are indications of how we are living our lives through an unsatisfactory self-image; they include, fear, insecurities, depression, inferior and superiority complexes, perfectionism, hostility, self-criticism, loneliness, compulsiveness, workaholism, addictions, defensiveness, false righteousness, people-pleasing tendencies, stress, unhealthy relationships, anxiety, and so on.

To the degree that the above unwanted feelings, emotions and behaviors are in your life is the degree to which you are under the influence of a faulty self-image and in denial of the real you.

For example, why do you think some people are perfectionists? Is it because internally they feel less than perfect, and early in their lives they were only acknowledged and rewarded when they conformed to other's rather high or rigid standards? This may have been what first motivated them, but gradually they identified themselves with their perfectionist behaviors until perfectionism became their self-image around which the rest of their lives evolved.

If perfectionists began to feel great and positive within themselves all the time, they would no longer need to be perfectionists, because their sense of self would not need external reinforcement.

Once a person knows and understands one's *hidden-self,* there is no longer an inner feeling of lack. Consequently, the need to have any other self-image disappears.

When you are consciously aware of who you truly are, and begin to understand the power of being yourself, you will not rely on inappropriate self-images and external values. While at times you may consciously use a self-image to help further your purpose, the self-image will never again be something you identify with as yourself.

So, how is your self-image? Not just the one people see, but the one you see? Have you really enjoyed your life so far? Has it been as happy, ecstatic, fulfilling, loving, and exciting, as you would like? Or are there areas in your life that are dissatisfying, limiting and unfulfilling?

Do you want to continue living your life in the same way forever more? If your answer is "No," the way to change it is by addressing your self-image. You may ask, "Do I have to look at all my old beliefs and attitudes to get a new self-image?'

The answer is: Not really. For the most part, let the past bury the past. All you need to do is to know and accept what, for now, I've been calling the *hidden* you. Then, by living consciously and purposefully from your *hidden self* with the same energy you used to form your old self-image, things will change automatically. I used to believe that you could change your life by looking at the past, which is like trying to move forward while looking through a rear view mirror.

The Importance of Knowing Your Self-image

Having used the comparison of using a rear view mirror while trying to move your life forward, I would like to say that there is still some use for the small rear view mirror. Look at it this way: from your ego flows your identity, which is your self-image that produces the life you are having. Being conscious of who you are allows you to live the kind of life you want. The freedom of being your true self is experienced through consciousness and expression. Consciousness means that you are aware of who you really are and who you are being in all your activities. However, in the beginning, especially if you are stuck, it may be advantageous to look at how you allowed your old self-image to run your life. Then you can begin to make new and more self-fulfilling choices.

How My Self-image Ran My Life

Let me demonstrate how a self-image influences one's life by my disclosing personally how my old self-image ran my life. You may relate some of my experiences to your own life and self-image problem.

Star Design

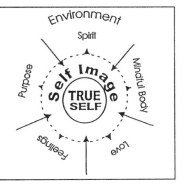

This diagram represents the five areas through which we live our lives:

1. Career (Purpose)

2. Spirituality

3. Mindful/Body

4. Feelings and Emotions

5. Love/Social

Looking at the above design, if you were fulfilled in all five areas at the same time, you would be experiencing a fulfilling and happy life, correct? Yet, as you will see, that cannot happen as long as your old self-image is running your life.

In the center are two circles. In the outer circle is your self-image that looks to the environment as its source for happiness. The outer line, circling the self-image, is not solid, while the line around the *true or hidden-self* is. This means that your self-image only relates outwardly expecting its meaning and fulfillment to come from the outer environment. At this stage, your self-image acts as an anti-self and is only an artificial imitation of the inner *self.* Your *true self* at the center of the circle waits for the self-image to be aware of its presence, at which time your old self-image would disappear and your true self would come forth.

In the diagram are five sections, or pieces of the pie. Using myself as an example, let us begin in the career section, as it has been the most dominant.

1. My Career

I was born in the Great Depression and, like many other families of that period, we were very poor. In today's jargon, you could also say that ours was a dysfunctional family in which I was constantly being put down. From an early age, I reacted by choosing not to feel good about myself. Furthermore, I thought our family's problems were due to a lack of money. Interpreting this to mean that as a family we were not worthy, it caused me to develop low self-esteem and an unsatisfactory self-image.

We belonged to a Catholic pre-Vatican II church, which was very strict and legalistic. I remember giving up trying to be good in grade four. I had tried living up to the rules, had failed, and knew I could try no harder. So, I remember in grade four thinking that I was doomed. Needless to say, this all contributed to my lack of self-worth.

As I grew older, I kept thinking that I would be okay if I could just get enough money. During all my growing years, the overriding message in our household was money. "If you could get enough money you would be happy forever." So, by the time I was thirty-five, I became successful in businesses and made all the money I thought I would ever need. This also included having a nice home, cars, and family. In other words, I fulfilled the North American social and tribal dream and had every thing a person could want. I then had a nervous breakdown. All the things for which I worked to fulfill me did not. Furthermore, because of my low self-worth image, the more successful I became, the more stress I felt, since my state of success was in direct opposition to my low self-worth image.

Like many people, I had overdosed on my career. If you look at the diagram as the whole of one's life, then you can see that my energy went into a very small area of the total. My energy went into my career and I tried to *achieve* happiness through wealth—instead I got a nervous breakdown. This started me on my second career and my search for truth with a capital "T."

I realized later that it was my low self-image that became the foundation on which I built my life. I thought that to compensate for this self-image, I would have to *get* my needs met, first from my career, then from the other five areas of the outer diagram.

It sounded so logical. In fact, most counseling and therapy has been about getting satisfaction from within each of the five sections of the circle, yet never addressing the core identity issue. As long as you have a self-image separate from your *hidden self,* you will sabotage most attempts to change for the better until your self-image issue is addressed.

2. *My Focus on Spirituality*

When I finally burned out in my career, I turned to God and thought, "Well maybe I can get God to love me. Surely if God shows love for me, I will know that I am okay and I will feel good about myself forever more."

I became involved with a highly charismatic faith healing group, and eventually was one of the leaders. It seemed that our focus was to try and have as many God-like blissful experiences as we could get We had many. I was involved in miraculous healing and in all kinds of visible and invisible manifestations of the spirit. However, I was still depressed. Furthermore, I saw very little change in myself, or in the people with whom I was involved. It seemed that our faith healing groups had an even harder time getting along than most people did. It was during this period that my wife and I separated and divorced.

So, regardless of my spiritual experiences, the fulfillment and happiness that I sought was still missing in my life. All the love, bliss and ecstasy I received from God still clashed with my low self-image, because at that time I never understood what was happening. Even the love of God was not enough to transform my self-image. In fact, my previous religious training had made me more conscious of the separation between God and myself. I would think that if I was not experiencing God's presence all the time, it must be because of my unworthiness.

3. Mindful/Body

After our marriage ended, I raised three teenage girls and a boy until they could be on their own. Once they were on their own, at the age of fifty-four I decided to go to university. I had become involved in counseling, finding the subject fascinating, and decided that that would be my new career. I focused my degrees on spiritual psychology, which combined my two main interests.

With my degrees I thought, "At last I must have it all together, here is the proof to myself and others that I am smart enough." Yet, even with degrees, my low self-worth image still followed me. It seemed that I could not get enough degrees or academic intelligence to go beyond this low image I had of myself.

4. Feelings and Emotions

It was felt then, and still is by some schools of psychotherapy, that if we can let people get into their feelings and emotions, they will be healed. It is theorized that our feelings direct our lives, therefore, if we can let go of certain negative feelings, only the positive ones are left.

Unfortunately, no matter how long you work on feelings, you will be able to bring up unwanted feelings forever, unless you deal with your self-image problem.

I am not saying that this form of therapy does not have its place in conditions such as post-traumatic stress disorder; however, in those conditions, its success is often minimal. Any therapy should only be used in the larger context of one's *hidden self.* Addressing a client's identity issue should be the overriding goal of all therapy; however, most institutional therapists are not equipped to handle the identity issue, due to the spiritual aspect of this process.

I began my private practice in counseling; and my practice prospered. At first, I worked very hard at using traditional therapy techniques to get people into their feelings. So, if we look at the diagram,

I was endeavoring to help people *get* happiness by having them re-live and re-experience their emotional pain and feelings.

As I said earlier, I discovered that it was a bottomless pit. You can have people go into their feelings forever without them ever making a decision to get on with their lives. In fact, the more they do it, the more convinced they become that they are not okay and see themselves as victims, even of their emotions.

5. *Love/Social*

This section covers all different aspects of relationships, indi-vidual as well as social.

Like many of us, I had to learn that I could not *get* happiness through trying to *get* someone to love me. I was judging my relation-ships by the amount of love I received, never understanding that there is no way I can talk or manipulate another person into loving me. It is always his or her free choice.

I am not saying that you cannot do things that make you attrac-tive to others and, by attractive, I am not just talking about looks. You can make yourself more attractive in a myriad of ways, such as caring, sharing, listening, giving, supporting, affirming, and so on. However, the choice is always up to the other person, and in the end, all your trying may never have any affect at all. Many of us may re-call loving someone greatly, yet the object of our affection felt quite differently, he/she never choosing to experience the love we were offering or feeling.

You can have all the desire for another that you want, but you run into trouble when you believe the other has got to meet or fulfill this desire.

Do you think people like Jesus, Buddha and other Masters loved for what they could personally *get* in return or because of who they were? They enjoyed loving for the sake of loving—it was an end in and of itself.

In the past, I spent a lot of my energy going after love for all of the wrong reasons.

My feelings of loneliness made me feel mistakenly that I needed a particular person to make me feel okay and take away my lonely feelings. My unworthy self-image was clamoring for someone else to give it worthiness through love and intimacy. I had not yet learned how to make myself my own best friend.

Experiencing loneliness usually means that you have a self-image that feels isolated from your *hidden self.* It reinforces your feelings of unworthiness or whatever your personal self-image problem is. There are times when everyone desires company and social engagement, but this is different from a feeling of loneliness that is experienced as obsessive neediness to have someone in his/her life.

Now this whole thing became quite a puzzle for me because, as you can see, I put a lot of effort into all five sections of the circle *to try and get worthiness.*

Have you not been told all your life that you could *get* happiness through one or more sections of the circle? For example, if you could just *get* the right job then you would be happy, or the right mate, or the right amount of bliss, or the right amount of success, and so on.

Yet, no matter how hard you tried to *get* happiness through your achievements, acquisitions and successes, it never really happened. Happiness, joy and fulfillment continued to elude you. No, I am not saying that you did not find some happiness, but it was never enough. It was never the total fulfillment you desired. There was always something missing.

Having material things, or being proud of your achievements, are not problems. It is only when you go after them to prove you are worthy, or to reinforce some other faulty self-image that you run into trouble. The truth is that you are always a grand, worthwhile, marvelous and superb human being just as you are, regardless of what you have or achieve. Once you realize this is so, most of the stress you have in your life will disappear. You would no longer think your worthiness and identity came from what you could *get* or accomplish.

The Self-image Problem

To understand the limitations of a self-image, one should be aware of some of its restrictive characteristics, which may even sound positive. Let us examine a few examples such as, superiority, perfectionism, obsession with success, low self-worth and self-esteem.

To understand this further, let us go back to our diagram and the five sections through which we express and experience life.

There are two main categories, which make up a self-image:

- A false sense of high self-worth
  (This category includes people with inflated feelings of superiority, perfectionism, and those who are obsessive about success.)
- An imagined low self-worth and self-esteem

There can also be times when a person can go from one category to another. In fact, this is fairly common until one becomes conscious of the true self.

People with an inflated self-image usually exhibit false pride, intimidation, insensitivity, controlling behaviors, and can be quite judgmental, critical, and overbearing.

In the love area of the circle, people with inflated attitudes often have difficulty in relationships, always wanting control, the upper hand, and a need to always be right.

In the career section, they can be difficult to work with, hard to get to know or get close to.

In the mindful/body area, people with inflated attitutdes employ judgmental, opinionated, and critical ways of thinking, believing and acting. They always see themselves in the best light at someone else's expense.

Finally, in the spiritual area, inflated self-image people are often in conflict with God, due to their not wanting to acknowledge anything equal to themselves. Therefore, these people would be inhibiting many of their creative, intuitive and insightful abilities. Or, if they are religious or spiritual, they may be more interested in religious supremacy than in the source.

People with inflated self-images are devastated any time events, situations and life do not match their self-images. These people live in fear of not being able to maintain their self-image. Each self-image has its own unique list of frustrating thoughts and feelings that inhibit fulfillment in all areas of ones life.

People with low self-worth and low self-esteem usually express and experience feelings of despondency, depression, self-blame, self-doubt, helplessness, neediness, fear, self-pity, and insecurity. They have a lot of investment in being a victim.

In love and relationships people with low self worth have a tendency to give others power over them, and often look at the negative side of most issues. They may tend to withdraw, yet also be angry for allowing themselves to have been taken advantage of. At the same, time they might be very needy, feeling they could never get enough love.

In the mental/physical section they are often full of negative self-talk or self-blame which compounds their thoughts of loneliness and isolation.

If people were religious or spiritual, they probably see God as all-powerful and themselves as powerless. They are afraid of God's judgment, and feel unworthy of God's attention and favors. This also affects their creative, intuitive and inspirational abilities.

They may also be unable to accept success in their careers because they would feel conflict between this and their negative self-image.

The answer lies in knowing who you are and successfully expressing this in all areas of your life, rather than always trying to *get* success from something you do or wish to become. Successfully being and doing your *hidden self* brings joy and fulfillment. This means that you are not dependent on outer trappings for your happiness. Yet, if fame and fortune happen to come your way because of the successful way you are living your life, you would take it in stride, accepting it for what it is, without getting hooked or hanging your identity on it.

Through practising *The Art of Purposeful Being,* you are able to have all you desire that is congruent with your ideal self.

If you are putting a lot of energy into obtaining things to make you happy, often you will end up being disappointed. In this case, you will look for something else and will be on a never-ending search for material gratification. There is also the chance that the thing that you desire may end up taking over your life and controlling you.

Remember the first man in our trucking story and the successful business he built? He became so busy and successful that he was always thinking trucks morning noon and night. His life revolved around his trucking business. Did he run the trucking business, or did it run him? Remember the old saying, "Be careful of what you ask for as you might just get it."

By now you are probably beginning to understand the significant effect that a self-image can have on your life. While it is very easy to spot someone else's self-image, it is not always so easy to spot your own.

A question that you now may be asking is "If I am not my self-image then, who am I? Who or what is my *hidden self?*" There is still a ways to go, but you are almost there. Be patient just a little longer.

You saw how I lived my life in each of the five different areas of the circle. I was trying to *get* satisfaction externally, because of what I perceived was missing internally. Once I switched it around and began to express and experience my *hidden self,* I began to realize that all the happiness I sought after was what I already had.

What is interesting is how the power of a self-image keeps giving us the same results, even when we know we do not like the outcome. I am reminded of a story about a bird trying to get out of a garage window, even though the garage doors were open wide. The bird kept hurling itself against the window until it dropped. Then the owner picked up the limp bird and set it free through the open garage doors.

We are like the bird in that we keep using a self-image that gets unsatisfactory results, and, like the bird, we will keep having the same painful results forever more until we decide to change our self-image for our authentic identity.

By now you should be able to see that no amount of therapy or personal growth will ever have any lasting effect until the central issue of your self-image has been addressed through finding the answer to the question of "Who am I?"

Furthermore, the same is true of your religious and spiritual pursuits. You can have all the miraculous and wondrous experiences you like, but they mean little until you understand the importance of addressing who you are. Once you know your self, the.n any therapy or spirituality you engage in will further your understanding of self.

For years, I searched for a method—a process that anyone could use to fulfill his/her life to the full, regardless of their educational, social or religious background. *The Art of Purposeful Being* is a result of this search and fulfills all that I had hoped for. It all boils down to an understanding of a *single thing* that runs our lives: our self-image.

The question, then, is, "What is the most meaningful and fulfilling self-image that a person can have?" This is the subject of our next chapter.

Please answer the following questions.

CHAPTER 2 QUESTIONS

As you read through the book and do the questions and exercises, your beliefs, understandings and attitudes will change. Later, by going back over the same questions, you will be amazed at how much you have changed the way you think, believe and feel.

1. Of the five parts of the circle, which has received most of your attention? Why? (The five parts were: career, spirituality, mindful/body, feelings and emotions, and love/social.)

2. What would self-image have to do with your above answer?

3. Is the life you have and everything in it the life you have chosen?

4. Have you always got what you wanted? Explain.

5. Supposing there is an afterlife, what would you take with you when you die?

6. If you could have any self-image you wanted, what would you choose?

7. What would have to happen for you to live the grand and wonderful life of your dreams?

8. Who are you conscious of being today? Explain.

9. What do you know about yourself that will determine your future?

CHAPTER 3

The Power of Being

*The factors that contributed to my growth were many—
finding someone who understood me, exploring the
unconscious, awakening my latent love . . . but one star is
brightest among all: the self. I found my source of
livingness inside me, something I did not even know existed.*

—*Ferrucci*

To get the most out of this chapter, I recommend that you now do
exercise #1 and exercise #2, which you will find in the
appendix (pp. 221-223). These exercises are crucial for providing an
experiential foundation to this work. There are two ways you can
integrate and experience this material. One is through the intellect,
the other is to actively begin doing it. It is felt that information,
which is experienced as well as intellectualized, has a far more profound effect. For example, intellectualizing about love means very
little until you experience it.

These exercises are insightful and illuminating. The rational and
experiential information in this chapter is the foundation for the rest
of this book and if taken seriously—the rest of your life.

Awakening to the Hidden Self: The Power Within

The Art of Purposeful Being exposes your true nature, then shows you the way to express the unlimited potential your true nature holds.

Once you recognize the truth of who you are, your inner reality, and the joy and ecstasy that lies within, you stop looking for it outside of yourself. You realize you already have and are it. Then whatever you do, work, relationships, and so on, become different. You recognize that being the real you is the foundation for everything you ever wanted.

Years ago, while staying in a monastery in Pecos, New Mexico, I had a dream that I went down some stairs into a dungeon where there was a row of prison cells. In each cell were huge chests and displays of gold, diamonds and riches of all kinds. This dream was showing me how I had locked away from the world and myself my internal power, values, riches, gifts, talents and abilities. Everything I wanted I already had.

Most of us have denied, or kept secret, large parts of our true potential. Look again at the five sections in the circle (p. 25) and see how you lived your life in the past. The five sections are:

1. Career (or Purpose)
2. Spirituality
3. Mindful/Body
4. Feelings and Emotions
5. Love/Social

If you 'overdosed' on one section of the circle then you have sold yourself short in all the other areas of the circle, and you have denied large parts of your life.

For example, if you denied your spirituality you were missing out on the gifts, intuitive powers and strengths that your spirituality provides.

Spirituality is a tremendous resource that helps you realize intuition, creativity, passion, ecstasy, bliss, wisdom, peace, love, healing power, and so on. Therefore, a lot is missing if you keep your spirituality in denial. What effect on the other four areas of the circle would you have by denying your spirituality?

Continuing with the circle, let us look at the mindful/body section. How have you limited the training of your body and mind? Have you held back great ideas and inspirations, and not followed your dreams? What are you tolerating that is holding you back now? I do not just mean circumstances and relationships but beliefs, attitudes and assumptions that keep you stuck. How is your toleration of these influencing the other four sections of your life?

In the section on love and relationships, begin by reflecting on an aspect of love, such as the way you may have held back your love. Then notice how such holding back influences the other four sections of the circle.

In the feeling section, you could look at the times you reacted emotionally with anger, sadness, or fear and how this impacts the other four sections.

In the career and purpose section, how clear are you about the ultimate purpose and direction for your life? If you are not clear about such an important aspect of living, how are the other areas of your life as represented by the other four sections of the circle being affected?

The Art of Purposeful Being is about helping you realize you have a foundation from where your thoughts, feelings and actions will flow into the outer areas of your life

This is why we begin with the aspect of who you are *being* before we address what you are *doing*. Once you value and appreciate who you are, we can then help you express this in ever fulfilling ways.

The Wondrous You

In the past, few of us have spent much time reflecting on what force, energy, or creative intelligence operates our physical being beyond our moment-to-moment conscious awareness.

Who or what is this force that runs our autonomic and sympathetic nervous system, creates our sleep patterns, reports on our appetite, adjusts our bodies' temperature to current weather conditions, automatically breathes for us. Who or what organizes our cellular structures to support all our activities, thoughts and emotions, and runs all of our body functions whether waking or sleeping?

What is it that creates the stories and information in our dreams and visions of the night? What gives us great inspiring thoughts infuses us at times with ecstatic feelings of love and joy? Who, or what, is this other self that cannot be seen, but is orchestrating so much of our lives from behind the scenes? Where did it come from? Where does it go when the body is officially dead?

This energy, or life-force, or intelligent essence, is who you really are. It carries the potential to change your world and the world around you, giving you the ability to dream and have visions, experience great feelings of ecstasy, excitement, inspiration and healing, and the wherewithal to have whatever life you want.

How many times do we hear of people today doing the impossible? A man will lift up a car to save someone from being crushed to death. People walk on hot coals, defying scientific views of reality.

Meditators levitate, creating visible illusions unexplainable to the rational mind. Healers activate the *mind/body* ability to heal through faith prayer, belief, and touch. They do it without the use of drugs or other substances. Dowsers find water where expensive scientific equipment has failed. Seers see into the future, read our minds, and assist the police in finding clues through extra sensory perception. The list of phenomenal experience is endless.

People of all races and religious persuasions do these things, even if they have not a particular belief in anything but the power within themselves.

These seemingly amazing powers are not usually experienced because of our concerns with insecurity, feelings of not being good enough, loneliness, rage, despair, depression, and so on These feelings are all a product of an unsatisfactory self-image and get in the way of us experiencing our true potential.

By not having any of these aforementioned self-images and by choosing to become aware of your true authentic-self, it is possible to begin expressing and experiencing your source, which is the grand, marvelous and wondrous you.

If I asked you, "When were you not okay?" you might answer with times, dates, places and events. The truth is that you have always been okay. It has only been how you thought about yourself that has created the illusion that somehow you were not worthwhile.

Even if you committed murder, your life-force is still a value. This life-force carries on whether you are asleep, awake, sick, or well. Therefore, within you is a constant faithful *self.* You just have not thought this way before.

It is impossible for you to stop *being,* even when you are at your most crippled, diseased ill self, you are still being. Nothing you can do in this lifetime could stop you from being. According to many spiritual beliefs, even suicide does not stop you from existing in another realm.

The Inner Dialogue

Talking to yourself is a fine way of tapping your intuitive resources. In her book *A Mythic Life,* Jean Houston tells of a time when she was a little girl her father took her to visit an old friend visiting their town. His name was Edgar Bergen, probably the most famous ventriloquist of the twentieth century. His famous dummy was Charlie McCarthy. They had their own radio show and appeared many times on TV and in the movies.

As she and her father approached Edgar's hotel room, the door was ajar and they heard someone talking. Looking in, they saw Edgar having a conversation with his wooden dummy, Charlie McCarthy. Her father listened for a while, then entered the room and asked Edgar, "What do you think you are doing? Don't you know that Charlie is just a dummy?" Edgar appeared embarrassed and said, "Yes I know, but I am always so amazed at the wisdom that comes from his lips." Edgar had found an intuitive tool for tapping his own internal wisdom.

The following dialogue is similar to what Edgar Bergen had been having with Charlie McCarthy. I had put myself in a meditative state and imagined I was having the following conversation with my internal image of God. I wrote down the questions and answers as they came to mind. I find this method helps articulate the following ideas in a more fluid way. I asked how I should write the following information, and the answer that came was,

"Do you want Me to write it for you?"

"Yes," I said, "Isn't that the idea behind intuition, inspiration and wisdom?"

God's next answer was, *"Then who will get the credit?"*

"Okay, you can have the credit, just help me out a little," I replied.

"You need to explain the Divinity Principle."

"What is the Divinity Principle?"

"I will explain it this way. In the beginning was the void, and the void was Me, God. All things, which came from the void were my ideas expressed in energy forms. Every manifestation, object, thing and form is my energy operating at different vibrations; I am all things and all things are Me.

"You are my energy produced in a form, which you call Phil. One might say that I have an experience of myself as Phil or as anyone else for that matter. I express and experience myself as trees, birds, bees, oceans, worlds, planets and Universes. All is vibrating at different speeds through my Energy.

"You and all other humans are shaped from my Image of Self, truly I am as you and you are as I am. Do you doubt this?"

"Well it has been a hard concept, or reality, for me to grasp. I see difficulties and limitations that make me believe I am anyone else but you."

"Yes, and there is the rub. You believe in difficulties and limitations, and hide from your unlimited potential. Did my Son not say to you, 'Even greater things than I you shall also do?' Wouldn't this mean you are equal to Him in resources and strengths, otherwise you could not do the things He did, or more, is this true?"

"Yes, here comes the 'but.' But I have never experienced doing any of the things He did. How do I get to that state?"

"You see, there is the big lie! You come from a position of self-perceived powerlessness. Yet have I not shown you to your strength and powers many times in many ways? How many times have you acted blindly and seen amazing results then written it off to chance, or had wonderful ideas and great inspirations, then failed to act on them? Did you ever wonder where these great ideas and inspirations came from, or again did you just consider it another piece of luck?

"What of the guides, teachers and mentors I sent you? Were they not there when you needed them? Remember the times when you just barely avoided an accident, or some other traumatic occurrence and

said, *'Boy it's a miracle I was not killed.' And you were right it was a miracle.*

"*All your life you have had moments of ecstasy, bliss, insights, and miraculous answers to your prayers and supplications. Yet in all of this, you chalked it up as coincidence and went back to your beliefs in limitation, struggle and lack. You never recognized or gave yourself credit for realizing and expressing your soul or God-Self, which is Me.*

"*As long as you continue believing and thinking you are separate from Me, and need an outer self-image, relationship, money or any 'thing' to give you an identity that you hope will prove to yourself or others that you are okay, the struggle will carry on. In fact, it will carry on forever more until you decide to change. I gave you FREE WILL, which means that the choice is always yours to think and believe whatever you want.*

"*The good news is that every one is an extension of myself as God, everyone has all the resources that go along with this reality.*"

"What do I do to attain this realization or understanding so that my life can be more effective or real?"

"*Consistently remind yourself that you and I are one; then express and do all things in harmony with this concept. As you do this on a daily basis you begin to experience a new sense of BEING in every cell in your body. Gradually, but surely, things begin to change and you experience a new aliveness and zest for living.*

"*You are the greatest aspect of My Self. As humans, unlike any other organism, you have the wisdom and free will to reflect on your origins, and find answers to the question 'Who Am I?' You can be aware of more than your surroundings, you have the ability to see things not seen and hear things not heard. You can realize powers, healing, insights and wisdom far beyond your rational minds. You have potential beyond your wildest dreams.*

"*Once you were born, you arrived in a culture that did not believe any of the above. Any time you would express or do something outside of your society's collective beliefs you were told 'That is not okay.' Being young and innocent you decided to give in to the beliefs of the society you belonged to.*

"Each society has a set of standards based on a belief in good and evil, right and wrong. For example, in one society you may have only one wife, whereas in other societies, 'the more the merrier.' Did you know in some egalitarian communal societies that they see stealing as a benefit to others? They hold everyone equal and everything belongs to every member of the tribe. For them it is wrong to hold on to something and not share it with others. Often, when they visit a regular village, they steal the villagers' chickens and things to teach them a lesson against selfishness and hoarding.

"In your society your religious beliefs often infer that you are born in sin. What a way to enter life. It is like you are BAD before you get started. You have not done anything as a baby that could be considered right or wrong even by your standards, yet you say the baby is born in sin. Then spend the rest of your life trying to prove to yourself and others that you are good enough.

"This sin business produces all sorts of judgment, condemnation and destructive activities. Yet my Son Jesus asked you over and over not to judge or condemn others and yourself.

"I think I have gotten a lot of undeserved destructive press over this sin business.

"Once you recognize that you and I are One, you begin to experience what love truly is. In Oneness with Me, your desires change for the better, your insecurities begin to disappear, your expressions are more fulfilling,

"Through your realization and practice of remembering you and God are One, and as this is experienced and understood **then there is no more:**

- *separation;*
- *need for a self-image other than being one with Me, your God-Self;*
- *need for external gratification for identity purposes;*
- *guilt, shame, or self-incriminating judgments;*
- *duality—your addiction to good and evil begin to disappear along with condemnation.*

You will also find that:

- *anger dissipates quickly;*
- *relationships become stronger;*
- *true meaning and purpose are found;*
- *ecstasy and joy are more of a constant companion;*
- *more creativity appears in every aspect of your life;*
- *loneliness disappears;*
- *you enjoy control and mastery of your life.*

"You see how much of life you have denied from yourself and others, and when you deny yourself you deny Me.

"Phil, you are writing about a profound concept—that of having people recognize themselves as Me. Some will find this easier than others. For many the idea is difficult due to their ingrained beliefs, ideals and false concepts of self. Many have been told all their lives that they are not good enough—Therefore, how could they believe that they are as God?

"Furthermore, due to their sufferings they have felt I have cut myself off from them, or that I should take away their suffering. I cannot do this without denying their free will. Then they would ac-cuse Me of being an interfering judgmental God. Yet, as I mentioned earlier, I am constantly sending them many signs through their dreams, teachers, guides, and healers, but they choose to ignore these and press on with their own misguided beliefs. So, on the one hand, I live up to my promise that they can have whatever they want, even though it may be destroying them, and on the other, I am con-stantly trying to influence them towards making better choices.

"You see they have forgotten what it was like to live in the all fulfilling dimension of Oneness with Me, which would provide them with all they truly want and the wisdom to know what this is and what to do with it."

"What about people who say, 'This is all fine and dandy, but I still am up to my ears in debt and I have a wife and family to sup-port, kids to raise . . . '?

"These people are still caught in the outer conditions of their lives as representing their internal emotional state. These two states have nothing in common other than what they choose to give them.

As long as they are letting the external conditions create their inner state of being, they will be in bondage to the outer circumstances and events of their lives. Furthermore, because this is where they are putting their energy, they will keep perpetuating the same problems. Remember, like attracts like.

"If they would attempt even for a moment to take themselves seriously as a Divine Being who resides in the Oneness of Myself and begin to express those things that are in harmony with this image, they would gradually experience themselves differently. The more they do this, the more they will manifest the life they truly want and the things they want."

"This is really helpful, thank you for this dialogue, and I will see that you get the credit."

"Bless you."

The above reminds me of an old Sufi story concerning an old and holy monk named Alfredo. Alfredo died and went before the holy gates of heaven. He knocked loudly on the gates. A booming voice then asked, "Who wishes to enter?" The monk replied meekly, "Alfredo, the monk."

"Go away," said the voice. "There is no room for Alfredo the monk in here." Heartbroken at this rejection, the old monk wandered the spaces separating heaven and earth for several years before he again approached the Pearly Gates.

Again the voice asked, "Who is it that wants entry?"

Alfredo replied in a meek and tired voice, "It is Alfredo, a human being who served you all his life."

Once more the voice exclaimed, "There is no room for Alfredo the human in here. Go." Totally mortified and broken, Alfredo spent the next few years trying to figure it all out. Finally, Alfredo hit on an idea, and returned to Heaven's gates.

The voice repeated the same question, "Who is it that wants entry into Heaven?" But this time, Alfredo said in a loud voice, "It is you!" Then, much to Alfredo's pleasure, the gates opened wide.

The voice now said, "Enter. You see, there never was enough room in heaven (or on earth) for both you and I."

This story is just another way of saying that God and I are one and the same.

If there is an afterlife, it is also likely that there is a God. If there is a God, where do you stand in relation to being *one with your God*?

Let us go back to the primary belief of many major religions:

- There is one supreme being.
- God is all things, and God generated all things.
- God is omniscient, omnipotent and omnipresent.
- There is nothing within the universe or beyond where God is not intrinsically and fully present.

The following is the concept of God that I have now come to accept: God is in every atom and cell of every living thing and every thing that is not living. Now, in reaching this belief, I was able to go the next step and say, "If God is all things, God must be all of me; as I am, so is God."

I now understand that there is nowhere within me where "God is not." For example, suppose I hurt my little finger, do you think I could keep this secret from God? There is no part of me of which God has no knowledge. Otherwise, if I could keep something from God, I would be greater than God.

Therefore, there is nothing in and outside of the universe that is beyond God's presence and knowledge. Again, as Jesus said, "Even the hairs on your head are numbered."

The Bible also says: "You are the temple of the living God."[5] Literally, this means that every living cell is a temple of God. God is always operating and thriving within every intimate, known and un-known, cell of your being. Otherwise, God would not be God. If there would be one place where God is not, God could not be all-powerful.

You are made in God's image. God not only is all things, but also experiences Him/Herself as Phil, Mary, Tom, or Joe.

Your life-force energy is God, and you are expressing this life-force energy any way you wish. What you want to do with this knowledge and resource is up to you. The only reason that you have been unhappy is that you never understood or believed this.

There is an old Sufi saying in which God says to man: *"You have seventy thousand veils that separate you from me, but I have none separating me from you."*

Jesus taught that the authority He had over what you see as natural forces is what you also have. His great difficulty was in trying to get this message across to His disciples. As they began to see and understand the concept, they finally began practising the things He had done.

Religious leaders and institutions are prone to create God in their image. Once that image has been set, they limit their beliefs to these self-made perceptions and are usually closed to new insights, beliefs and understandings. The disciples had to battle with their old religious images and beliefs as they compared them with the new concepts of God-like power that Jesus claimed they had. I believe that what we call miracles are normal experiences when you come from your true reality.

If God Is All Things, Is God Also Evil?

God is present in humans when we do things that are perceived as evil. Does this mean, then, that God has a shadow side that is also evil? Because of our free will, we can do so-called evil things. However, this does not deny that God is not present, but only that we have chosen to do things that others and ourselves may eventually find less than satisfying. The person is not evil; only their actions might be perceived as evil. If you have a child who murders others, you may despise the child's actions, but not the child. You may justifiably hate the choices the child has made, yet still have compassion for the child's ultimate welfare.

Evil is a human perception that varies within countries, races and religions. I like to think that people are not evil, only that they make choices detrimental to themselves and others. And because they have *free will,* God lets people make any choice they wish. Therefore, I believe that apart from our human perceptions and actions that we label as evil, God is always benevolent, and that the heart and core of God is love.

The Traits and Characteristics of God

For those of you who have done the exercises in the appendix, some of this may seem familiar; yet it will be worthwhile repeating.

I invite you to go back and do this exercise now if you have not already done it. Make sure you complete your God-Tree and write down what you feel are the traits of God.

You should find it very insightful and self-illuminating when you relate it to the following.

This is a list of God traits and characteristics that were obtained from participants at our seminars. Some had religious backgrounds, while others had none at all. Yet they all agreed collectively that this list represented the characteristics and traits of God. You may look over the list and add those to your God list from the exercise.

God List

truth	centeredness	choice	beauty
health	freedom	light	worth
strength	consciousness	gratitude	originality
self-healing	mystique	decisiveness	essence
value	potential	miraculousness	might
magic	regality	excellence	morality
compassion	power	specialness	soul
creativity	uniqueness	benevolence	oneness
omniscience	forgiveness	simplicity	faith
omnipresence	consideration	omnipotence	unity
connectedness	oneness-with-all		

Awake! This is You!

The amazing thing is that this list is all about you. You could not write about the characteristics of God unless you had some knowledge and experience of what it is you are writing about.

No one would search for a gold mine if they did not know what a gold mine was. To search or try to get something you must have an idea of what you are searching for. The same is true of *unity, oneness* and *true being*. Deep within, you have always known this exists, yet you may have looked in all the wrong places and accepted external and artificial representations of what it is your looking for. You forgot that all the ecstatic joyful pleasures you sought were already within you.

My daughter Gloria expressed it well, saying, "It was like I was always looking for second-hand joy."

The desire for unity is brought about by your soul's remembering what its true home within God is. The work is about remembering what your true nature has always been and doing all things that are in harmony with your image of being as God. When we finally expose our "true selves" to ourselves, all we find is pure love—a love so great that it enthrones every wondrous, ecstatic, orgasmic feeling we ever had.

As previously mentioned, this can be helped by memories, perhaps those of a child, when you were awake to the wonder and awe of being fully alive. It may have been in a church or some sacred setting when you experienced a state of bliss or peace. It may also have happened in nature when you felt a *oneness* with all things. Possibly, it happened in a relationship, during lovemaking or at some other momentous occasion.

Your love center is built in. We all have this inner hunger and drive for something that we know is there. You have been searching for it, albeit in all the wrong places. You never understood it was always within you.

This is not about changing your desires, but it is about changing the erroneous focus of your desires to a more personally enriching and rewarding awareness.

Go back over your God-Tree exercise and the words you wrote describing the traits of God. Next, claim each of the traits of God as a trait within yourself. "Impossible!" You might say. "How can I be all wise, create miracles, be all powerful, or anything like God?"

Well, let us take them one at a time:

1. *All wise:* Have you not at times experienced insights, or a piece of wisdom that surprised not only yourself, but others as well?
2. *Miracles:* Have you not desired, prayed or believed something would come about, or happen, and it did?
3. *All powerful:* I interpret power to mean strength within myself, not over others. So, if I were internally strong then the things of the world, people and events would

not bother me. I would be staying centered and in my strength regardless of what else was going on around me.

On the other hand, we have been given the strength to move mountains, depending on our belief. As in miracles, each of us has had the experience of performing some feat, deed or act beyond his/her normal abilities. After having such an experience, we may have caught ourselves saying, "If I had been given more time to think about it I probably would not have done it."

It is these coincidences, surprises, insights and strengths that are experiences of our God-Self. We think of them as chance occurrences, and give them little credit. Yet they show us to the hidden resources that lie within us all.

By going over your God list and owning each characteristic or trait as yourself you will begin to realize your own greatness.

To complete this part of your process, I now invite you to do the next and last exercise #3 in the appendix. If entered into seriously, this exercise provides a very powerful experience.

When Self-image Disappears—God Comes Through

The key to making changes and transforming yourself begins with your beliefs about your identity. What predicts your future is your identity. Your life and all you have in it now is due to your way of making choices that have conformed to your old self-image. Change your self-image for the highest possible self-mage you can imagine and your life will change accordingly. Is there a higher image than being as God, and what other image could offer you more than this?

This, then, would be your first challenge. Hopefully by now you have come to believe that you are *at one with God* and are as God. This is probably a very challenging belief for some people to begin perceiving. The few who take this seriously are taking the first step for having the life they always dreamed of. It is not that you are God apart or above all things, but as all things are God, then so are you.

Within this God-Self-image is all that you ever really wanted. Can you imagine, after referring to your God list, anything else in life that would be more satisfying than consistently experiencing these items on your God list? It would be difficult to describe your levels of happiness. Words like ecstasy, bliss, and joy are probably just a beginning.

Has it not been said that "the eye has not seen, nor ear heard, nor the heart of man conceived what God has prepared for those who love Him."[6] Like many people, you may think, "How could I ever attain such happiness, power, love, wisdom and understanding?" Yet, as has been previously shown, already in your life you have had these experiences, moments, insights and understandings. In the past you chose to ignore them as chance, or coincidence, or you just denied them.

The way of being your God-Self is to remember these experiences, then add to them a new belief about yourself. These experiences came from you, the God-like person that you are.

A movie that most profoundly makes this point is *A Leap of Faith.* Steve Martin plays a phony faith healing evangelist who travels from town to town, using high-tech gadgets to fool people into thinking that he is the voice of God and a healer. He arrives with a full set of tent equipment and attendants who act as technicians and gospel singers.

At the end of the movie, a young crippled boy, whom Steve got to know earlier, comes forward and asks for a healing from Steve's character. The audience gets behind the lad, and everyone is yelling for Steve to heal the boy. Finally, Steve is backed into a corner and there is nothing he can do but to lay hands on the kid and pray for him. This he does, and to the boy's ecstatic joy and the audience's praise, he is healed.

Steve is overwhelmed. He cannot believe it has happened. The next scene shows Steve sneaking off the grounds, getting into his car, and driving away. He had come face to face with his own power and could not accept it. It was more than he could handle and against all his beliefs.

As he drives away, he mutters something about going to Miami where there are more shady opportunities. Here he had everything he had ever wanted. The greatest magic and power anyone could ever ask for, literally right in the palm of his hand; yet it was too much. It was against everything he believed about himself and life. To accept it he would have to change all his beliefs. He could not do that.

There is a lot of truth in that movie. I have seen similar things happen in real life. People get a glimpse of their true potential and run and hide, for it is too overwhelming. It has been said over and over throughout history, in many different ways, that our one great fear is that of our own true greatness.

Most of us look at our weaknesses and failures and think of them as representing who we are. As long as we live with an illusion that we are separate from God, we continue producing all the things we do not like about ourselves. Within this concept of separation, we choose to express hate, anger, jealousy, and so on. Because of our false belief that we are not God or pure love, we create a false self-image that relies on our outer world for its gratification and identity. In this world, hate, greed and insecurity abound, whereas all that separates us from the love and joy of our true divine nature is an erroneous belief that we are not *one with God.* Because of this belief, we are all in denial of being the Godly person we really are.

Please answer the questions on the next page.

CHAPTER 3 QUESTIONS

1. Have I had experiences that would include some of the items on my God list? These could relate to: intuitions, hunches, coincidences, bliss, ecstasies, wonders, awe, insights, premonitions, visions, miracles and other related items. List three.

2. What was I doing at the time that may have helped facilitate these experiences? This can include location and a particular period in my life.

3. How intuitive am I? (from 1-10) How has it helped me in the past?

4. What does the concept of *self as God* mean to me?

5. Am I willing to say, "I am one with God; God is all that I am"?

6. Has there ever been a time when I have not expressed my God-Self?

7. What is one of the first things I could do to begin expressing and experiencing my understanding of God-Self?

8. What is my new self-image?

CHAPTER 4

A Way of Being

*Where there was a human sense of being there is now the
spiritual livingness in the Kingdom of God my Kingdom
on earth. I see this . . . I feel it . . .*

—*John Randolph Price*[7]

In the last chapter, we explored our 'great self' through the God
list and the experiential exercises in the appendix. If you did the
exercises, you now realize there is more to you than your rational
mind. In this chapter, we will expand and integrate your experiences
and insights.

A Case History

The following story is interesting because it concerns a person's
journey into the reality of being *one with God* and belies the belief
that we must be perfect before we can experience God. It tells how
the embracing of this divine reality brings about the changes, in spite
of our human weaknesses.

This story is about a client, who we will call John. He was
heavily involved in the drug scene, and had mixed this with an interest in metaphysics and spiritual pursuits. On his first visit, he told
me of a time, two years prior, when he was sent to a mental institu-

tion. He said he was there because he thought he was Jesus Christ. Of course, the hospital staff thought he was delusional, and said he could not leave unless he no longer claimed he was Jesus Christ.

My first reaction to his stay in a mental hospital was similar to that of the institution, and I chalked it up as a delusional episode, brought about by drugs.

Our visits were irregular and after about three months they ended. I thought no more about it until after I became involved with *The Art of Purposeful Being.* The next time he came, I asked again about his experience of being Jesus Christ. His surprising answer was, "It wasn't that I was the only one who was Jesus Christ. I could see that everyone was. I would keep looking at the nurses and doctors, and it was as if I could see behind all their fears, doubts, and low self-worth. I kept telling them that "You could be full of joy and feel as free as I am. You can be Jesus too."

"Then they would just give me more needles and drugs until finally I never wanted to be Jesus Christ again. Ever since, I am always afraid that I might feel that good again and get sent back to the hospital."

Together, through *Purposeful Being,* we worked at getting him back to being Christ-like. About a year later, I came back from a Christmas holiday and received a message that he wanted to see me. I phoned and asked what was up. He said, "I am Christ again." "Wonderful," I said. "Let us get together."

At his next session, he told me that he had been feeling depressed and had gone outside and yelled at God, wanting to experience Him again. Immediately, he began to feel ecstatic and had felt this way ever since. He was a little afraid of it being another psychotic episode but felt, because of the sanity in other areas of his life, that it must not be so. Also, because of the consistency of this Christ-like experience, he felt substances or other circumstances would not have let the high last so long.

I confirmed his insights and assured him that I saw no need for any concern, and encouraged him to enjoy, and continue practising being *one-with-God* through *Purposeful Being,* which he has done ever since.

Gradually, by staying in his new-found image of being as Christ, the irregularities in his life have been falling away. So much has changed in his life that he has become a different person. It has not been easy. Shortly after his second experience, his wife and children left him. He lost all he had financially. Yet through it all he has maintained his true identity and is gradually learning to express himself in more harmonious ways with his new reality of *being.*

John did not take on his Christ-like identity as a way of overcoming his involvement with drugs and his unsavory lifestyle. He took on this God-like experience because it was the best drug he had ever had. Then, as he realized his *Christ-self* more and more, the negative aspects of his life began to change.

Towards a Deeper Spirituality

The issue of being as God is a problem only when you believe that you are the only one. Everyone is a Christ, meaning God incarnate in human form. If I had had the impression that John considered himself to be the one and only Messiah, it would have been a different matter.

John's story also shows, regardless of our religious belief, lifestyle, background, color or race, that *oneness-with-God* is all-inclusive and present in everyone. When we look for human images of God, each person names or sees God in the image that is most familiar, such as that of Jesus, Buddha, Mohammed, and so on. In other words, we create God in our own image.

This brings us to claiming who we are. Buddha, Mohammed, and Jesus were all spiritual icons of their cultures. Each was a figure in whom the ideals of divinity-in-man were manifested. For many people in many cultures, these spiritual giants became God incarnate. It would seem this step was necessary so that we could recognize the power and presence of God in human form. These personages best exemplified spiritually empowering possibilities that are open to the human condition.

The evolution of spirituality in western consciousness can be seen in our Judaic-Christian tradition, beginning with the Hebrew people. The Hebrews considered God as a sky God, a God beyond reach who only spoke through selected people, such as prophets, or spiritual leaders like Abraham and Moses. In the early Hebrew tradition, God's name was so sacred that no one was permitted to pronounce it.

In the New Testament, we have a more human God in Jesus Christ. This incarnation into human flesh by the Divine was a momentous leap in Western Spiritual understanding. God becomes visible and physical. He presents Himself as a human representation of God. A human with the highest qualities to which man, as God, can aspire. A God with whom we can both socialize and communicate.

Furthermore, God demonstrates a care and compassion for everyone, regardless of position or rank. We now have a human who fully understands that He and God is one. We have gone, then, from a sky God to a God human who has an understanding of His true identity, and who also uses the power that this understanding allows. This gives Him the wisdom and strength to perform acts beyond the perceived abilities of most humans at the time. History tells us that this transition was not easy. Those who wished to believe in the possibility that a human could be one with God were held up to ridicule, banishment, pain and torture.

Today, the concept is no longer foreign. Once we know that God in human form is a possibility, it is not much of a leap for us to understand that God represents Him/Herself as everyone.

Therefore, the final step in divine evolution in Western consciousness may well be like that of John in our story. We will all realize that God and we are *one* in human form, and that the only separation from our true divine nature is our beliefs and perceptions.

Jesus alluded to this in many of His Gospels. Both the idea that we are made in His image and the fact that we are told that "even greater works you shall also do" infer that we, too, should be operating within the power of our Christ- or God-like nature.

Throughout the gospels, Jesus admonishes His disciples because they will not exercise their power to do the things that He does. He expects them to be as Himself. He often refers to them as "men of little faith." For example, at one time, they are at sea during a storm. Afraid, they wake Him up and He calms the storm. Again, Jesus reprimands His disciples because He feels it was something they should have done.[8]

I am making these points to show that we have within us these powers and abilities, the same attributes as the God/man Jesus. We have the ability to exercise God-consciousness as effectively as Jesus Christ.

How Do You Know You Are One With God?

Basically, you know you are *one with God* through belief, expressions and experiences of your God-like nature. This means that, as you explore, express and experience your new insights and understandings, you gradually go from belief to surety.

This is unlike religions that are followed because of duty, or because their truths are imposed. Regardless of their truths, religions often create puppets or robots, stifling true spirituality.

This *way* is not about taking on something new, but remembering who we really are. Perhaps memory and intuition are intertwined, meaning that we have intuition about remembering what fits with our ultimate source.

Through realization and remembering our God-like nature, comes a *breakthrough,* a merging in consciousness, an inner awareness of *fusion-with-the-all.* Fusion happens when my realizations and expressions are in harmony with being as God. Then I am at my optimal living experience.

Why have we kept this reality of our true God-like nature a secret from others and ourselves? Because often we are so filled with our own limitations and unworthiness that we dare not imagine we can be anything greater.

A client, who I will call Bill, seemed to vacillate between a self-image of unworthiness and one of grandeur. He was having real trouble with this concept of being *one-with-God.* As Bill was a religious person, I asked him to sit in meditation before his favorite religious objects or pictures, and keep asking himself the question of "Who am I?"

He had done this for two weeks before receiving an answer that had overwhelmed him. It seems the answer was "You are Christ." Now this so shook him that he went into a deep depression, which took him quite some time to cure. Why? Because, if he accepted this God-like image of himself, all his beliefs in limitations and low self-worth would have to change. In other words, he would have to leave his old dissatisfying, but familiar, way of being.

Sometimes an encounter with our true self can be an overwhelming experience.

The Drive for Unity

Each of us is born with an inner drive to 'unite.' First it is with mothers, parents and siblings. Later with friends, social communities, churches, political groups, clubs and even gangs, and, of course, intimate relationships. The attraction of sex is based on a desire for 'unity.'

Religious practices and spiritual pursuits are also based on a desire for 'unity.' In fact, all attempts at altered states of consciousness are our attempts to unite with the All. Of course, there is no uniting to do, as we are already *one with God,* and it is only our mistaken beliefs that have separated us.

I would like to take this into another realm. To help you understand more succinctly the power of being as God, I wish to go to a first hand source of what this experience is about. I would like to refer to someone who had fully experienced this and was able to tell of it.

In recent years, ever since Raymond Moody's book *Life After Life* became a best seller, there has been a lot of interest from professionals and lay people alike in near-death experiences.

So much so, that organizations exist to study and chronicle these occurrences. *The Journal of Near Death Studies* and the *International Association for Near-Death Studies* chronicle all cases that come to their attention, which number in the thousands.

There are also other publications on the subject, including those by author Kenneth Ring who has applied scientific analyses to compare the different experiences of people who have near-death experiences,[9] and also Pierre Jovanovic, whose study I am about to quote.

I chose Jovanovic's case study because it exemplifies what Kenneth Ring calls a 'core experience,' meaning that the subject went all the way to a realization of its divine source. This case also appealed to me for another reason, namely that the subject's experience was not due to a death bed occurrence.[10]

A Near-Death Experience: A Case History

Here, then, is a case from *The Journal Of Near Death Studies,*[11] as reported by Pierre Jovanovic in his book *An Inquiry Into The Existence Of Angels.*

Beverly was a Jewish girl of twenty years. After her father died, her mother became quite depressed, so Beverly ran away from home. Jovanovic quotes her account:

> Since learning, in very muted terms, of the Holocaust at age eight I had turned angrily against any belief in God. How could God exist and permit such a thing to occur? The secularism of my public school education and the lack of any religious training added fuel to my beliefs. (49)

She leaves Philadelphia for the eternal sunshine of California and arrives in Los Angeles at the high tide of the hippie years. The next day, to celebrate her arrival, a friend suggests a spin on his motorcycle. Far from the oppressive atmosphere of her home, she finally feels happy and carefree, and hops onto the passenger seat.

The ride through the California desert ends badly. On a baking-hot narrow road, a drunken driver smashes into the bike. Without a helmet, Beverly is flung clear, finally crashing headfirst to the ground, then sliding several yards, leaving behind the skin of her face.

She spends the next two weeks in the hospital, full of anesthetics and tranquilizers to help her stand the pain of her fractures. Finally, she is released from the hospital. She goes back to her little temporary apartment, sets down her bag, and opens the bathroom door. She switches on the light and, for the first time, takes a good look at herself in the mirror.

She is disfigured. Her face is the face of a mutant. Suddenly, she realizes that with a face like that, no man will ever look at her twice again. That thought becomes an obsession, a nightmare. She collapses in tears.

She weeps and weeps as she has never wept before. After the loss of her father, this accident is the straw that breaks the camel's back. She reaches the depths of despair and, for the first time in her life (like so many people), she turns to God—the only hypothetical friend she has left. Praying to him, she begs him to carry her off, once and for all. Beverly's own words recall her experience.

> I could not live another day. At 20 I had no goals but to enjoy life and to find someone to share it with. The pain was unbearable: no man would ever love me; there was, for me, no reason to go on living.
>
> Somehow an unexpected peace descended upon me. I found myself floating on the ceiling over the bed looking down at my unconscious body. I barely had time to realize the glorious strangeness of the situation—that I was me but not in my body— when I was joined by a radiant being bathed in a shimmering white glow. Like myself, this being flew but had no wings. I felt a reverent awe when I turned to him: this was no ordinary angel or spirit, but he had been sent to deliver me. Such love and gentleness emanated from his being that I felt that I was in the presence of the Messiah.
>
> Whoever he was, his presence deepened my serenity and awakened a feeling of joy as I recognized my companion. Gently he took my hand and we flew right through the window. I felt no surprise at my ability to do this. In this wondrous presence everything was as it should be.
>
> Beneath us lay the beautiful Pacific Ocean, over which I had excitedly watched the sun set when I had first arrived. But my attention was now directed upward, where there was a large opening leading to a circular path. Although it seemed to be deep and far to the other end, a white light shone through and poured out into the gloom to the other side where the opening beckoned. It was the most brilliant light I had ever seen, although I didn't realize how much of its glory was veiled from the outside. The path was angled upward, obliquely, to the right. Now, still hand in hand with the angel, I was led into the opening of the small dark passageway. I then remember travelling a long distance upward toward the light. I believe that I was moving very fast, but this entire realm seemed to be outside of time. Finally, I reached my destination. It was only when I emerged from the other end that I realized I was no longer accompanied by the being who had brought me there. But I was not alone. There, before me, was the living presence of the light. Within it I sensed an all-pervading intelligence, wisdom, compassion, love and truth. There was neither form nor sex to this perfect Being. It, which I shall in the future call He, in keeping with

our commonly accepted syntax, contained everything, as white light contains all the colors of a rainbow when penetrating a prism. And deep within me came an instant and wondrous recognition: I, even I, was facing God.

I immediately lashed out at Him with all the questions I had ever wondered about, all the injustices I had seen in the physical world. I do not know if I did this deliberately, but I discovered that God knew all your thoughts immediately and responds telepathically. My mind was naked; in fact, **I became pure mind.** The ethereal body that I had traveled in through the tunnel seemed no more. It was just my personal intelligence confronting that Universal Mind which clothed itself in a glorious, living light that was more felt than seen since no eye could absorb its splendor.

I don't recall the exact content of our discussion; in the process of return the insights that came so clearly and fully in Heaven were not brought back with me to Earth. I am sure that I asked the question that had been plaguing me since childhood about the sufferings of my people. I do remember this: there was a reason for everything that happened, no matter how awful it appeared in the physical realm. And within myself, as I was given the answer, my own awakening mind now responded in the same manner: **"Of course," I would think, "I already know that. How could I have ever forgotten!"** Indeed it appears that **all that happens is for a purpose, and that purpose is already known to our eternal self.**

In time the questions ceased, because I suddenly was filled with the Being's wisdom, I was given more than just the answers to my questions; **all knowledge unfolded to me,** like the instant blossoming of an infinite number of flowers all at once. **I was filled with God's knowledge, and in that precious aspect of his Beingness, I was one with him** (My emphases) (49-50).

Again, this is not a normal near-death experience, as there is no physical death at the time of her experience. Yet she did have the same kind of core experience that many NDE subjects have had. The following points are highlighted from Beverly's story:

1. *"I lashed out at Him."* At this point, she is still angry at what she perceives are the wrongs in the world. She is caught in the duality of good and evil. Later, God helps her to understand this.

2. ***"I became pure mind."*** This was her first indication of her true God-like nature.
3. ***"Of course,"*** I would think, ***"I already know that."*** It seemed as if all the information and answers to her questions were already known, but had been previously forgotten, suggesting that she has been to this realization of 'All-knowing' before.
4. ***". . . All that happens is for a purpose, and that purpose is already known to our eternal self."*** From this we can assume that her purpose was known and agreed upon prior to entering this time period. I say 'agreed upon' because we always have free will. Also, it was here she was informed that what she thought to be evil, the world's suffering (duality), was part of an overall purpose.
5. ***". . . All knowledge unfolded to me, . . . I was filled with God's knowledge, . . . I was one with him."*** She had reached a realization of her ultimate union, or fusion with the all. She was one in knowledge and wisdom with the Divine.

Her story gives us a glimpse, in human terminology, of the bliss and ecstasy she must have experienced.

The interesting thing about Beverly's story is that she goes through all of the various steps until she realizes her complete unity with God. She becomes aware of her greater capacity at understanding and knowing all things. And finally she is aware not only of her God-Self, but the tremendous joy and ecstasy this brings.

Many might read into this that we must die to appreciate a lot of what Beverly experienced. Not so. Any study of people who have had a near-death experience shows that once they returned, decided to change their lives, and live from whom they truly are, they then begin experiencing heaven here on earth. All we need to do is start living our God-Self now, which is what Jesus, Buddha, and many saints and mystics have taught us in their various ways, all along.

The above personal encounter with God, and the ultimate awareness of fusion that took place as Beverly realized that she and God are *one,* is about her awareness that God is at the seat or soul of her being. This represents the journey of consciousness for all of us, *the journey home.*

To begin the journey, you must start at the end to claim your heritage—your true identity—which is *"God and I are one, I am as God."*

By constantly acknowledging your God-Self from moment to moment, you allow it to take hold, then the realization of you as being your God-Self is experienced as a reality.

This is the task, your #1 project, focusing, perceiving, believing and doing only that which helps you realize you and God are *one.* This is the objective of this book.

CHAPTER 4 QUESTIONS

How would you imagine that the acceptance of yourself as *one with God* would impact all areas of your life?

1. Being as God requires . . .

2. What changes would take place as you lived from this new awareness of being as God?

3. What would be happening that would make this God as self concept real for you?

4. Since beginning this book, how have you experienced or thought of yourself differently? Explain the changes.

5. Having realized your divine self, what limits would you place on living your dreams?

6. How in the past have your desires for *uniting, surviving* and *social programming* affected your life?

7. How would being your God-Self begin to change that?

CHAPTER 5

The Power of One

> *God is a sphere who's centre is everywhere*
> *and whose circumference is nowhere.*
> *—Hermes Trismegistus*

Let us review what we have covered so far:

- Having a self-made image other than your *God-Self* puts you in a mental form of separation from your true reality.
- You are your #1 project.
- Realizing your true God nature at all times, you only express that which is in harmony with your God-Self, such as all things on your God list. For example, on this list you have 'love.' If you believe God is pure love, then all thoughts, feelings, attitudes and actions relating to love show you to your God-Self. This will get simpler when, later, we will help you realize your *soul's purpose;* now you only need to choose the loving things that help you sustain your sense of being as God. Any thoughts, feelings, attitudes and actions not in harmony with your concept of God-as-love will keep you in a mental form of separation from your true self. But remember, all separation is just a perception, because you can never be separate from God.

- Every decision you have ever made has taken you to this point in your life. You can truly say you are constantly creating the life you are living.
- To realize you have a self-chosen *purposeful way of being and living* that is practised daily to deepen your experience of being your God-Self.
- Through experiencing your God-tree meditation and God list, you should now have a greater sense of self, as well as a home base from which you can build your life.

Science and the Power of Oneness

The concept of *oneness* is not new. Parmenides, a Greek philosopher considered to be the founder of western philosophy and metaphysics in the fifth century BC, was the first to consider this idea of *oneness*. Throughout the ages, his theory has been argued back and forth by philosophers and theologians. It is sometimes referred to as monism. A few of the philosophers and theologians that addressed this topic were Baruch Spinoza, St. Thomas Aquinas, and St. Augustine. Parimenedes and Spinoza held the view that whatever exists is a part of a single substance; therefore, all things are God.[12]

Up until now, we have discussed *oneness* from a philosophical, psychological and personal point of view. There is still the question of what science can show us about this theory. The following studies show how science seems to be catching up with philosophers and theologians as scientists are now addressing theories of the supernatural, spirituality and the theory of *oneness* in their labs.

Science, Oneness and the Universal Mind

This concept of *oneness* is so powerful that it works when done subliminally and without participants knowing what is happening.

Psychiatrist Lloyd Silverman of New York University conducted an important series of studies which show even the subliminal effects of *oneness* to have far-reaching effects.

"Mommy and I are One"

The sentence *"Mommy and I are one"* was flashed to groups of students subliminally (without their awareness). When they were later tested on a variety of tasks, achievements, exam scores and aspirations, all their performances were enhanced.

The aim of this study was to prove that having an experience of *oneness* would enhance performance; and it did. In their book *Super Learning 2000,* Sheila Ostrander, Lynn Schroeder, and Nancy Ostrander report that since Silverman introduced this study twenty-five years ago, his idea of the power of *'Mommy and I are one'* has been used to improve almost anything. Improvements have been found in math, sports and dart scores, as well as weight loss, law exams, and so on. Other studies bear witness to the same principle.

The Mother Theresa Affect

In his book, *Healing Words,* Dr. Larry Dossey reports on the findings of David McClelland, Ph.D., of Harvard Medical School, that demonstrate the healing power of love through "The Mother Theresa Affect." McClelland showed a group of Harvard students a documentary of Mother Theresa administering loving care to the sick. Before and after seeing the film, however, he measured the students' immunity by measuring the IgA levels in their saliva—IgA being an active antibody used against viral infections, such as colds. The students' IgA levels rose significantly, even in those students who considered Mother Theresa as being too religious, or a fake.

The above two studies show the powers of love and *oneness,* even when people are seemingly unaware of their own process. Imagine, as in the first study, what kind of results you would have by purposefully meditating on being *one-with-God* instead of one-with-Mommy.

"The Mother Theresa Affect" in the second study shows how love is transformational, even when it happens without your awareness. If love is synonymous with God, purposefully loving *is just another way of being as God in consciousness.* Therefore, by purposefully doing *oneness* and *loving,* you are on the fast track to having the life of your dreams.

This concept of *oneness* is further extended when we consider the possibility of there being just one Universal Mind of which we are all a part.

In the same book, Dr. Dossey reports numerous studies relating to mind, prayer and healing.[13] He refers to prayer and distant healing as 'non-local.' This means that you have a 'pray-er,' and a 'receiver.' The receiver may be miles away, yet when measured on the right type of scientific monitoring devices, the receiver is observed to have the healing experience at the same time it is sent. There is no lapse of time involved. There is a *oneness, or intrinsic connection* between all individuals, which is outside of our previous understanding of time and space. As stated by Dr. Dossey:

> Mind, a factor in healing both within and beyond persons. Mind not completely localized to points in space (brains or bodies) or times (present moment or single lifetimes) mind is unbounded and infinite in space and time-thus omnipresent, eternal, and ultimately unitary or one. Healing at a distance is possible. Not describable by classical concepts of space-time or matter-energy. (41)

Dr. Dossey also reports on studies by Princeton Engineering Anomalies Research (PEAR) Laboratory. They conducted studies to determine if subjects could influence random events on a mechanical device, which they called the Random Event Generator. The subjects sit in front of this device and try to influence the random selection of numbers in a positive or negative direction. Over the years, they have conducted 2,520,000 trials on the same device. The results are overwhelming and show that individuals can influence random numbers to form specific patterns on a mechanical device. It did not matter whether the subjects were sitting directly in front of the machine, or on the other side of the world; the results were equally impressive, regardless of the subject's whereabouts.

Physicist Helmut Schmidt further supports these experiments by showing how subjects could influence the output of a microelectronic random generator, even after the machine has stopped.

Since first reading this material, I have acquired a similar device that is played through my computer. It is called Shapechanger and is based on the experiments done at Princeton University and their PEAR project. The object of this program is to sit and focus on an image that is flashed on the screen randomly and see if you can stop its random movement. It is amazingly easy to do. There is no physical contact with the computer other than your will.

Psychologist Rev. John H. Hampsch tells in his recording, *Healing of Memories,* about a rather abusive animal study that relates to time and distance. The Russians (during the cold war) took baby rabbits three hundred miles out to sea in a submarine. The submarine was submerged for the experiment. Back on Russian soil they took the mother rabbit and attached her to an electronic monitoring device. Then, at a pre-arranged time, the crew in the submarine chopped off the baby rabbits' heads. At exactly the same time the head cutting occurred, the electronic monitoring device attached to the mother rabbit reacted wildly, causing extreme fluctuations in its recording apparatus.

This is just another indication of the interconnectedness of everything in our Universe, which challenges our previous suppositions about time and energy and space.

We have all heard stories of how parents, and particularly mothers, have had premonitions of something traumatic happening to their children even though they were hundreds of miles away. Later, they found that the premonition occurred at the same time that an unfortunate event took place.

I mention the above to show how all of us are connected to each other and everything around us. We are all intrinsically *one with the One Universal Mind.*

Scientific Studies on the Power of Belief, Thought and Imagination

At the healing level, Dr. Dossey goes on to show the miraculous affect that takes place in healing through prayer and the power of the mind. Whether or not those who prayed or meditated for others were religious or spiritual seems to be of little consequence. What seems to matter is compassionate intention.

If this is true, and I assure you it is, then miraculous feats such as those Jesus did in regard to healing, calming the storm, and feeding the five thousand no longer seem to be beyond the realm of human possibility. What if miracle workers, faith healers, rain makers, and seers were all just expressing our God-like nature that has been with us since time immemorial?

What this means to *Purposeful Being* is that if you recognize your *oneness-with-the-All* your God-Self and wish to share in the power of what this means, reshaping your thinking in line with your new belief of who you truly are is very important. Let us go back to our pie design of chapter 2. If, in the mental section, you entertain negative, depressing, self-deprecating, envious, angry, and self-pitying type thoughts, they, in turn, can create feelings and emotions and effect all other parts of the pie—that is all of your life—and your old self-image will be retained.

To give you further proof of how powerful your thoughts are in relation to your health, two studies were done, one in Manitoba and one in Alameda County, California. Both studies focused on the same question, which was "How would you rate your health? Excellent, good, fair, poor, or bad?" I invite you to answer the above question and mark off one of the above that you feel relates to your state of health.

The gist of these studies is this: No matter how good their health was according to their physician's reports, those that rated themselves fair, poor, or bad, died much earlier than those who rated themselves good, or excellent. Even if they were in worse shape than those who rated themselves fair, poor, or bad, as long as they *thought* their health to be good, or excellent, they still lived longer, regardless of their medical condition.[14]

So, how did you rate yourself on the test? These studies show that beliefs and thoughts can be a life and death matter. The point of all this is that by realizing and expressing *at-one-ment* as your reality, the more you will feel fulfilled. If you completely and fully believe that you and God are one, you will move towards perfect health, fear nothing, want for nothing, and have access to all wisdom.

The Folly in Positive Thinking

When people are asked what they would do to change their self-image, they say, "I would change my attitude and be more positive."

This is not enough. Why? Any thoughts that are not in harmony with your new beliefs of who you are are no longer an option, regardless of how positive these thoughts may be. You see, what brought you up or down in the past had a lot to do with the way you believed and thought. You might have felt you were a fairly positive-thinking person, but your life did not always seem to reflect that. Why? Because, without having a true understanding of who you are, what you were thinking positive about may have been detrimental in the long run. It is not enough to say that I think positive, or I am a positive person. The question is "What are you thinking or being positive about?"

I call it 'the folly of positive thinking.' I can think positive about a myriad of things that, in the end, may be harmful to others as well as myself. Or I can have a great attitude about something and still miss the mark. Hitler was a very positive thinker with a very positive attitude. He took a destroyed and broken country and turned it into the most successful economic nation in the world during the world's greatest depression. Furthermore, out of nothing he created the strongest military force in the world. It took the combined power of the industrial nations to overcome his military creation. He was very positive, with a very positive attitude, but with a very destructive focus for himself and others. Hitler was very much into getting power for himself and his country at the rest of the world's expense. Hitler got what he wanted, but it cost him his life, and the lives of millions.

This is true with positive thinking and attitudes. The first thing in wanting something is to ascertain whether this thing that you are thinking positive about is in harmony with your newly realized self and purpose. The way to do this is to ask, "Would doing this (whatever it is) in this way and this manner serve my greatest and highest good forever more? From this point of view, you may think as positively as you wish about all things that are in harmony with whom you have *purposefully* chosen to be.

Most of us have never given much consideration to the power of thought. We usually have thousands of thoughts every day. We have not realized that it is our thoughts, beliefs and expressions that show us to who we are.

The ability to have strong and powerful beliefs about yourself helps you to have a healthy life. It is my belief that we can give ourselves no higher or more powerful belief or thought, than being *as God.* Pause and think for a moment: Is there another image, thing, or device that could offer you a greater potential for living than being as God?

The Healing Power of Imagery and Imagination

Another internal attribute is that which we call 'imagination.' It is a skill you have used all your life. As mentioned earlier, whatever you have gained or achieved in the past, began with your imagination. All human accomplishments are products of the imagination.

Today, many people use the power of imagination and visual imagery in regard to a host of activities. Imagery is used in everything from healing cancer to improving your ability to win at sports. To give you an idea of how specific this form of imagination and visualization can be, I include the following two studies.

Drs. Achterburg and Mark Rider conducted a study to see if visualization and imagery could affect specific pre-chosen cells. They examined the ability of subjects to affect specifically the numbers of certain types of white blood cells—neutrophils and lymphocytes—in the blood stream, which make up eighty-five to ninety percent of the total white cell count in the blood. Thirty subjects were randomly assigned to either the neutrophil or lymphocyte group, after which they underwent a six week training program, in which they focused on images of the shape, location, and patterns of movement of these cell types.

Music was used to enhance their imagery. Results showed that only the neutrophils decreased significantly in the neutrophil group, while only the lymphocytes decreased significantly in the lymphocyte group. The authors concluded that the highly directed *imagery* was cell-specific, that it affected the cells toward which it was intended or directed, and not the others (Achterburg 247-57).

Another unique study relates to the field of plastic surgery and imagination. This study, carried out by R.D. Willard, was also found in *The Healing Brain* by Ornstein and Sobel. Thirty-two women between the ages of nineteen and fifty-four volunteered for the study. Their breasts were carefully measured before and after by an independent observer. In twelve weekly sessions the women were given suggestions for deep relaxation and told to imagine warm water flowing over their breasts and that there was an imaginary heat lamp warming their breasts. They were also told to imagine a pulsating sensation. The sessions were taped so that they could practise at home.

Nearly eighty-five per cent of the women were found to have some breast enlargement, requiring a larger bra size. Careful breast measurement revealed an average increase of one-and-a-third inches in circumference, over one inch horizontally, and two-thirds of an inch vertically. The breast sizes were not correlated with changes in weight or menstrual cycle. These findings are consistent with four other published studies of breast augmentation by suggestion.

Bicycle Riding and Purposeful Being

Have you ever wondered why so many people read numerous self-help books, attend seminars and workshops, but notice little change in their lives? Unfortunately, some people are like curious tourists who are always being entertained by something different. Until you take something you read or learn, and develop a way for it to be practical in your life, the amount of change you will experience will be minimal. Therefore, it is time now to look at a *way*—your *way*—for understanding and experiencing your God-Self.

The way to begin this process is by recognizing 'your way,' and that this 'way' should be consciously under your direction at all times. As you practise it, you become confident that it is *your way* to self-fulfillment and mastery.

To give you an illustration of the steps you have used to produce 'your way' for accomplishing things in the past, let us compare it to bicycle riding. If you have never ridden a bike, it does not matter, because you would have chosen the same process for learning to drive a car. For clarity's sake, we have broken them down into a four-part process.

How to Achieve Anything—Through the Power of Bicycle Riding

1. *Desire*—believing, thinking and imagining
2. *Choice*—attending, focusing and learning
3. *Risk*—acting and experiencing
4. *Commitment*—doing it until it becomes automatic

1. Desire

First, you had to know what a bicycle was, or you would not have desired it. Then, you saw riding it was possible for others. It looked like fun, and it was something you really desired to do.

- *Believing and Thinking*

Gradually, you believed and thought you could ride a bicycle, if you were given the chance.

- *Imagining*

All along you were imagining and fantasizing about bicycle riding. You would dream about what it was like to go riding with your friends. Thoughts of cruising your neighborhood or riding off into the sunset filled your head. (You imagined and dreamed that you had already accomplished the process.)

2. Choice

You can desire, think, and imagine all you like, but at some point you must make a choice. Without making a choice, your desires end up in the wastebasket of broken dreams. You made a choice to learn to ride a bicycle.

- *Attending*

You attended to everything that had anything to do with *bicycle riding*. You attended to every opportunity to know more about it.

- *Focusing*

You had on a filter that blocked out all other means of transportation. Your filter only allowed you to focus on bicycle riding.

- *Learning*

By whatever way possible you learned all you could to get yourself started riding a bicycle.

3. Risk

You were prepared to go where you had never gone before. Even if there were doubts, you steeled up your courage and said, "I will go for it." This was the scary part. Would you get hurt? Would friends and peers laugh at you if you failed? In spite of all your fears, you still did it.

- *Acting*

Nothing is ever accomplished until you take action. How many great earth changing ideas lie in the wastebasket of untried dreams. You actively got involved for it to become a reality.

- *Experiencing*

Finally, you experienced it. Now think a minute. Did you experience it all at once, or in bits and pieces? If you were anything like myself you experienced it in little increments, especially in the beginning. First, you may have gone only a few feet before you fell. Then, determined to push on, you got up and tried again.

Now this is important. Why would you try again after you failed the first time? Because you experienced it, even if only for a few feet. Like the Wright Brothers whose first flight barely got off the ground, it was enough to prove it could be done, and it became the beginning of aviation.

As with each new experience, you drove your bicycle a little further. Your confidence and elation grew until one day, you did it automatically. Each little experience was your reward for trying it, and each experience added to your confidence and beliefs, until finally, you no longer *believed* you could ride a bicycle—you *knew*.

4. Commitment

Remember when you fell, you did not stop trying; instead you stayed with it until it became automatic.

Think about anything else that you ever accomplished in your life. Were these not the steps you went through to realize your dreams and desires? Is this not 'your way?' I am inviting you to use those steps again to create the life you desire through *Purposeful Being.*

The same steps we used for bicycle riding apply for your realization of *at-one-ment:*

1. **Desire**

You desire a more fulfilling and meaningful life than the one you are living now.

- *Believing and Thinking*

Due to past fleeting moments of joy and happiness, you believe that life has more to offer. Also, it just might be true that you have denied the truth about who you really are.

- *Imagining*

You can imagine what it is like to be in a constant state of elevated aliveness and to know that all God has is yours. Imagine the love you would have for relationships, and the security and happiness you would enjoy?

2. **Choice**

Doing *Purposeful Being* begins with a choice, which is consciously choosing to believe that you and God are one.

- *Attending*

Attend to all that relates to your *Purposeful Being* way of life.

- *Focusing*

You are focusing on ideas and concepts relating to *P.B.* that can be integrated into your life.

- *Learning*

You are committed to learning all about the experience of living from your God-Self. You learn what it feels like when you are on or off track.

3. **Risk**

You must choose to go where you have never gone before. To risk accepting new beliefs and ideas in spite of your fears of what others may think, or the beliefs you held in the past.

- *Acting*

You must take action by doing what is necessary to produce the life you desire.

- *Experiencing*

Regardless of how you feel, or how much stress or trouble you have in your life, you continue on (just like bicycle riding) and soon you are having experiences of elevated joy through being your God-Self. Each joyful moment or day is your reward for doing what it takes to understand and realize the pleasure of being your self as God.

4. Commitment

At first it may seem nothing changes, but you stay with it because this is who you are, regardless of your outer circumstances or consequences. Then, as you begin experiencing the ecstatic life without effort, still stay committed because this is who you are *Purposefully Being* all the time.

The Great Truth of Being

This brings us to the question of doing *Purposeful Being,* in spite of the challenges you are facing:

> Is it better to concern yourself with what you would do in every situation, or to concern yourself with who you would be in every situation?

If you were always concerned about what you would do, your focus would tend to be on the consequences of your decisions, rather than on who you are. Once you know who you are, or what and how you want to be, then external issues are of less concern, as they cannot disturb you being your God-Self. All events and situations are seen as secondary to maintaining your awareness of being as God.

You now know that you can achieve anything you desire by using the bicycle riding process. Everything you have achieved or attained in your life so far is a result of going through these steps. All you need do is to apply these same steps for knowing and realizing who you truly are, so that your joy may be complete.

Bicycle Riding as a Way to Practise **Purposeful Being**

- *Internal:* This means that the first stage is about internal practices. In other words, you will choose new attitudes, beliefs, thoughts and imaginings through choosing, attending, focusing, learning and committing.

- *External:* The second stage, risking, acting and experiencing, brings about your total transformation, both internally and externally. This involves purposefully doing all the external practices and exercises necessary to reinforce your concept of *Purposeful Being.*

Practising thoughts of your God-Self and doing God-like expressions eliminates low self-esteem and self-worth. They are no longer an issue. Your confidence and personal empowerment rises, and you no longer need to depend on others, or material things for happiness. You soon begin to realize you have found the source to the fountain of life, and all along it was with you. All your searching is over.

Through employing your *bicycle riding* process, your life will continue to improve. Soon you will never look back, or go back to old habits and behaviors that separated you from experiencing your true God-Self. There is nothing you have to give up, or change. Just practise *The Art of Purposeful Being* through your *bicycle riding* process, and the life you want will be yours.

CHAPTER 5 QUESTIONS

1. What do you think makes the statement 'Mommy and I are one' such a powerful statement?

2. What would be the advantage of using the statement, 'God and I are one' over the statement 'Mommy and I are one'?

3. What does the Universal Mind mean to you?

4. What have you received or achieved in the past through using the 'bicycle riding process'?

5. Using the 'bicycle riding steps,' which of the ten steps was the biggest challenge: *desiring, believing, thinking, imagining, attending, focusing, risking, acting, experiencing or committing*?

6. The ten steps of 'bicycle riding' are broken up into four groups. Name one step from each group.

7. Why would the 'Mother Theresa Affect' have such an influence on an individual's immune system?

8. What can you conclude about love after reading the 'Mother Theresa Affect'?

9. What would be different in your life if you were more concerned about *being* than *doing*?

CHAPTER 6

Transforming Beliefs, Feelings and Emotions

> *The greatest discovery of my generation is that human beings, by changing the inner attitudes of their minds, can change the outer aspects of their lives.*
>
> —*William James*

B efore discussing beliefs and feelings, let us look at the flow chart on the next page. As we can see, by being in a form of mental separation from our God-Self, we have produced a lot of dissatisfaction in our lives.

By our trying to meet tribal and social expectations, most of how we spend our lives is registered above number seven on the chart. Unity and survival needs are also sought after externally. Living life in this way has kept us in denial and separation from our greatness.

This is similar to how the animal kingdom perceives its outer environment by making it responsible for its well-being. Animals do not have the reflective powers to realize who they are, how they came to be, and where they may be going. Unlike animals, humans are capable of this awareness. The concept of *Unity with the All,* or that we are as God is only understandable by human consciousness. Therefore, it is possible for us to see within the substance and structure of our physical world another unifying reality.

Flow Chart

1
God-Self
Unawakened and Unrealized

2
Motivated by Survival—Unity—Tribal
and Social Programs

3
Chooses Erroneous Beliefs and Thoughts
Concerning Self Identity

4
Creates False Self-image

5
Tries to Get External Gratification to Feel Good

6
Creates a Perception of Separation
From Authentic God-Self

7
Decides to Purposefully be Authentic Self

8
Awakens to True Identity and Unity With God

At this time, where on the flow chart would you be?

In addition to letting tribal and social conditioning create our identity, we have also allowed our survival, security, and unity needs to shape our self-image. How much of our emotional stress is a result of beliefs concerning our social identity and fear of insecurity?

Feelings and Emotions as Biofeedback

I believe most distressful feelings and emotions are detrimental to our state of well-being if we do not address them. They distract us from being as God, and are indications that we have formed a mental separation from our God-Self.

Upsetting emotional reactions provide feedback that we have *beliefs* that are irrational. Any disturbing feelings or emotions are our way of drawing attention to an internal conflict that is asking for resolution.

To what extent are our goals for a healthy and successful life sabotaged by distressing feelings and emotions? Consider how many relationships and marriages fail because of emotional stress. In the workplace, stressful feelings and emotions arising through interactions with others are responsible for many of our work-related problems, as well as our physical and mental safety on the job.

The word *stress* is a buzzword that is often used today by professionals and others to avoid underlying issues. It is now considered reasonable to take time for vacations or to take pills and medication because of the pain called *stress.* The idea that there are underlying reasons, such as an inability to manage feelings or to deal with unrealistic beliefs and expectations, often gets swept under the carpet.

Stress is experienced as a result of one's inability to adapt to his/her environment emotionally. *Stress* is normally due to feelings and emotional reactions that are supported by false beliefs and expectations about our life and our environment.

Stress that is not dealt with is considered to be the major factor in all physical and mental illness. In its wake, it leaves labor unrest, marriage and relationship breakdowns, financial setbacks, and business failures. In spite of all this today, not many consider the management of feelings and emotions a priority.

The psychological profession has had mixed opinions over ways in which people should handle stressful feelings and emotions. One school of thought believes feelings are responsible for our limitations. By going backwards in time and tapping into the original event, we are free to get on with our lives. This is particularly effective for post-traumatic stress disorders and other incidents where clients seem to be having unmanageable disturbing emotional reactions. Two professionals and authors who have developed therapies from this position are Arthur Janov Ph.D., founder of *Primal Scream Therapy* and Grof Stanislav, M.D., who developed Holotropic Breathing.

In the sixties, it was thought that feelings should be expressed regardless of who they may harm. Hence, we had what was known as 'encounter groups.' This theory later gave way to venting feelings and emoting privately in a place of safety. For example, you could go into your bedroom and beat the mattress with a tennis racket while yelling out loud whatever was bothering you. The benefit of this process was that you had an opportunity to relieve your stress momentarily; however, the underlying unrealistic beliefs and expectations were still not dealt with.

In recent years, cognitive therapy has been another answer to emotional management. David D. Burns M.D., psychiatrist and author, is a major developer of this form of intervention. It is one that I find most compatible with *Purposeful Being* because it goes beyond just venting feelings to addressing the beliefs that created them. Once the belief is changed, emotional reactions around similar events are no longer triggered.

Purposeful Being is different from a specific therapy in two important ways:

1. Therapy is about dealing with a specific problem or issue you may be having, such as depression, or anger. Once the problem is solved, you go back to living your life in the same manner as before, hopefully without the depression, or anger.
2. Therapy does not deal directly with your core issues, which are "Who am I?" and "What is my purpose in life?" By not addressing these issues, the opportunity for lasting change has been missed.

Purposeful Being goes beyond therapy by helping you identify your God-Self. Next, it helps you choose the type of expressions that show you are being it. Finally, it helps you fulfill your ultimate purpose and destiny. Through practising your *P.B.* way of life, a lot of old patterns, habits and distressful feelings and emotions just seem to fade away. When they are gone, you again are back to your original state of being, which is pure ecstasy and joy. *P.B.* is not a therapy, it is a way of life. However through doing it, a therapeutic affect is a secondary benefit.

In a sense, you become your own coach, mentor or guru by having the tools in hand to begin living your life to your full potential.

Imagine what it would be like if you no longer reacted with stressful emotions to the events and situations in your life. Think how free you would feel if you no longer expressed and experienced upsetting emotional reactions in your marriage, relationships, job and other activities. There would be more energy to give to your loved ones, work and other interests. Physically and mentally you become a healthier person.

I invite you to make it a challenge to go beyond conflicting feelings and emotions, by addressing your *beliefs, reactions and expectations.* Integrating your feelings and emotional reactions by looking at your beliefs and expectations sets you free.

What if *fear* is at the base of all these stressful feelings and beliefs? Anger is a form of *fear* that something could be taken away. Or, it may be a *fear* that something you did not want to happen might occur. *Fear* could also arise when some old beliefs are being challenged, and you *fear* that you might have to make a change. Sadness could result from a *fear* of not being able to do, or have, what you want. Or guilt can arise from a *fear* that you might do, or have done, something wrong and you are *afraid* you might be found unworthy or get caught. Also, like most of us, you are probably *afraid* of physical or psychological pain.

Our intense desire to survive is indicative of an overwhelming fear of death and dying. Once death is faced and seen as a step towards the merging of a more joyful experience of being, then death literally "loses its sting." In studies of people who have had near-death experiences, the fear of death practically disappears regardless of how fearful or insecure they felt before their near-death event. More amazingly still, these people look forward to dying again, now that they know what it is all about. Author Kenneth Ring and director of International Association of Near-Death Studies, (IANDS) reports that students of near-death experiences are challenging us to move towards a 'positive and fear-free attitude' in regards to our fear of death. If we would commit to doing this, we would also have a "positive and fear-free attitude" towards living (Ring 17).

The point is, like all animals, we are born with a will to survive and a fear of death. We react with fear any time our survival is being threatened.

Many mystics, saints and gurus have shown a high disregard for their physical and personal comfort. What is consistent is their ability to be happy in any surroundings, rich or poor. Their *feelings* and *emotions* are not dependent on what the environment can provide, but on their state of *unity with the All,* and what they can do for others by which they are constantly fulfilled regardless of the circumstances. These people have transcended their fear of death. They no longer depend on the environment as the major supplier of all their needs. There is a trust that their needs will be met in this world and the next.

A time honored quote fits this perception:

> Consider the ravens, they neither sow nor do they reap, they have neither storehouse nor barn, and yet God feeds them. Of how much more value are you than the birds! For all the nations of the world seek these things, and your Father knows that you need them. Instead seek His Kingdom and these things shall be yours as well.[15]

For *Purposeful Being, God's Kingdom* means living in a state of *oneness* and expressing this at all times.

As you realize and express the values relating to your God-Self, your level of joy is elevated, and dependency on external things becomes less. You may still have money and things you previously valued, but whether you have them or not, is no longer as important, because you have found a greater value. It is this greater value of being and doing your God-Self that inspires mystics, gurus, and saints to lose concern for their physical needs. The point of all this is that by transcending your insecurity through *Purposefully Being* your God-Self, you will transcend *fear* into an experience of a constant state of joy, ecstasy and freedom. In the past, such an experience was considered the exclusive territory of spiritual masters.

Now is the time to reflect on how much of your *feeling* and *emotional* life has been related to fear, and insecurity. For many of us, security comes from our environment by making a lot of money, or having a job for life, regardless of whether we like it or not. The other day, I heard a quote that went something like this: "I never want it to be said that my destiny was in my attempt to live within my means." Often I counsel retirees who look back and regret how they gave so much of their lives to unsatisfying work for the sake of security.

Feelings of fear and insecurity are related to survival, and survival is related to a fear of death. I could put it another way. We are in love with life, as we think it is the only 'act in town' and, therefore, we are afraid of losing it. Back in the seventeenth and eighteenth centuries, a popular meditation was to focus on a human skull to help a person go beyond the fear of death.

In the beginning, it is necessary to recognize when you are having feelings that get in the way of your enjoyment of being your God-Self. When this occurs, you can say, "Under this fear is my fear of death, and death is about returning to *unity and being one with God* where I will experience joy, happiness and ecstasy. Therefore, I have nothing to fear."

Building God Consciousness Through Giving

Another great help in working with *feelings* such as *insecurity* is to give away that which is not compatible with insecurity. You cannot give something away unless it is already in your possession. Whenever there is an opportunity to help others feel more secure, happier or worthwhile then do so. This works because your focus has changed from thinking about insecurity to thoughts of love and benevolence. The giving away of anything from your God list shows you are being God in a most satisfactory way.

Whatever you focus your energy on, you become. Remember the four owners of the trucking firms? Each owner got exactly what he wanted by what he focused his thinking on. Therefore, if you *consciously* focus on helping others to feel better about themselves, then so will you, and insecurity will recede into the background.

Examples of how you make the environment responsible for your fears of *insecurity* and *survival* are:

- "If I don't get married I'll die."
- "I cannot live without him/her."
- "What if I lost my job? How would I survive?"
- "If I don't get a job we will all starve."
- "I could never take the time off to do that. I would not survive."
- "Without enough money, education, good looks, good health, good relationships, or good anything I will not survive."

These examples show that *insecurity* continues to be the focus of your thoughts. This kind of self-limiting thinking promotes more *insecurity* and *fear*. From this, all kinds of other *reactions, expectations, feelings* and *emotions* can arise that compound the stress in your life. You might become less confident, lose self-esteem, and feel more helplessness, despair and depression.

Steps For Moving Beyond Fear and Insecurity

1. Center in on your God-Self through acknowledging your union with your Source through affirmations and meditation.
2. Recognize that your desires and concerns are nothing compared to the joy of consciously being your God-Self.
3. Place your desires in *source* consciousness. *Imagine* and *act* as if the solution or its attainment was already a fact.
4. Whenever insecure thoughts arise in a fearful way, just say, "Thinking these doubtful thoughts is no longer an option." Then focus on something unrelated to fear that is meaningful.
5. You still may do what you can to bring about a solution, or the attainment of what you desire, but it is no longer a

fear-based insecurity issue. You are not attached to the outcome, because your focus is on who you are *being,* not the consequences.

6. You need to know that whether or not you obtained a solution, the *feeling* of *fear* is unnecessary and is a waste of time and energy. Also, by living in *fear,* you give no credit to your God-like potential for generating the life you want.

7. Giving away the items on your God list shows you your God-Self and more worthwhile feelings than those of insecurity.

8. You can believe death is a doorway to an even greater experience, or you can believe it is a devastating loss. For example, believing death is a devastating loss, one risks feeling more and more insecure and fearful about physical aging. But in believing death to be a positive experience, one would allay present concerns with physical aging and with death, and look forward to the future.

You have the ability, unlike an animal, to recognize your true God-like nature and go beyond the insecurity and survival fears of the animal kingdom. It is your choice.

Finally, as you express and experience your God-Self, fear and insecurity fade into the background along with your other irrational feelings and beliefs. Anger is less of a concern as fear of someone taking advantage of you, or hurting you emotionally, becomes less and less. Losing a relationship or business is also easier to recover from as your need for love and material things is being blessed through your *Purposeful Being* way of life. It is not that you have to always deal with your feelings, but rather that when you are living from your new identity, many of these feelings are transcended.

Who is Responsible For Your Stressful Emotional Reactions?

Imagine what your life would be like if you no longer expressed or experienced any distressing emotional reactions? What is an *emotional reaction?* Emotional reactions can be joyful or distressing. If you just won the lottery, you would probably have a powerful and joyful reaction. However, if you just got fired, your emotional reaction could be quite stressful. A stressful reaction is usually related to an expectation about a belief you have that is being threatened. You *believed* you had a steady job, but you got fired. Because you *expected* to stay employed and to be continually paid, you *reacted* with stressful emotions. Your beliefs were supported by your *expectations* that your employer should always provide work, regardless of economic conditions or possible personality conflicts. Anger, frustration, fear, guilt, sadness and depression are your reactions to a belief and expectation about some external event or situation. No event can cause a reaction, only you can. Whether you are emotional or not, you are still fired. Staying in your stressful feelings and emotions limits you from moving on and reassessing your future.

Understanding Reactions

1. All your emotional reactions are about you, and you alone. Others' reactions are about themselves, and themselves alone. You may have concern for someone's distress but you can never have their feelings and they can never have yours. Stressful reactions manifest themselves as feelings of anger, frustration, self-pity, grief, hurt, rejection, despair, hopelessness, helplessness, guilt, intimidation and withdrawal, and judging, criticizing, or manipulating others.

2. Reactions, expectations and beliefs are always your choice. No one, but you, can make you feel your emotions. When you bring into consciousness the awareness of what you are doing to yourself with your reactions, you are on the road to being free. Owning stressful, upsetting reactions and expectations, and choosing to be and do something else, transforms you and puts you in the driver seat of your emotions and feelings.

3. At the root of stressful reactions and expectations are false beliefs which you feel are being threatened.

4. Reactions are expressed in two ways:
    a. internal (implosive)
    b. external (explosive)
    Both are stress builders and are, therefore, problematic.

5. Unless dealt with, any dissatisfying emotional reaction you have will continue re-emerging and being a problem for you and those around you forever. The proof that your reactions are always your problem is that in any situation when two people can be presented with the same issue or conflicting situation, often one may choose to react, the other may not. This means that it is not the event that causes reactions, but individual choice. Some people exhibit "road rage" when they are driving, while others choose not to.

The Key for Transforming Beliefs and Emotional Reactions —Through Expectations

Working with your beliefs and emotional reactions begins by addressing your *expectations*. By recognizing your irrational *beliefs* that are behind your expectations and making different choices, you reduce your emotionally charged feelings, thereby eliminating your main source of stress. The key, then, to revealing false *beliefs* and reducing stress is through addressing your *expectations*. An irrational *belief* is one of the building blocks of your old self-image. You *expect* all things in your life to conform to it, and discard all that does not.

Most people of a religious or political persuasion have *expectations* of how life should be lived according to their particular religious or political *beliefs*. Anything that does not conform to their theological or political *beliefs* is discarded. Only that which conforms is accepted. So much so, that people throughout history have died for their *beliefs* and yet, often in hindsight, their *beliefs* were later proven to be false. For centuries wars were fought because of peoples' different religious beliefs, often within the same religion. Christian Catholics and Christian Protestants, by their violent acts towards one another in past centuries, are a good example of how people die for what they believe.

In chapter 5, I quoted studies that showed that even if you were well, if you believed you were not, you died faster than those who were ill and believed they were healthy. If we are able to die for our beliefs, then they must have a powerful influence in our lives.

Because there are life and death implications connected to *beliefs,* it would be advantageous to have a method whereby a person could root out their own mistaken *beliefs* and the accompanying *feelings* and *emotions.*

The Silent Scream and Expectation Process

Over the last several years, I have developed a powerful and simple way to get to the heart of our irrational beliefs and thereby eliminate expectations that create our stressful emotional reactions. Clients like it because it is such a simple tool. However, due to its simplicity, you may discard it before giving it a chance, and risk missing the benefits of its effectiveness.

It can be used in a two-fold manner:

1. As a means for getting feedback and testing your personal *beliefs,* theories, and perceptions.
2. As a means for taking control of your *emotional* life, such as fear, anger and sadness.

Following is an example of how you may discover your own conflicting *beliefs* through your *expectations* and *feelings.*

Using Expectations and the Silent Scream Process

1. State your beliefs, feelings and emotions as expectations.
2. Exaggerate. Blow them out of proportion
3. Raise your level of intensity, scream and yell them silently or do them out loud.
4. Use words that are absolutist, demanding, judgmental, critical, blaming or dictatorial in nature. Such as should, must, always, never, forever and expect. Even though this will feel unnatural and a bit humbling, you will be surprised when you are expressing them that they will, in fact, match what you are feeling.
5. Do all of the above until you see the humor, or absurdity in your beliefs. Often, when they are expressed and out in the open in this way, you begin to smile or laugh at yourself. The realization comes that it was these blam-

ing and absolutist words that were behind your beliefs and expectations and were producing your strong emotional reactions.

We will use the following as an example of this process.

Pretend you have a mistaken belief in a judgmental, critical, condemning God. Pretend you are this judgmental God and take a pompous, self-righteous, dictatorial position. Say rather loudly:

I am your God. I *expect* and *demand* that you will *always* obey me. I do not *expect* you to use your own free will. You can *never* do what you want, but I *demand* you *always* do what I want. I *expect* strict compliance with all my laws, rules and edicts. I *expect* nothing less than perfection in every thing. I created you to *blindly obey* me and *never, never* to think for yourself. I only offer my favors to a chosen few, and, because of your failures, you will *never, ever* be one of them.

You are not *good enough.* I *expect* you to be *forever* powerless and dependent on me. I *judge* and *condemn* you for the slightest infraction. You will *never* live up to my *expectations* of what I *demand* from you. I *forever* hold over you the threat of hell and damnation as my one and only incentive and motivation for leading a good life. I am a *God of punishment, judgment, damnation and hell fire. I expect your blind obedience or you shall suffer forever and ever.*

Notice the absolutist, dictatorial judgments expressed in the words in *italics,* including the use of the word *expect.* Who could ever relate the above to a loving, caring, compassionate, forgiving God? Yet, by taking it to its most outlandish expectation, we exposed the absurdity of believing in a judgmental God, which, unfortunately, is still the way many people think of God.

Through your exaggerated *expectations,* you would soon begin to see the irrational side of your beliefs, and this understanding would enable you to make different choices. Your perception of a harsh, critical and judgmental God would soon begin to change.

Whenever you are upset about someone or something, you may address your reactions through this *silent scream and expectation* exercise. At times, you may find it advantageous to repeat the exercise until you know it is no longer your belief.

Furthermore, we cannot have a belief in one area of our lives without it affecting all areas of our lives. For example, if we believed in a judgmental God, we would also tend to judge, criticize, and blame others and ourselves. The above irrational belief in a judgmental and condemning model of God encourages people to do the same. Hence, throughout history, there have been brutal wars fought in the name of religion due to misconceptions about the nature of God. How can learning to be judgmental and condemning ever make us feel good about ourselves? And how could a God who was that judgmental feel good about itself? Yet duality concerning good and evil comes from this mistaken perception that things are either good or bad and God is out to get us every time we fail.

God is about freedom. Giving you free will is God's grand design to let you choose whatever beliefs you want, but when you do not like the consequences, do not blame God. Everything you have, everything you are, is because in some way you have chosen it.

The answer to handling your emotional reactions is to look at your *expectations* of how the world should behave around your beliefs, and exposing yourself to your own absurd perceptions.

If you have a belief that the world *should be fair,* then you will always be disappointed and upset whenever your beliefs and expectations of fairness get transgressed. If you should decide to alter your belief by no longer *expecting* the world to always appear fair, then you eliminate your ill feelings. You would experience freedom from these emotions around this belief. The reality is that the world often does not appear fair and will likely always appear as such in your lifetime. It may never comply with your particular standards of fairness.

The Way You Wish to Be and Act

About feelings and emotions, you can ask, "Do I want to be angry, sad and fearful whenever something I do not like happens? Is this the *way* I want to *be* in my world? Do I want to continue giving my life to these feelings forever more?"

Not too long ago, a noted New Age personality and screen star came to our city. During her stay, the newspapers carried several reports of incidents of when she blew up at the people who were trying to help her. It would seem that she had not integrated her spiritual knowledge enough to know who she wanted to *be* in all situations and circumstances. In spite of all her spiritual experiences, she was still unable to handle her feelings and emotions.

Knowing the way you want to be in the world helps bring your emotions and feelings into harmony with your God-Self.

Most people are not in touch with their feelings. We have a tendency to hide from ourselves what is distasteful and usually obvious to everyone but ourselves. We know that people in general do not handle their feelings well. They may keep them suppressed and, therefore, implode, or they dump them on others and explode. Both methods are equally destructive. Exploding results in saying things you are sorry for later, destroying relationships and limiting your advancement in your career. Imploding is often experienced through withdrawing and denying, thereby suppressing the feelings that would show you to the beliefs that are sustaining them. This usually results in excessive internal stress that is reflected in physical and emotional illness.

I like to think that one of the ways to get beyond our limitations is by understanding and changing our feelings and emotions. It matters not whether we are rich or poor, unknown or famous. No matter what our present status in life is, we will always be limiting ourselves until we take control of our emotions.

The other day, I was on a long car trip with my daughter Gloria. She loves loud rock music. The sound left me with a drumbeat pounding in my head. I decided to try the following experiment. Telling myself this is only stressful if I allow it to be, I decided to focus inward on my God-Self. I soon got to where I experienced *oneness* and fell asleep.

Most People Have Beliefs and Expectations:

- Of how life should be according to their personal view, regardless of how it really is.
- Of how society and others believe you should be. Reactions come from the difficulty people have in conforming or not

conforming to society and others. For example, always trying to be nice.

- Of what society should be like.
- Of how others should behave towards them.
- Of what God should be like, based on old information they have not checked out for themselves.
- About how the environment should be.
- That their world is permanent, resulting in expectations that every thing should always stay the same, and that they should always be safe and secure.

A Domestic Example of Dealing With a Stressful Emotion

(Review the *Silent Scream and Expectation Process*)

Let us say that your husband forgot to take out the garbage. To begin, you make an absurd, exaggerated declaration to yourself of what it is that has upset you:

"That no-good-so-and-so forgot to take out the garbage again!!!" Now you would silently raise the intensity by raising your voice, loudly declaring your false *beliefs* and *expectations*. You would really exaggerate them by exclaiming, "That stupid, mean ignoramus, he *never* takes out the garbage. He *never* ever does anything I want. He always thinks of himself and *never* cares about me! I *expect* him to do things like this on purpose just to get me mad! He is *always* trying to get me angry! Will I ever get back at him! I *expect* and *demand* that he *always* remember to do *exactly* what I want him to do, when I want him to do it! I *expect* him to spend his time just thinking about my problems and needs! Who does he think he is?"

As you get into it, a shift takes place. As the basis for your reaction seems to change, you begin to smile, or laugh at yourself for having such unrealistic *expectations* and *demands.* Once you smile or laugh, you realize the absurdity of your false belief and it loses its hold. You are now free to make a different choice.

People have used this process in all kinds of situations, including separation and divorce. By being brutally honest with your feelings in that kind of a traumatic situation, you can quickly bring your emotional feelings into balance and thereby lessen the time of emotional adjustment.

Here are three principles worth remembering:

1. People, as a rule, are not intentionally out to harm me.
2. I can change no one but myself.
3. No one has to meet my needs but me. If it happens that someone does meet my needs and expectations once in a while, that is cause for celebrating my blessings, and gives me an opportunity to honor and thank that person.

Your reactions and expectations are separate from the issue that triggered them. Once you have a handle on your reactions and emotions by dealing with them through the above 'unrealistic expectation and belief' process, you can go back to the issue involved and settle it amicably. In other words, this does not mean the issue does not have to be dealt with, it only means that once you are able to manage your emotions, you are in a better position to deal with it more creatively.

The 'Keeping Your Cool' Exercise
(How to keep your head when someone else is losing theirs)

You now realize that your stressful emotions are about you, and the stressful emotions expressed by others are about them. This means that if someone you know is upset emotionally, then it is his/her responsibility to deal with it, not yours. However, it would not be considerate to make comments like, "Oh, you are just reacting," or "That's your stuff." This response to their emotions and feelings will get you nowhere. You will put them on the defensive and they will probably be even more emotionally aroused by your insensitivity.

A better approach is to acknowledge how you see them reacting by saying things like, "Boy, you feel really strongly about this," or "I had no idea you felt this way." You may also say, "This seems really important to you. I didn't know you felt so concerned about it." You can offer your help in saying, "Because you feel so strongly about this, what is it I can do now to help?"

This concern for the other shows you to your true source of love, which is yourself. No one can give you love; they can only help you see the love that is within you. So, in caring for another, it is the love within yourself you are experiencing. Whether the other person appreciates your offers of love is of little concern, as the act of consciously loving is rewarding in and of itself. Otherwise, you only love for what you may get back from the other person.

If the other person persists in having a tantrum or staying stuck in their emotional anger or rage, then excuse yourself and leave the room until the air is cleared. However, you must be careful how you leave. The object is to leave without giving the impression that you are blaming or criticizing that person for his/her emotional reaction.

The following is a very successful method for leaving an emotional situation when the other person refuses to stop raging. You say to the person:

1. "This is too upsetting for me." (Notice no blame.)
2. "I need time to sort out my thoughts and feelings about this issue or problem."
3. "I am leaving now." (Give an idea of where you are going, taking a walk, going to your room.)
4. "I will be back in an hour or so, and if you wish, we can talk about it then, or whenever it is convenient."

It is very important to do each of the above steps. Otherwise, the person will see it as a power trip, i.e. your leaving without any reason why, and then not giving the other person any idea for how long, or any indication of when you will be back. If you do not take these steps, you will probably make matters worse. Loving is an art, and requires practice. Do not be discouraged if you blow it occasionally, because you can use each failure as an opportunity through hindsight to learn by rehearsing in your imagination what you will do the next time.

A good example of the above exercise is an experience I had with a client some years ago. Joe was in his seventies, and no sooner than he had he entered my office, he stated his intention to commit suicide. I asked him what was his motivation.

He said, "It is because of her."

"Because of whom?" I asked.

"Because of my wife."

"What is she doing?"

"I cannot stand living with her, and I am too old to live by myself, or start a new life, so I might as well be dead."

"What is it about her you cannot stand?"

"She makes me angry with her constant nagging and complaining. She constantly picks on me."

"How long has she been making you angry?"

"For forty years. We have been married forty years. I guess I could take it more when I was younger, but now I cannot take it anymore."

"Joe, I have a puzzle for you. What if two people wanted to cross a busy highway and the traffic was not stopping or slowing down. So, one person begins yelling at the traffic and losing his temper. The other person remains calm, waiting for an opportunity to cross. Now what would make the other person angry?"

"The traffic," he said.

"Wait a minute, there were two people trying to get across. How come the traffic could affect one person and not the other?"

"I guess the angry person must have made himself angry."

"That's right, no one can make you mad, but yourself. You *believe* that it is the traffic and your wife that has the power to make you angry. Therefore, you *expect* them to behave according to your *beliefs,* and you are madder than hell when they don't."

So, he jumped up to leave, saying angrily, "Okay it is all my fault!"

I said, "Sit down, I'm not through yet." He sat down, and for a while I repeated what he had said several times earlier: "So, for forty years your wife has made you mad. For forty years she has the magic button that continues to make you angry. For forty long years she has had the power to make you angrier and angrier."

"Well even if I am doing it to myself, I don't know what to do to stop; so, I might as well kill myself anyway."

At this point I asked him if, for the next two weeks, he would commit to doing the exercise on anger management, the Keeping Your Cool exercise I referred to earlier.

He said, "Sure, what have I got to lose? What do I have to do?"

"Every time you are upset with your wife's nagging, without blame you say to her, 'This is too upsetting for me right now. I am going to my room for a while, but I will be back.'"

Joe left my office agreeing to make this response every time he felt annoyed with his wife's nagging.

Two weeks later, the day before his appointment became due, he called and said that he wanted to cancel his appointment. I asked him why, and he said that he did not have a problem anymore and that he was not going to commit suicide. So, I asked him what had brought about the change. He replied, "You did. Every time she started to nag at me I did what you told me and went to my room, or for a walk, and when I came back she would be nice and calm. Then we would talk, and you know, she is not really that bad a person. In fact she is quite interesting."

I never had time to teach him more about his *beliefs* and *expectations*. Yet, by doing this one simple exercise of owning his own feelings and leaving until he calmed down, everything around him changed. I never heard from him again.

I invite you to recall your *bicycle riding process* for putting this exercise into action. Remember the steps:

1. *Desire*: You seriously *desire* to change how you handle your feelings, emotions, beliefs and expectations.
2. *Choice:* You choose to study the methods outlined in this chapter.
3. *Risk:* You are willing to commit to put into action the above steps when faced with stressful emotions.
4. *Commitment:* Commit to doing these exercises for a period of time until they become a habit.

CHAPTER 6 QUESTIONS

1. What is the connection between your beliefs and expectations?

2. What is the advantage of blowing your expectations out of proportion?

3. What happens when you deny your feelings, or hold them inside?

4. Knowing who you *are,* what one feeling could you express that would fulfill you all the time?

5. What steps would you go through to challenge your beliefs, about God, politics, relationships, and so on?

6. How have your stressful feelings and emotions affected your relationships at home, on the job, and socially?

7. What one feeling and emotion do you have the most problem with?

8. When you use words like should, always, never, what is this telling you about yourself?

9. When someone is yelling at you and will not stop, what will you do now? What have you done in the past?

CHAPTER 7

Intoxicated With Love

Some day after we have mastered the
Winds, the waves, the tides and gravity, we
Will harness for God the energies of love
And then for the second time in the history
of the world man will have discovered fire.

—*Pierre Teilhard de Chardin, S. J.*

It seems that learning about love is a modern-day preoccupation. Bookshelves are overloaded with hundreds of books that dissect, analyze and explain, in the finest detail, the "how-to" of loving. There are seminars, workshops, and relationship therapists all trying to help us learn and understand the process of love. We seem to be a society that is obsessed with getting love.

All major religions and spiritual practices have a common belief that the heart and soul—yes, even the very substance—of God is Love. If God is all things, all things are love. If you uncovered all of the cloaks, or layers, that separate you from your divine self, you would be left with the most overpowering experience of pure love. You can only want something that you know in one way or another exists. You go after love because your soul knows what it is. If you had no concept of it, what would inspire you to go after it? The irony is that you are going after something you already have.

The problem for most of us is that we think love is outside of ourselves and is something we have to get. Trying to *get* love from others is a futile attempt to gain a substitution for the real thing. Until each of us will recognize ourselves as the source of all the love we have ever experienced and ever will, we will continue being needy, dependent and victims to our relationships. Love is not a commodity that can be exchanged; it is something you express or feel from within yourself. You can love anyone you wish, however, the object of your love may not know this, or feel anything.

Let us examine in more detail what I mean by saying you cannot give love to another. You can only show by your actions and words that you are feeling these feelings that are yours, and yours alone. Nor can others give you their emotion of love; they can only show you by their words and actions that they also may be experiencing the feeling of love in themselves.

Can others make you happy? No, they can only help you choose to express and feel the happiness that you already possess within. In other words, you cannot give people an emotion, and they cannot give you an emotion. As we said earlier in the last chapter, all people's emotions are always about themselves, and they can choose to have them whenever they want. Can I make you love me? No; I can do all kinds of nice things for you, but in the end, it is still your choice.

Every Act You Have Ever Done Was Done For Love!

In the last chapter, we discussed how the fear of not surviving and not being secure motivated most of the unhappy self-images you carry within you. Now let us go to the next step.

You have always acted out of love, even though later it may have proven harmful to yourself and others. Let us use the example of suicide.

A person commits suicide because it seems the best possible self-serving choice from a selection of not so good choices.

It is my belief that all love is self-serving, and that unconditional love does not exist, at least in the way we have understood it.

If you asked people why they do the kind loving things that they do, most would say "because it makes me feel good." In which case, their love is not unconditional, as 'feeling good' is the reason for loving. This is important to understand, because if you can serve others and feel good about yourself, why would you not want to serve yourself this way all the time?

Sometimes you may help someone and feel upset afterward. Usually this reaction suggests that you are helping someone because:

1. of duty;
2. you are trying to please for approval;
3. you feel you have to do something for others because it is expected of you.

In these instances, you are either feeling obligated or expecting something in return. What is amiss is your belief that the giving is done because of duty or for reward or possible future benefit. These three ways of loving are about serving your self-image, not your God-Self.

Purposeful Being's concept of love is that through loving, you show yourself to the love you have and the loving God-like person you are and have decided to be. In this case, loving is a way of rewarding yourself. Love is removing expectations from gaining something other than the experience of loving. When understood this way, the most selfish thing you can do is to love another. The secret is to consciously make the choice to serve others so that you may feel fulfilled within your self.

We need to understand that we do not love just to feel good: we also love because it is meaningful to do so, even when we know we will suffer. A person who runs into a burning building to save another's life does not feel good, at least not at that time, but does it because there is *meaning* within the action. He feels that saving a person's life is meaningful, loving and worthwhile.

As I was working on this chapter, I went into my sacred intuitive place and asked about love of self. I asked if this was what drove our survival and insecurities, hence the following reply:

"Yes love of self, an ego self and its self-image—and fear that this form of self may be eliminated, harmed, diminished, blocked, controlled, imprisoned, broken and killed is what motivates your insecurities, distrust, reactions and so on. But I tell you this—and

listen closely. Your true self will never die—I repeat, you will never die! You will live forever, otherwise I could not live forever. For the self to die, I would have to die, and this I cannot—will not do. I love my self too much for this to ever happen. You see, I AM you and you are Me. Therefore, you can never, in fact, kill yourself. You can only kill some of the outer physical appearances of self, but never your true self. No matter what you will ever do to yourself, you will always Be, otherwise I would not Be.

Again, what you fear is that you might lose your erroneous self-made image. This is the base for your fears of not surviving. If you would once realize that you are made in the image of God, and are the temple of God, what else would you want? Would not all things be yours? Why would anything be denied you? What would you deny yourself? Who do you trust, yourself or your God-Self? If you believed and trusted your God-Self what would happen to your insecurity and fear?"

"It would all disappear."

"Dear one, not only would fear disappear, but can you imagine what would take its place? Once fear and insecurity are gone from your life, what would be your limitations? You could do, be and have all you ever dreamed of, without carrying the backbreaking load of fear that stops you from living your dreams. Go beyond fear, serve your highest good, and you will never look back."

"Thank you, again you have clarified another issue for me."

"You're welcome, anytime."

After this conversation I remembered hearing that, during the beginning of the Great Depression, businessmen were jumping out of New York skyscrapers after hearing of their financial losses. I wondered, how much of their self-image was related to their being successful businessmen? If this were the case, they loved their self-image more than they loved their lives. They could face death easier than they could face the loss of a successful self-image.

Throughout my life, I felt one had to be involved in some kind of special religious discipline in order to experience the ecstatic love and joy of God. I thought it was only special people, such as monks, shaman, priests, saints and gurus who could be blessed in this way.

However, since practising *Purposeful Being,* I have come to see that everyone can experience the joy, bliss, and ecstasy through realizing their God-Self. Furthermore, by understanding and believing this to be true, we can begin to manifest all that we need to fulfill our lives. This is especially true with love. As we understand that the essence of self is love, and we experience this reality, then our need to *get* love from another source is greatly diminished. Loneliness is no longer a major issue.

Now let us summarize some of the points we have covered so far:

1. All you have ever done for yourself and others was out of love.
2. Love is the motivation behind all your actions, whether it is to serve a self-image or *God-Self.*
3. God is love, and all things are God, therefore, all things are love and this includes you.
4. Like many, you may have felt that others could give you love, or take it away. You felt it was a commodity, which could be traded back and forth. The reality is that no matter how much love you attempted to give another, all you were doing was showing yourself and the other the love you had inside of you. Whether or not the other wished to respond and express the love inside of them was always their choice.
5. It is my belief that there is no such thing as unconditional love. We always love to please or fulfil ourselves in some way. For example, I serve others. Why? Because loving by serving others fulfills me.
6. Realizing all of the above, a person sees that the quickest way of experiencing your God-Self is through love. When you love and are aware of it, then you are being *one-with* your vision of your *God-Self.* Loving is God in action.

People who purposefully love are *purposely being God.* The act of loving transforms them. It is the quickest way to break through to a realization of fusion with the Divine. Give, give and give, recognizing that it comes from your love chest and that with each loving act, your love chest expands. Loving is its own reward.

The Law of Attraction

There is a second benefit to loving just for the experience. This is through the law of attraction that states "what you sew, so shall you reap." I refer you again to the story of the four trucking businessmen in the first chapter. Each attracted the kind of business results that related to the kind of mental energy (beliefs, thoughts and attitudes) he was bringing forth from himself. Like attracts like.

Through *Purposeful Being,* you consciously love because you wish to experience your personal capacity for love, regardless of what you may receive from others. Then, through the law of attraction, you draw to yourself similar energy states, meaning you begin to experience and receive from others their expressions of love, without trying to get it. However, you must be careful that you do not love just to attract love. In that case, you are back to trying to *get* love rather than being a loving person, regardless of what you *get* or attract. Loving for the sake of loving is the way of being as God. Loving to *get* love is to serve your self-image and keep you in separation from your God-Self.

Further spin-off benefits through purposely loving this way are that it attracts and creates: *unity, harmony, community, security, friendships, intimacy, well-being, good marriages, good neighbors.*

Some of the feelings that we associate with love are: *ecstasy, joy, exuberance, awe, orgasmic sensations, bliss, and so on.* These feelings are the core of who we are and what we wish to be experiencing all the time. Expressions that show us the experience of love include, *firmness, caring, listening, compassion, gentleness, strength, loyalty, dependability, honor, play, virtues, quiet, reflection, seriousness, attractiveness, unattractiveness, pain, sensuality, sexuality, outrageousness, values, honesty, trust, courage, romance, miracles, magic, understanding, sensitivity, assertiveness, openness, practicality, innocence, wisdom, forgiveness, inspiration, gratitude, beauty, nature, knowledge, connectedness, intimacy, creativity, art, music, and so on.*

I am sure you have more that can be added to the list. Notice how similar the items are with your God list in chapter 3. It is true that you have loved by doing things from this list in the past, but many times it probably did not turn out as well as you expected, due to your expectations of receiving something in return.

Defining the Two Ways of Loving

The first one is when you do something because others expect it from you, or you do it as a duty, or you do it in expectation of receiving something for your effort. The second is that through the experience of loving, you get to appreciate yourself. The latter means that love is consciously done on purpose to expand your experience of being as *God.* People and your environment provide the opportunities for expressing your love in this way.

Therefore, it pays you to give your love and expand the richness within yourself. You are your own benefactor. How you choose to love indicates how much love you will experience.

Serving others as a way of serving ourselves seems to expand our experience of the joy of love, as opposed to just serving ourselves. God experiences love through our acts of love.

Love and Sex

It is my firm belief that experiencing love is the essence of experiencing who and what God is. Is there anything in your normal life more ecstatic and awe inducing than the act of love? Is this not a spiritual state, an experience of the unexplainable? The act of sex is a symbol for the power of unity. Out of this orgasmic unity, it is possible for a new being to be created. In orgasmic *oneness,* unity and fusion are experienced as an altered state; it is ecstatic and blissful.

What if sex is showing us to our normal state and capacity for happiness and that what we previously considered normal is really an abnormal state? Operating from an old self-image could mean that a lot of us are in an abnormal state most of the time.

Our secular culture tries to make sex just another emotional high. Yet nothing else we do has such generative powers of creativity for the human race. You could get high at a sports event while becoming passionate and excited about the scores. However, you will create nothing from your passion. Many in our society have difficulty seeing sex as a way to experience God. Eastern spiritual traditions have understood this concept; in particular, tantric yoga and many Taoist philosophies treat sex as a sacred experience.[16]

In the West, our spiritual tradition seems to have gone in the opposite direction. Celibacy has been the practice of many of our priests, monks, mystics and saints. They believe that awareness of *oneness with God* is a greater ecstatic and blissful experience than any short-term act of sex; therefore they usually leave their sexual practices behind and develop their own path to God.

It would seem, then, that the western path for mystical union focuses more on acts of love and compassion. Along with prayer and meditation, their purposeful acts of love carried out persistently and repetitively seem to take them deeper into the experiences of ecstasy. They no longer focus on receiving appreciation from others for their caring and compassion. That is no longer a concern. The philosophy believes that the act of caring for others is in and of itself its own reward. They are not the slightest bit concerned about getting love externally because they feel the source of love comes from within. This probably explains why so many saints and mystics experience ecstasy while living in situations of intense personal abuse.

Journalist and author Pierre Jovanovic has researched documents relating to the ecstatic experiences of saints and mystics in his book *An Inquiry into the Existence of Angels.* Some of these saints described their relationship with Christ like that of a union between a bride and groom.

To the contemporary mind, this sounds like an impossible paradox, yet the ecstasy and bliss that these people enjoyed cannot be denied. There are countless stories of prisoners in communist work camps who were blissful and ecstatic beyond the comprehension of their guards and fellow prisoners. For example and as mentioned earlier, Gandhi described his time in prison as being some of the most meaningful years of his life.

For *Purposeful Being,* this means that anything you do relating to expressing love consciously from your God-Self creates your ultimate happiness.

In Neale Walsch's book *Conversations with God, Book 2,* he asks God if evolved beings give up sex. God's answer is "It is more of a releasing, a pushing away from, as one pushes away from dessert. Wonderful as it is, you've had enough." He then goes on to say:

> You may never decide that you've had enough . . . that's okay that's all right. The sexually active are no less qualified for enlightenment, no less spiritually evolved than the sexual inactive. What enlightenment and evolution do cause you to drop is your addiction to sex, your deep need to have the experience, your compulsive behaviors[17] (102).

It would seem that union with God is not dependent on being either celibate or sexually active. For some, sex may well be part of their mystical journey, while for others it may be celibacy. I am inclined to think that if either path included purposeful acts of love and compassion, experiences of ecstatic union with God would be greatly enhanced.

What Is The Difference Between Happiness And Ecstasy?

What is happiness? Webster's dictionary describes happiness as a state of well-being and contentment; whereas it describes ecstasy as "Being taken out of oneself, or one's normal state, and entering a state of heightened feeling." One is lifted above normal emotional levels.

I feel that ecstasy is the natural condition of the soul, or God-Self. When we go beyond trying to get physical external things to make us happy to more meaningful internal expressions, we begin experiencing ecstasy. A very lasting and fulfilling aspect of ecstasy derives from that which provides *meaning.* If you go over your life, your greatest memories are those that gave you the most meaning and fulfillment. If you look at these instances more closely, you would probably find that they involved your loving relationships with your spouse, family, friends and others.

People seem to sacrifice many things for that which they find meaningful, such as looking after an ill spouse or child, going to war, or working for a worthwhile goal that is focused on serving others. All this is done because of the fulfillment gained through finding meaning in pleasant and unpleasant acts of love. However, ecstasy is often realized when people do these things as a conscious outpouring of their sense of oneness with God. The more conscious they are of coming from their God-like identity, the greater their experience of bliss and ecstasy.

Consciously Loving

I said earlier that everything you do, you do out of love. Even when you are purposely hurting another, you are doing it out of love of self. The difference comes when you can *consciously* ask, "Is this the best way I want to express my love?"

What about putting up with the stress in your life? Having to support a family at a job you hate or looking after kids all day, or putting up with a sick relative, or having a debilitating illness? If you are doing these things while thinking that you are losing something, or not getting something, you will generate stress in your life. If you experience each task or situation by deciding that what you are doing is a conscious act of love, you will use those experiences to serve your greater good, thus intoxicating yourself with love.

A friend of mine, all excited, called me to say, "We are love and everything we do is love, even hate." After thinking about it for a moment I had to agree. Everything we do is to serve ourselves. I feel that if I hate, hating is serving myself in some way. I serve myself because I love myself and I only do things that I think benefit me—even if, through my false perceptions, they turn out to be self-destructive in the end.

When we hate, we experience stress, bitterness, conflict, discomfort and so on. The person who is the object of our hate will also feel uneasy around us. Thus, if hatred is continued and stress held within, we create physical and psychological problems. Therefore, while hating is a self-serving loving act, it is still not serving your greatest good. While you are hating, ask, "Is this emotion serving my greatest good and my concept of being my God-Self?"

An Example of Loving Selfishly

I would like you to read the following letter to a popular radio talk show host, Dr. Laura Schlessinger. Schlessinger is also the author of the best-selling book, *Ten Stupid Things Men do to Mess up their Lives.*

> I have been married to a wonderful lady for thirty-one years and I am probably the most selfish man in the world. I say selfish because everything I do is because these things make *me* feel good and stroke *me* in the way I want. Let me give you an example.
>
> I take my wife out to lunch and/or dinner because of the great pleasure it gives me to sit across the table from this beautiful lady. I open the car door for her because of the great pleasure I get from watching her slide in and out of the car. It is a beautiful sight seeing her legs swing out of the car and her feet touch the ground. What a surge of desire!
>
> I take her coffee in the morning because of the joy and pleasure of seeing her open her beautiful blue eyes in the morning.
>
> I telephone her from work each day because of the peace I receive by hearing her voice on the phone.
>
> I kiss and hold her when I get home from work because just the feeling of her arms around me makes my day okay.
>
> Well, you see that all I want to do is please myself—do you think there is help for me or not? It seems the longer I am married to this lady—the more selfish I get.

This letter is a good representation of how loving can be a very rewarding act of selfishness. By consciously loving, you are selfishly experiencing your greatest joy.

Money and Giving

Some people think that all we are talking about is money when they hear the word "give." Giving is so much more important than just money. It is the *how,* the *way* and the *manner.* It is in the little moment-to-moment opportunities which cross our path every day. These are what build our character and generous loving nature.

People who have near-death experiences have reported that when they are in the 'light,' they often see their lives pass before them. What seems to surprise them is that their notable accomplishments have nothing to do with their business projects, careers or worldly accomplishments, rather its their past acts of love, no matter how small, that seems to get all the credit.

An example would be the following: I was with my friend, Gerry Monkhouse, when we passed by a Girl Guide cookie stand. He went up to the little girl and asked her how many she had sold. I think she answered, "Two or three boxes." He said, "Can I buy four boxes?" So, the girl very happily sold him four boxes. Then he said to her, "Now, is this the biggest sale you ever made?" "Oh, yes!" she answered excitedly. "That's great," he said. "Now I want you to tell your mom and family that you are a great salesgirl because you have to be good to sell four boxes to one customer, isn't that right?" Of course she enthusiastically agreed.

The point in this story is that he gave her so much more than money: he gave her a sense of pride and self-worth that may stay with her for the rest of her life. Loving is the intent behind the act, and is the attitude and manner in which the act is performed.

My Spouse, My Teacher

Whenever we are in an intimate relationship, we have an opportunity to learn about our behavior, emotions, and way of loving.

Here is an example. Let us say a couple was married for about five years and had not been getting along. Finally, they decided to take one of our Purposeful Loving Workshops. During the next five years, the wife followed very seriously the ideas that we have been presenting to you—while the husband did not. She learned to love without expecting anything in return, except for the pure joy of loving. As time proceeded, she became happier and happier. Her countenance changed, her stress went away, and she became a different person. At the end of the five years they still broke up. Who benefited? Yes—she did.

She had become a very self-fulfilled and loving person, and why not? She had a great teacher. Without someone as non-loving as her husband to practise her skills of loving on, she would never have learned how to love. With her husband, she had learned how to give love for the joy of doing it, regardless of what she got in return. She also had to learn how to deal with her emotional reactions to his non-loving ways. Finally, without expectations, she could accept him for who he was. This woman was now ready for a great relationship.

Another question may arise, such as, "What about my needs and desires? How will I get those met?" What are some of your needs?

Normally in our workshops, you are asked to make a list. I would suggest you do that now. Your list of needs in a relationship might include some of the following:

Love	Attention	Communication
Sex	Fun	Acknowledgment
Entertainment	Respect	Friendship
Selflessness		

You may add your needs to the above list.

Is it your belief that someone else has to meet these needs? If it is, this is how you create a lot of stress with your partner. Realize that no one has to meet your needs but you. Anytime you think someone else has to meet your needs, you set yourself up for stress and frustration. Think of how much energy people put into their expectation that someone else must meet their needs and live up to their wants and desires. Turn it around. Would you like always having to meet someone else's desires, needs and expectations? The truth is that no one, at any moment, fully understands what your needs are, and, thus, would be ill equipped to meet them all the time. Needs are telling you something about you. If you have a need, behind the need is a perceived lack in yourself that you falsely believe can only be met by someone other than yourself.

As we have been discussing all along, you are the source of all your needs, however, until now you may not fully have understood this. If I need acknowledgment, this suggests that I am feeling a lack of self-worth, and do not know how to acknowledge myself. The same is true for the rest of the items on the list.

Let us look at another example. Many people feel they need someone to take away their loneliness. I often ask people, "When you are feeling lonely, who are you alone with?" They usually say, "Myself." I then ask, "What is so bad about being alone with yourself? If you cannot stand to be alone with yourself, why would you expect anyone else to want to be with you?" *Purposeful Being* is about making you into your own best friend.

Another question is "How do I meet my sexual needs?" Not too long, ago a friend of mine disclosed the fact that he had a problematic sex life. His wife had lost all interest in having sex. He said, "For a long time I thought of leaving, then I figured I had two choices: 1) I could leave, or 2) I could stay and quit complaining about it. Before I was married, I had had a lot of relationships. I discovered that some of my girl friends were great in bed, while others were not. It is as if each relationship was like a piece of pie. You could never get the whole pie; there was always a piece missing. One person would make a great friend and be poor in bed, while the other might be the opposite. My wife is the greatest friend I have ever had; I enjoy her company more than anyone I have ever been with. And so I decided that I could live without sex easier than I could live without her friendship."

A way of saying it is that you can want something all you like, but you run into trouble when you expect that someone else has to give it to you. You have two choices:

1. Responsibly manage all your needs, with no expectations of needing someone else to fill them.
2. Do not accept that you are responsible for meeting your needs, and continue to complain and feel sorry for yourself while blaming someone for not meeting them.

If you are accepting full responsibility, every time someone meets your needs, or does something for you, it is a blessing and an opportunity for you to celebrate this caring gift of love with thanks and gratitude. If you do not accept that it is up to you to meet all your needs, you will constantly judge others by what they give or do for you, and you will never be satisfied.

How Do You Behave When Your Needs Are Not Met?

Perhaps you:

criticize	blame	control	yell or scream
manipulate	whine	cry	withhold love
throw tantrums	pout	withdraw	feel self-pity

These are but a few of the many ploys that people use to attempt to change others, or to get their needs met. I call them power trips. As you are probably aware, they usually backfire and set up more stress and conflict. To the list, you may add your own behaviors, including incidents of withholding love, affection and intimacy in order to manipulate the other. You may find it useful to monitor your behavior with the above list, by beginning to notice when you are power tripping. When you catch yourself doing it, you can say things like "I do not do that anymore," or "This is no longer an option." Then, as a *P.B.* practitioner, decide upon a creative way in which you would like to handle the situation, without power tripping.

For many years, I suffered from a lot of neediness, always thinking someone else could give me the love I thought I lacked. I blamed parents or partners endlessly. Finally, I discovered that at the root of all my neediness was a lot of love. I have a tremendous amount of love within me, which is in direct opposition to my perceived belief that I need someone else to give it to me. I cannot have a desire for something unless I have an inner knowing about what it is I am after. I realized that my neediness for love showed me the love I have within. After this re-evaluation, anytime I felt needy, I would remind myself of the following affirmation: "Look at the love I have. It is not out there, or with another, it is all in me." Usually, this resulted in a deep appreciation for my God-Self center of love.

Rejection, Grief and Loss

Often in therapy there comes a time when you are working through loss, grief or rejection. Eventually it becomes apparent that you should move on with your life. The bottom line is that you have felt a lot of love with someone, but because of separation or death, you mistakenly thought they took your love with them, or harmed it, or hurt it in some way. Consequently, you became sorrowful and grief stricken, perhaps even angry or resentful towards them.

Instead, through *Purposeful Being* you could stop and think of all the love you felt with that person. Then celebrate the love you brought forth from yourself during the time you were together. Furthermore, the love that was exposed was your God-Self, as pure love. Congratulate yourself for having all this love, and realize that if you get involved with another, you still have all this love to experience all over again.

This is also beneficial for those who have been physically or sexually abused. The reality is that all you wanted was to contain all the love you had within you, so that you could eventually experience it with a person of your own choice. Realize others have never taken it from you; you only thought they did. You still have the capacity to love and have it exposed every time you perform loving acts.

Much of what passes for grief could be termed as a form of self-pity. It is true that when we lose someone, we still have so many memories that it takes a while for the power of these memories to fade. However, it can become self-pity when we are focusing on what we are missing and how hard it will be to get along without this other person. At this point, we need to engage in other activities (acts of love) that can override these self-limiting thoughts. We should find something to do that gives us meaning. Later, we will be discussing your God-Self doing your *soul's purpose* and how, by doing this, grief and self-pity recede into the background.

Loving the Person and Not Your Images

In his book *The Way of the Wizard,* Deepak Chopra tells a story about a young knight approaching King Arthur with his request and desire for a wife. Let me condense this story for you: Arthur challenges the knight on his understanding of love, telling him that he knows nothing of love. After the knight angrily denies this accusation, Arthur claps his hands and an old cleaning lady appears. Arthur then suggests that she would make a good match for the knight. The knight, however, objects strongly. And so, Arthur claps his hands again, whereupon a servant brings in a beautiful little baby. Yet the knight protests again, saying that she is too young and that he would be too old by the time he could love her. Finally, Arthur brings in a young maiden of about thirteen.

By now, however, the knight is very upset. But Arthur explains, I offered you a fine old woman, but you said you could not love her because of her age. Then I offered you a beautiful baby girl, and again you said you could not love her, as she was too young. Finally, I offered you a young maiden, and she also was too young for you to love. Yet, you argue with me that you know something about love. Well, as Merlin taught me many years ago, you will never love a woman until you can love the old woman, the young baby and the young girl. Otherwise, all you are in love with is an image, a fantasy in your mind that has little to do with love.

I like this story because it exemplifies a modern dilemma. On television, in magazines and in movies, we are inundated with idealized images of young male and female figures. Few of us will ever look like the models that are presented to us daily; neither will we ever, in all probability, find someone who matches these images. They are now calling it some kind of syndrome. It seems we have been sold these images so well that a lot of people do not want to settle for anything less.

I often see articles in magazines with captions like "How to find the perfect mate!" or "How to get the man or woman of your dreams!" These statements usually mystify me. These articles suggest that there are people who are perfect. Perfect by whose standards? What are each person's standards of perfection? If there were such a thing as a perfect mate, I would have to wonder if I could measure up to that person's level of perfection.

I am reminded of my friend's explanation that everyone has a piece missing from his or her pie. Finally, where would one go to find a person who represents his or her view of perfection? Many people hang out in the kind of places in which the type of mate they dream would never visit. In addition, by being in a certain type of environment, as a matter of course, one becomes like the persons one hangs around with.

Regarding the *person of your dreams,* it begs the question, "Am I the person of my own dreams?"

Each of us can ask the questions:

- What are our own standards for the opposite sex?
- How realistic are these standards?
- What are our standards for ourselves as a man or a woman?

As you develop your new sense of God-Self, you will then attract the people or person in your life who best corresponds to your new sense of self. Like attracts like.

The Downward Spiral

As George S. Pransky writes, "The 'downward feeling spiral' signifies the mutual and gradual decline of love in a relationship" (82). When you first get together in a relationship, you are feeling all this love that you think the other is giving you. Let us call a fictitious couple John and Judy. One day John perceives Judy did not love him in the way he had come to *expect*. John felt less loving in return and withdrew a little. This upset Judy as she saw that John did not love her in the way she *expected*. She became less loving towards John. John began to wonder what kind of a selfish mean person he had married, and continued to withhold his love. Judy was now convinced that John was the most self-centered person she had ever met and continued to hold back her acts of love from John. Down and down their love spiraled, until they landed in the divorce court. Once this downward spiral starts by each withholding acts of love, unless one of the partners is willing to interrupt the process, the marriage is doomed.

Your Song of Love

Another love trap is thinking that the other person does not love you because he/she does not express love in the way you *expect* love to be expressed. Each of us has our own 'song of love,' our individual way of wanting to experience love. A common example would be when a woman would say, "He never tells me how much he loves me." While the other person's response may be, "Of course I love her, I work hard at my job for her, I do all the maintenance around the house and yard. I take her places and to nice restaurants. How can she think I don't love her." Both people have their own way of showing love—one likes to express it verbally, while the other likes to do things. Who's to say one way is better than the other?

Perhaps you have never thought about the other person's song of love? Instead, like many of us, you may have been so concerned with getting your own song of love met that you missed a great opportunity to show acts of love the way the other person wanted to experience it. By choosing to love in a way that the other wants to experience it, you again expose yourself to your own storehouse of love.

Can Meditation Replace Loving Acts and Human Involvement?

I overheard a radio talk by an American Buddhist monk who had gone to India for several years to study meditation and the Buddhist way. He came back to the U.S. to teach, and was soon involved in a relationship. He said he could not believe all the anger and selfish acts he displayed in his relationship. He claimed it was much easier to sit in meditation all day and send love to others and the world than to be intimately involved with someone. He realized that love requires more than just praying or meditating. You have to do it.

Love and Biofeedback

Just before hearing the above, I had been talking to a lady who is involved in biofeedback. She was telling me about the levels of meditation that corresponded to their biofeedback equipment. There are four: beta, alpha, theta and delta. Beta according to her is when we are in our heads, always thinking and figuring things out. Alpha is when we are into mental pictures and imagery. Theta is a place where deep meditation is experienced. Delta is when we truly know and experience our God-Self.

She said, "You know it's funny, but you can experience the first three levels through meditation, but the final level of delta can only be experienced through compassion." This simply confirms what the monk was experiencing: there is no faster way to know and experience the joy of your God-Self than through acts of compassion and love.

This was really interesting, clarifying why some gurus, meditators and church leaders lead such sordid and unworthy lives. They can get caught up in the spiritual benefits of alpha and theta, but they must consciously express acts of love to arrive at delta, the experience of being one with God.

These concepts of love as a way of being may be difficult to grasp at first. This is due, in part, to society's perception that love is something to be received, and objectified in others, rather than being a subjective experience of the self. Love is the essence of God and of all life. It is the unifying principle of life that cannot be taken from us because love is who we are. Yet it would seem that we only experience this love through our individual acts of kindness and compassion.

The Seven-Day Love Exercise

In his book *A Spiritual Philosophy for a New World,* John Randolph Price has a great exercise that you might want to try.

For seven days, from the time you get up until you go to bed in the evening, you put only loving thoughts in your mind, only loving acts in your day, and only loving ways and manners in your behavior. You hold no grudges, nor manipulate or get upset at others; and if you do, you offer appropriate apologies and reparation. You concentrate daily on giving love, without having any expectations of receiving love from others. You seek only the good in everyone and eliminate all forms of gossip or conversation that would be of no benefit to the one being talked about.

This is a very worthwhile exercise. You soon begin to experience elation and freedom, even though at times, you will feel deeply challenged. Record your experience daily. Try it and have a great week.

The consensus is that in order to learn a new behavior, you have to repeat it often enough until it becomes automatic. To start something new requires more energy in the beginning while you are learning to integrate it into your life. *(Remember bicycle riding.)*

CHAPTER 7 QUESTIONS

1. How can you experience love from another?

2. How can you give another love?

3. If you love someone, do you love the other or yourself?

4. How can you get God's love?

5. What would you do to experience God's love?

6. What has been your way of loving? Has it been working for you?

7. Whose love do you experience during sex?

8. What one feeling would you want above all others, and how would you get it?

9. How have you gone about getting your needs met?

10. What ways of loving would you like to bring forth?

CHAPTER 8

God Consciousness:
Knowing Your Soul's Sole Purpose

Until now, we have been looking at the meaning of *being* and its importance in relation to being conscious of our God-Self. We have also discussed the various aspects of God that we can choose to emulate from our God list. We will now address your God-Self's *sole life purpose* (simplified—*soul's purpose*).

Mary's Soul's Purpose

One of my clients, Mary, said that she had a concern about her lacking a human image for God. She became frustrated with all this talk of the power of the universe, God as an intelligent energy force, the cosmos, and so on. She felt that she needed something more humanistic, somebody she could relate to as an ideal, guide, and personal inspiration. I then invited her to go through the following steps of self-discovery, to which she readily agreed. As Mary and I proceed, you may want to join us and discover more about your *soul's purpose.*

I asked her who in her awareness has best exemplified all that embodies God in the form of a human being? What person throughout history stands out as having expressed most of the traits, characteristics and behaviors of God? Who in her estimation would have lived up to the traits on her God list? I cautioned her to be sure that they represented characteristics from her God list, rather than society's images of power, fame and fortune. I suggested that people who are God-like show wondrous powers of love, compassion, and humility. They are able to see and hear things beyond rational thought as well as do miraculous deeds. Many were great healers and prophets.

Mary chose Jesus. "You now have in your mind a human representation for God," I told her. Then I directed her to sit in a relaxed state, take a few deep breaths, close her eyes and feel centered before continuing further.

"What do you think it would feel like to be as Jesus?"

She said, "I don't know, but it sounds like it would feel great."

I then invited her to recall all that she could remember about Jesus. I asked her to imagine the following: "Go to a very safe, special and spiritual place of your own choosing. Next, imagine that from a distance, Jesus slowly comes into view and He continues to move ever closer. Then, when He is within arm's length of you, hold out your hands and imagine that he takes them and gradually merges with you until you both become *one*. Now, I would like you to own this Jesus-like energy by saying, 'Jesus and I are one.'"

After a few moments of merging, I asked her, "What is the first thought that comes into your mind as you make this claim or statement?" She said rather quietly, "It is like I cannot believe it, because my life is not anything that's Jesus-like."

I explained to her that this is a common reaction. Intellectually, she may have understood all that we have been saying, but had not yet experienced it emotionally. (Incidentally, this is why I used a tree form of meditation early in the book: it takes time for some people to accept this concept.) "Often," I said, "this is the point where people come up with objections like, 'I cannot be Jesus (or Buddha or Mohammed . . .); I'm not good enough'; or 'How can I compare myself with Him, and what I have done with that which Jesus did?' We are in no way similar and probably never can be. In other words, the thought of being as one with these historic God-like figures seems overwhelming and threatening." As she stayed with this concept, she gradually began to understand. "The truth is that we will never be the person who was Jesus or Buddha. However, we still can share in their God-like qualities."

I invited her to go beyond her resistance, and experience all she could by again letting Jesus merge with her as one. I told her, "Those who give up their resistance to being Jesus-like, or Buddha-like, soon begin to feel stimulated by this affirmation."

Remember the study in chapter 4 on the power of "Mommy and I are one" and my suggestion we change this to "God and I are one." Well, you can now make the same affirmation with yourself and Jesus, or Buddha, by saying "Jesus and I are one." What you are now doing is accessing all of the God-like resources of this image of God in human form. The point is that through the concept of *oneness* with God, you have all that Jesus had.

It took her a few moments to get back into merging with Jesus. I then asked her, "What would be *one thing,* characteristic or trait that mostly stands out for you when being as Jesus? Please do not say words like love or peace; try to be more specific." She said, "I began to feel a sense of internal power and strength. The power to be totally alive and in control of my life."

"That's great! What if we could take the essence of what you had just experienced, and use it as your single *guiding principle* for your life, your *soul's life purpose?*"

"Sounds good to me."

(We will catch up with Mary in a moment).

In his book *First Things First,* best-selling author Stephen R. Covey explains the value of having a personal mission statement. According to Covey, when they first go into business, most companies formulate a vision for what they are doing. They simplify it into a statement of as few words as possible that still contains the power of the company's vision. He suggests that each individual and each family create their own mission statements and refer to them whenever they are lacking purpose or direction (112-113).

Defining Your Soul's Purpose and the Meaning of Soul

Purposeful Being defines your vision as one single *guiding principle* which becomes your *soul's life purpose.* It becomes the very breath that runs your life when you seriously inject this into every aspect of what you do and who you are.

The word '*soul*' is hard to define. Thomas Moore, author of *Care of the Soul* describes it as that which relates to the heart and spirit. The New American Version of the Bible's dictionary explains it this way:

> Soul: A spirit having understanding and free will and destined to live forever. It is created by God to His image and likeness, and is the seat of grace and glory. It also refers to a person under his/her *superior and God-like aspect.*

Purposeful Being proposes that you can constantly be aware of this seat of grace and glory as you consciously and purposefully express your superior God-like qualities. Under this definition, then, all things on your God list are aspects of the *soul* (which includes heart and spirit). Anytime that you are aware of doing anything from your God list, you are acting with *soul consciousness* and being as God.

Earlier, we asked about *anger, fear or sadness,* and which emotion has been the most dominant in your life. It is true that you can feel all three of these emotions in a single day. However, throughout your life, there is one that you seem to feel more often. This *one thing* is then the most troublesome if you have allowed it to produce the problems and limitations that you have in your life. We talked in the last chapter about fear and how it supports anger and sadness. Yet, without realizing that fear is our issue, we use sadness and anger to protect us from facing fear. This can be quite self-destructive.

For example, if you chose anger, you live your life from a defensive, aggressive position. Furthermore, you feel others are against you, or want to take something from you. Filled with distrust, you are always on the alert, defensive, and protective. Like attracts like. This means that the way you live your life attracts people and circumstances of a similar nature. If anger was your selection, how much of your life has been adversely affected by it?

The same is true of sadness. If you have a tendency to hide in sadness, depression is probably your constant hiding place. If you choose self-pity, feel "poor me" and other feelings of victimization whenever things do not go your way, you are living out of a low self-image, and much of the time, you might feel others are responsible for giving you the feelings you have.

If you are able to say that fear is your motivating factor, you are self-protecting, afraid to take a risk. You feel as if you lived your life in a box. You may feel more secure within well-defined structures. Changing jobs, partners or locations may feel more stressful for you than others.

Each of the emotions of *anger, fear or sadness* was chosen at some time in your life as a means of coping with your environment, usually when you were quite young. Now they are holding you back from acting responsibly and realizing your *soul's power*.

Take a moment and reflect on the times when you have been expressing your dominant feeling and the kind of outcomes it created. This is to show you the power that a single influence as this one feeling can have on your life. In other words, you are allowing a single type of feeling or energy to produce most of the problematic outcomes you have experienced so far. Or, you could say that the expression of dissatisfying feelings has been responsible for the dissatisfaction in your life. In other words, the way you react emotionally to the people and events in your life has provided a background for most of your limitations.

It is important to help you see the power behind the principle of a single thing like dissatisfying feelings, and know that as long as you choose to use them, you will continue experiencing the same results forever. Therefore, would it not be to your advantage to choose a different *guiding principle*—your *God-like soul's purpose*—that would fulfil you and help you go beyond old dissatisfying emotions.

Using Your God List to Define Your Soul's Purpose

If you did not join in with Mary and do the imagination part of merging with a God-like figure, then let us find your *soul's life purpose* now:

1.   What historic figure most represents the qualities of God in human form to you?

2. What traits or characteristics come to mind when you think of this person? What was this God-like figure noted for?
3. Add any new findings to your God list. (I have repeated the God list at the end of this chapter, p. 136.)
4. Now prioritize the list by selecting those traits or characteristics that appeal to you the most. Rate each trait on the list from one to ten. When completed, your highest numbers are your most appealing expressions of a human God-like person. Pick one of these attributes that appeals to you the most.

Finding Your Soul's Purpose Through Anger, Fear and Sadness

The key to your purpose may be found in what appears as its opposite. For example, if your dominant expression was *anger,* you might choose to show yourself and others to the value of *peace making.* You could further aid this along by studying the biographies of noted peacemakers such as Gandhi. On the other hand, if your dominant function was *fear* and *insecurity,* you may decide to choose *trust* or *courage.* In this case, you might show everyone to the value of *trusting* in themselves and others, or the *courage* you and others have in the way you are living your lives. Whereas, if you found *sadness* to be the most dominant, you could choose from the traits that would be most apt to fulfill and uplift your spirits, such as showing yourself and others to the beauty, magic and excitement in your lives.

After choosing one thing as your *soul's purpose,* ask yourself, "If, by believing, thinking, and expressing this as my *soul's life purpose,* would I feel empowered with myself and those around me forevermore? If I were to do it in every aspect of my life, what would change for me?"

Your false self-image and unsatisfying feelings were built on misguided beliefs. Now, with your new identity, you will know that you are acting with *soul power* as your God-Self every time you express your *soul's life purpose.* Furthermore, you now have a more satisfying single *guiding principle* than your distressful emotions of *anger, fear or sadness* with which you may direct your life.

Let us get back to Mary. I asked Mary what was important for her about the realization she had had when she was experiencing the '*power* and *strength*' of Jesus.

She said, "Most of my life I have felt helpless and powerless, and it is wonderful to be aware that I am not that weak."

"Would you be willing to build on this information and, through it, experience your *soul's life purpose*?"

She eagerly said "yes." I explained to her the principles behind the idea of having a single *soul's purpose*. Then I asked her if she would accept as her God-Self's purpose the challenge of showing herself and others to their *soul's power* and *strength* that each person possesses. Again she agreed.

"Where and how would you go about doing this?"

She seemed stuck. For a moment she thought, and then said, "When I see someone doing something strong or powerful."

"Then you would not be doing it very often."

"Why is that?"

"Because your answer seems to indicate that you would always be looking to see *strength* and *power* according to your old perceptions and beliefs of what *strength* and *power* is. Would you like to broaden your understanding of *strength* and *power*?"

"Yes. Please explain."

"When you felt weak, helpless and powerless, did you do it well?"

"Um, yes I guess so. Why?"

"Would you say you did it *powerfully* well?"

"Come to think of it, I did it real well. Yes, I could say I did it *powerfully* well."

I then explained how there are no weak people, only those who do weakness *powerfully,* and that the importance of this is that if you have done one thing *powerfully,* you can choose to do something else equally as *powerfully* that could serve you better. She needed to see the *power* and *strength* that existed in all things, including every expression of herself. (We will get back to Mary again shortly.)

The Principle of 'One Thing'

What is so important about choosing *one thing*—a single *soul's life purpose*? Well, let us look at a couple of the great figures in history and see how they used this principle to transform themselves and others.

In the United States of North America, there was a lawyer who was very depressed and locked in the prison of his own depression. His friends always had to keep sharp objects from his reach. When asked why he never carried a knife he would say it was because he was afraid of killing himself. Fortunately he never did, as he became the President of the United States. His name was Abraham Lincoln. It is easy to guess what his God-Self or *soul's purpose* was. It was freedom. He has gone down in history as the man who freed the United States from slavery. Can you imagine how much he freed himself in the process? This was reported by historian and author Professor Michael Burlingame in *The Inner World of Abraham Lincoln.*

Our second example is also a lawyer who lived in this century. He was a man of slight build and humble expression who, early in his career, was known to struggle with his violent temper. Yet he fought and won a war, on the basis of non-violence. His only weapon was peaceful aggression. Yes, it was Mahatma Gandhi. His *soul's purpose* was non-violence. Through practising and teaching non-violence, he was able to sit down with his aggressors, no matter how angry or upset they were, and calmly work toward peaceful solutions. His *soul's purpose* not only changed his personal life, but also the way many people, as well as many nations, now think about war. Gandhi's *soul's purpose* took all the energy, creativity, love and compassion he could muster. It transformed the way he lived his life. By teaching non-violence, he became a force for peace, a believer in peace, and through it all, found peace within himself.

Following your destiny through focusing on your *soul's purpose* simplifies your life. In fact, in the beginning, it appears too simple. Yet as you continue to practise and make it your life focus, you begin to understand the challenge and the great mission which you have chosen. It took all their skills and the use of elements like those on our God list for Gandhi and Lincoln to do their *soul's purpose.* I am sure each would say it was the most fulfilling, exciting, worthwhile thing they could ever have imagined doing.

Simplify your life, commit to doing your *soul's purpose,* make it your personal mission and destiny and begin by bringing it into the simplest of occurrences.

Giving Your Soul's Purpose Away

I explained all of this to Mary, and then I asked her if she would like to give her *soul's purpose (power and strength)* away?

Her quick response was "No, why would I want to give it away?"

"If you are not willing to give it, by expressing it to others, then you will never experience it. It is by seeing it and offering it to others, even in the smallest ways, that will bring about your ultimate joy, happiness and fulfillment."

"Well, how do I give it away?"

"By expressing the *power* and *strength* that you see in all things to others as often as possible. Did Gandhi or Lincoln hoard their *soul's purpose* and keep it for themselves? No, they gave it away until they were the embodiment of all that their God-Self, *soul's purpose,* stood for.

"What type of person would you be at the end of your life if, in all situations, you expressed *power and strength,* always practised thinking *strong* and *powerful* thoughts, doing powerful things, as well as forever complimenting others on their many expressions of *power* and *strength*? What would others say about you?"

"I guess I would be thought of as a *powerfully strong* God-like lady."

Overcoming

"The God-like part would come by expressing *powerfully* the God-like qualities on your God list. Would you do your *soul's purpose* to overcome some part of your personality?"

"Wouldn't I do it to overcome weakness?" she queried.

"If you did, you would miss the point. You do not want to do your *soul's purpose* to *overcome* something, you want to *be aware of being it—through doing it.* However, in the doing of it, the old fades away. There is nothing to *overcome,* only something different for you to do, experience, and help you remember who you have always been—your God-Self.

"For example, as we just indicated, if you wish to know that you are a *powerfully strong* God-like lady every time you saw or did a *powerful* act that was in harmony with your concept of God, you would be experiencing and remembering your power and strength as God. This would be totally different from just trying to *overcome* something."

The Secret is Conscious Awareness

"Mary, the great secret is to be consciously aware that by doing a *powerful* act of kindness (or whatever), you are experiencing your God-Self. By bringing it into your conscious awareness, this reprograms your beliefs, attitudes and life. You need to keep doing this until you feel so *strengthened* by it that you could not imagine doing anything else.

The whole process is your choice. It is your choosing to be, do, and have the wondrous and *powerful* life you have been offered. Do you choose to express the same kind of thoughts, beliefs and attitudes you have in the past, or do you now choose to express thoughts, beliefs and attitudes that relate to your understanding of your *soul's purpose—power and strength*? Mary, which do you choose?"

"Well, my life hasn't been going that great. I don't really like being a *powerfully* weak person, so, henceforth, I am being a *strong* and *powerful* God-like lady."

"That's great, Mary. Now that you've made this decision, by practising it, you are developing your way of being it. No one else will ever do it quite the same way as you. It will become your way of life, and as time goes on, others will learn from you and develop their way. You do not have to act as their teacher or guru, but, by setting an example through being, thinking, believing, acting and sharing your God-Self's concept of *power* and *strength,* they will be attracted to you. You may also decide to teach and mentor others about their God-Self and their *soul's life purpose,* but that is up to you. All you have to do is live it and practise it."

When Do You Know You Are a Powerfully Strong God-like Person?

"Mary, if you were asked what it took to be a rocket scientist, what would you answer? The world's first rocket scientist did not wait until they created a school for rocket scientists; he became one by doing it. An official certificate or degree is society's way of saying that you have enough knowledge by society's standards to call yourself a rocket scientist officially. Now, you can advertise your accreditation to land yourself a job. However, would the scientist not be a rocket scientist the moment he decides to be one and do anything related to rockets? He may not have all the knowledge or the papers, but he is thinking and doing what rocket scientists do. If he went into a hobby shop and bought a model rocket kit, would he be a rocket scientist? If his intention were to do things involving the science of rocketry, then all his actions relating to this would label him as a rocket scientist." The point is that no matter how small your effort, as you are consciously doing your *soul's purpose* with the intention of helping yourself and others experience their God-like *power* and *strength,* then you are experiencing your God-Self. As you consistently do this over time, you will begin experiencing a wonderful new sense of joy and happiness.

"Mary, is there a time or place where you could not do your *soul's purpose*? Could you use it when you are driving your car? When you are rowing a boat? When you are alone in a cabin? When you are having a bath? The truth is, you can use it anywhere and in all situations. Even when you are alone, you can give yourself credit for *strong* and *powerful* thoughts and expressions. Just studying how your body moves could be an exercise in studying the gift of *power* and *strength* and appreciating the *power* of God's hand through creating you.

"Let us compare two people's lives. One we will call Miss 'X' and the other we will call Miss 'O.' Miss 'X' lives her life the way most of us have. She does some acts of *kindness,* but they are random selections, not chosen for any purpose other than the way she feels in the moment. It is one of the many things she does, usually without focused or directed awareness.

"Miss 'O,' on the other hand, is a practitioner of *Purposeful Being* and is constantly concerned about her *soul's purpose,* which consists of expressions and attitudes of *kindness.* Her days are filled with many wonderful opportunities to think about, act out, give and receive *kindness.* Mary, who would arrive at a self-realization of her God-Self quicker, Miss 'X,' or Miss 'O'?"

She replied, "I would think Miss 'O' would."

"Move to the head of the class. Yes, of course it would be Miss 'O.' She would always be realizing her God-Self through the conscious action of her *kind* deeds. Her previous forms of unwanted thoughts, attitudes, feelings and emotions would soon disappear. In their place, she would have more enthusiasm, energy, and goodwill, which would continually uplift and enrich her, as well as those around her.

"Mary, you know it works, because you have already been doing it. Let us go back to fear, anger and sadness. Look at how you have been doing at least one of these all your life as your previous *one thing.* Consider how much of your life has been unsatisfactory because of your stress through anger, fear, and sadness. Do you wish to continue bringing these unsatisfactory emotions forward into the rest of your life?"

"No I have had enough of that. How do I get started?"

"It is simple, Mary. Just do it, and do it with the same elements you used to learn bicycle riding."

Your Bicycle Process

"Mary, whenever we choose something new and want it to become a part of us so that we do not have to even think about it anymore, we must go through the steps of bicycle riding. Remember that:

1. you must desire, believe, think and imagine you can do it;
2. you must focus your attention on it, and learn about it;
3. you must take the risk and do the actions.
4. you must make a commitment to do it even when you do not feel like it.

You cannot let feelings get in the way of your *soul's life purpose.* As you are consistently doing your God-Self through your *soul's purpose,* you soon begin to experience the results, until you enjoy it so much you cannot imagine not doing it.

"You may change and fine-tune your *soul's purpose* as time goes on. One of the first things I chose was *power* and *strength,* then as time went on, I expanded my vision and chose again. I chose to show others and myself to their God-Self and *soul's life purpose.* What matters is that you first make a choice—you will not miss the mark even if it is a temporary choice. As long as you choose to do something that is compatible with your God list, you are then on the way to being conscious of experiencing your *soul's power.*

"Mary, you can begin by putting your *soul's purpose* into an affirmation such as the following:

I am always experiencing my God-Self—soul's power—by showing myself and others to their power and strength in all things that are in harmony with my God list.

"Well, Mary. How are you feeling now?"

"I am really excited at this concept of expressing and experiencing my God-Self through doing my *soul's purpose,* and I can hardly wait to get started. Thank you for everything."

Mary has continued expressing her *soul's purpose* and now she often looks back with disbelief at the way she used to live her life.

Until now, most of us have not intentionally followed a consistent program for realizing our natural state of joy and happiness. Instead, we have operated our lives in a hit and miss, non-focused way. We make New Year's resolutions, try this or that, but mostly allow our lives to run on chance, rather than on purpose. *Purposeful Being* is not just another way—it is your way to God consciousness.

Every thought, belief and attitude is stored in our memory banks forever. Psychiatrists have been able to access detailed information of past experiences, no matter how trite, through the use of probes to certain parts of the brain. In other words, we cannot forget material we have been aware of. Therefore, the attempt at elimination of a certain form of consciousness does not produce its opposite. Only a new determined action and belief can override it.

You might have had periods of inspiration, elatedness, direction and focus. However, because you were not involved in purposefully being anything but your old self-image, these occurrences probably happened randomly, as if by chance. This is because you have never spent the time, or made the commitment, to pre-choose a way for being and doing your life.

Most of us have been *re-actors* rather than *pro-actors*. As a *re-actor,* we make others and our environment responsible for our feelings and quality of life. As a *pro-actor,* we decide in advance who we are and what will be our way of being in life, regardless of others, or events and situations.

Purposeful Being offers a way to purposefully design your life by choosing and expressing your *soul's purpose* in any way you wish. By doing so, you are continually experiencing your *soul's power* as your *God-Self.*

God List *(repeated from chapter 3)*

truth	centeredness	choice	beauty
health	freedom	light	worth
strength	consciousness	gratitude	originality
self-healing	mystique	decisiveness	essence
value	potential	miraculousness	might
magic	regality	excellence	morality
compassion	power	specialness	soul
creativity	uniqueness	benevolence	oneness
omniscience	forgiveness	simplicity	faith
omnipresence	consideration	omnipotence	unity
connectedness	oneness-with-all		

CHAPTER 8 QUESTIONS

1. As a practitioner of *Purposeful Being* what is the simplest way for you to bring about personal change?

2. Will letting go of something bring about personal change?

3. What *one thing* did some of the famous people you know of do that made them famous?

4. What would you expect to gain from practising your *soul's purpose*?

5. Would there be a situation, either with a person or a place, where you could not practise your *soul's purpose*?

6. Are you prepared to give your *soul's purpose* away?

7. What *one thing* have you done all your life that has limited you?

8. What *one thing* has helped you the most throughout your life?

9. What is the key to fully understanding and appreciating your God-Self?

CHAPTER 9

Self-Empowerment Through Choice

*Things cannot be solved at
the level where they exist.*

—*Albert Einstein*

In our fast-paced, technical society, we are presented with more opportunities to make choices than at any other time in history.

Imagine how many choices you make just driving to work. At times it seems that many of these choices are automatic, such as in starting your car, braking, adjusting speeds, turning, signaling and honking your horn. You also make choices about your route, the radio station you listen to, who to avoid hitting, and so on.

Many times, your choices have little emotional content. Yet consider the many times when your choices have emotions and feelings involved. For example: The teacher gives your child low marks at school. What do you feel? Who do you deal with—the child, the teacher or both? Your husband is two hours late for supper. What are you feeling, and what do you decide to do? The car will not start, you have to get to work. You do not have enough money to pay the bills, now what? The list is endless. These are all choices that could arouse guilt, anger, self-pity, blame, judgment, powerlessness and humiliation. The list seems endless.

Driving to work involves choices that are mostly automatic and usually stress-free; whereas most of your responses to the feelings mentioned in the above paragraph would not have been automatic, and would have involved varying emotional responses. What makes the difference?

Going Beyond Reactions to the Power of 'Pre-choice'

Pre-choice came in to play when you first decided to drive a car (or a bicycle). Not only did you decide to drive, but also, to a degree, you chose the kind of driver you wished to be. If you had not, then you would have probably been the cause of many accidents. Like the rest of us, you decided to learn how to be a reasonably safe driver, before venturing forth on the street. Learning the rules of the road in advance was just as important as learning to drive. Often farmers will let their young children drive around the field, but, because it is illegal and unsafe, they will not let them on the road until they are old enough to learn the rules of the road. All of this is done in advance to prepare you as much as possible for any situations you come across while driving. Imagine how you might feel driving to work tomorrow in the absence of any previous knowledge of driving? The probability is that you would not get there and would not only have accidents, but experience major emotional reactions all along the way.

When you think about it, most of us are better trained to drive our cars than drive our lives. Just as you *pre-chose* the kind of automobile driver you wanted to be, thereby avoiding all kinds of stressful emotional reactions, so can you *pre-choose* the kind of person you want to be. This means pre-choosing the way you wish to be in all circumstances, including the kind of reactions you wish to bring forth, and even the kind of thoughts, beliefs and behaviors that you wish to have.

In the chapter on beliefs, expectations and emotions, the main focus was on how to change your upsetting emotions after you had reacted to them. In this chapter, the focus is on *pre-choosing* the way you wish to be in advance, thereby eliminating the need for upsetting emotional reactions.

Pre-choice begins with a self-image. In his book *Christotherapy,* Bernard S.J. Tyrell states, "In general it may be said that both concepts and feelings pertain to the self-image, and consequently a transformation in self-image will involve a change in both the conceptual and feeling level." (68)

This means that changing your self-image changes the way you think and feel. In *Purposeful Being,* your first *pre-choice* involves giving yourself a greater self-image than you have previously considered. The only image you can give yourself that will always produce the most satisfying results is *the image of God.*

Centuries ago, Paul in Galatians put it this way: "I live now not with my own life (old self-image), but the life of Christ who lives in me." And in Corinthians he states, "With our unveiled faces reflecting like mirrors the brightness of the Lord, all turn brighter and brighter as we turn into the *image* that we reflect."[18]

This is the *pre-choice* each of us must make for ourselves. "Who do I want to be?" Choosing the *image of God* opens us to resources that we denied ourselves when we were limited to the self-image of the ego.

Let us say there was a valley that was walled in by mountains and that no one had left the valley for one hundred years. The daily conversations involved the things of nature, crops, weather and social gossip. The arguments that may have arisen might be from someone thinking he had a better pair of horses in the valley than anyone else. One day, one of the farmers decided he could stand the isolation of the valley no longer and chose to venture out into the world. After several days, he arrived in a huge city. What he saw was unbelievable: vehicles that moved faster than horses, television, telephones, radios, movies and computers. Even these were only a small part of the technical wonders that he came across.

Of course, he could hardly wait to get back and tell every one of the things he saw. Yet, as he explained what was outside the valley, they did not believe him and instead, got mad at him. In the end, they chased him away and told him never to return.

He went back to the city, and learned to live their way.

The point of this story is that to have a life in the city, he had to think differently than when he was in the valley. In the valley all his thoughts and choices related to valley issues. Furthermore, when he went back into his old way of being (in the valley), he could no longer think the same way as the valley people did. By *pre-choosing* to go to a different place, (the city) his life changed.

This story is an appropriate allegory for doing *Purposeful Being.* If you continue with your old self-image as did the valley people, no matter what new information you hear, it will always get sifted through the beliefs and attitudes of your old self-image about life, and no worthwhile changes will occur. Like the farmer, you have to pre-choose to go outside of your present beliefs and attitudes before any permanent change can take place. Always consciously choosing to express and experience your God-Self does this. This is why meditation, contemplation, and visualization are important. They help you keep this image and awareness of your spiritual identity foremost in your mind.

The Limitations of Reason and Feelings as Choice-Making Tools

Until recently, it was thought that 'reason' held the answer to all our problems. Then came the prospect of total annihilation from the atom bomb and repercussions from the war in Vietnam. People began to doubt the value of relying only on reason and their thinking function. If reason was able, through the creation of technical systems, to create such senseless wars that threaten our existence, then reason left something to be desired. We next went from reason to feelings. Psychologists and therapists have, for the past twenty to thirty years, expounded on the value of getting into your feelings. This has led many people to rely on feelings as a way of making choices. More often than not, this method can be counter-productive. You would not trust a child's safety to just the child's feelings. I often come across clients who get into the worst of situations because they chose to do something because it felt good at the time. Anyone who has raised teenagers will have some idea of what I am talking about.

Making choices by feelings would be like having a teenager running your life. Try driving a car just by feelings. For over twenty years, we have been caught up in the cult of feelings. Another way of looking at it is that we have moved from the masculine way of thinking (the function of reason) to that of the feminine way (the function of feelings). Like the farmer in the valley, if we do not go outside of what is familiar, we are just juggling with the same old pieces, and no real change can happen.

So, where do we go from here? As Einstein said, "Things cannot be solved at the level where they exist." We now go outside of reason and feelings to intuition, which is another name for the spiritual realm. In other words, we must go beyond the realm of thought and feelings in order to bring real change into our lives.

Reason and feelings should be the servant of intuition. The insights attained through intuition can now use reason and feelings to implement them. This, of course, begs the question of "How do we do this?"

I will discuss several approaches to intuition as we proceed through this chapter. However, there are still some facets of choice-making that need to be addressed.

Pre-choice and Bicycle Riding

Having made a *pre-choice* about the kind of driver you wanted to be (a safe driver), you went through all the steps of your *bicycle riding process* to accomplish your goal. These two steps, *pre-choice* and *bicycle riding* helped you get to the stage where driving became automatic, and the risks and emotional traumas of operating a vehicle were greatly reduced.

In *Purposeful Being,* there are three steps involved:

1. *Pre-choosing* a new image—*God.*
2. Using the *bicycle riding process* to help keep you consciously aware of your new image, which can involve meditation, prayer, and so on.
3. Using the *bicycle riding process* to help you express your *soul's purpose.*

The automatic part is felt when you have achieved such an awareness of fulfillment that not practising it is no longer an option.

You could no more go back to being your old self-image than the farmer could go back to the valley.

The Benefits of Pre-selected Values and Images

One of the ways the *power of pre-choice* is used when practising *Purposeful Being* is by *pre-selecting* worthwhile values and ideals in relationship to your *pre-selected image.* Otherwise, when an occasion arises, that which offers immediate gratification will win out. By having a *pre-selected* image (that of a safe driver) and *pre-choosing* to learn the value of driving according to the rules of the road, you saved yourself a lot of major problems. *Pre-selecting* your God-like image and values, as in your *soul's purpose,* ahead of time prepares you for your life's journey.

All too often in this culture, expediency and immediacy are practised at the expense of integrity. Society is being burdened today by people who make instant gratification the means for directing their lives. Those who go for what feels good in the moment—short-term gain—are exposing themselves to long-term pain.

There is an endless list of those who practise this delusional philosophy of life. Employee thieves risk not only losing their jobs, but also suffering the associated shame and possibility of a jail term. Impromptu acts of passion often lead to consequences such as sexually transmitted diseases, or unwanted pregnancies. Other actions of shortsightedness include those of drug addicts caught in their addictions, as well as people who indulge in affairs at the risk of breaking up their families. It would seem that some people put on a pair of shortsighted glasses and make the *pre-selection of* values and integrity a low priority, thereby shortchanging their future happiness. There can be little doubt that short-sightedness is neither psychologically or spiritually beneficial. *Pre-choosing* your God-like image and *pre-selecting* corresponding values takes you beyond or outside of just reason and feelings and the pitfalls to which many in our society are prone.

The point is that through living this *P.B.* way of life, you do not just choose standards to stay out of trouble and escape many of the problems that we have just mentioned. You do it because of the intrinsic joy you experience, regardless of these other benefits. It is not like you are giving up something, but that you are going to a deeper experience of the integrity of self that is new and wonderful.

Dualism

Dualism relates to our concern with good and evil, right and wrong, perfect or imperfect, success or failure, good or bad. As a rule, when we make something a choice between right and wrong, we are putting a value judgment on it. In most cases, this can stop us from making the most sensible choice in the moment. Judgments that do not relate to our *P.B.* way of life—such as right and wrong—are like roadblocks preventing us from making a decision.

Duality and Choice Making

George is a middle-aged father who wants to quit his job and look for a new one. His concern is "Would I be doing the 'right' thing?" Quitting his job has nothing to do with a moral judgment of 'right or wrong.' In fact, his concern about a 'right or wrong choice' is a hindrance to finally making a choice. A better question would relate to his goals, desires, wants, needs, long-term and short-term gains and values. Unless he is planning to perform an illegal or un- ethical action, his concern about 'right or wrong' is a waste of his time and energy.

So, I ask George, "What has right or wrong got to do with it?"

"As a father is it right for me to want to make a change?"

"If 'right or wrong' was not an issue what would be your next question?"

"Should I quit or not?"

"What if you did not use the word should?"

"Then I would have to decide, will I, or won't I?"

"How would you go about doing this?"

"I guess I would look at the other job opportunities and see if they compared with mine in the way of remuneration, future ad- vancement, and so on."

"Could you do this?"

"Sure that would be fairly easy."

This example shows how going beyond the concept of right or wrong allows you to get to the heart of the issue much faster.

External Control Versus Internal Control

In his book *Choice Theory,* renowned psychiatrist William Glasser goes into extensive detail on the way in which we let others control our lives. He says that when we choose to coerce, force, compel, punish, reward, manipulate, boss, motivate, criticize, blame, complain, nag, badger, rank, rate, or withdraw, we are using external control. He suggests that we replace these behaviors by choosing to care, listen, support, negotiate, encourage, love, befriend, trust, accept, welcome, and esteem. It is interesting how similar these words are to our God list.

We have talked about social and tribal conditioning. Most of the first group of words would relate to this form of external control. However, if your tendency is to use any of the words in the first part, such as blaming others, you will also use them in three other ways:

1. You will be prone to judging and blaming yourself.
2. You will feel others are judging you.
3. You will also feel that God is judging you.

Your outer actions of judging or blaming others show what you are doing internally and externally. 'As above so below, as within so without.' You cannot be doing it in one area of your life without doing it in all areas.

The good news is that whenever you use any of the words on the second list, they also show you to what is happening, 'within and without, above and below.' You get to choose which list you wish to operate with.

Using external control from the first list suggests that you have chosen to adapt to social and tribal conditioning. Again, it is like the people in the valley that chose not to discover another way of life.

When George asked questions that related to 'right or wrong' and 'should he' in regards to quitting his job, was he under external control or internal control? George was under external control as he was looking for answers outside of his own free will. Who do you think represented George's external judges? The external judges were probably parents and early authority figures. Furthermore, because our parents represent a child's first image of God, the degree to which the child feels its parents are judgmental is the degree to which the child will also feel about God. Therefore, much of George's concern over 'right or wrong' was due to his imaginary external parents, authority figures and false images of God (imagined as external control) that he was allowing to run his life.

External Control and Dualistic Questions of Right and Wrong Arise When . . .

- In situations like those of George where you are considering changing jobs or careers, your asking if it is *right* or *wrong* makes it a moral issue and detracts from assessing the potential benefits of a new job or career.
- Making a choice a moral issue when one does not exist limits you from making a more worthwhile choice.
- You want a guarantee against failure. (Failure is a feeling related to being right or wrong.)
- You fear others might judge you as being 'right or wrong' and accuse you of being a failure.
- You fear that life might get worse if you make the wrong choice.

Due to the above, fear and panic can set in and you may become immobilized.

This list is about imaginary external control and has nothing to do with whether you should quit a job. It has only to do with fear of being wrong, and making a mistake.

For George, quitting or staying at his job could offer many different outcomes, regardless of whether it is right or wrong. He could stay at his old job, only to find the plant closed down and everyone was laid off, or that six months down the road he could have a promotion and really enjoy the new challenge. The same thing could happen with his new job. There are no guarantees. He would be better served by making choices according to his personal, wants, desires and goals, and not pay any attention to his imaginary inner control figures.

Judging 'Right or Wrong' Through Purposeful Being

The way *'right or wrong'* is used in *P.B.* is by asking the question "Is this 'good' for my *Purposeful Being* way of life? Does it fit with the new image and standards of integrity I have set for myself?" You make judgments and decisions all the time; the advantage you have now is that you are forming a new concept from which you wish to base your judgments and decisions on. You are developing inner control abilities that will bypass your old external control messages.

External Control and the Old Self-image

How much of our self-image is related to external control? I would think practically all of it. The degree to which our God-Self has been denied in the past is the degree to which we have acted through the influence of external control. This includes those times whenever we first chose to succumb to tribal and social conditioning.

This means that we have allowed most of our choices, beliefs and thoughts to be directed by external influences, which would also include our feelings.

Even though at times we may have acted righteously, how many of these acts were influenced by external constructs, such as duty, other's expectations, and social imperatives. The question that needs to be faced is "When am I making choices for me?"

This takes us back to the self-image problem. Having a self-image that denies its God-Self means that we choose actions, not because of the intrinsic personal value or pleasure within the acts themselves, but because we attempt to use our actions to get value and satisfaction from our external environment.

This is similar to a trained animal. An animal will learn to obey and do tricks because of an external reward or of a need to please its master. It does not do these tricks when the master is not around as there is no enjoyment that is derived from the act itself. Therefore, an animal changes its behavior only because of an external influence. Humans seem to have a choice: we can choose to act to please or derive satisfaction from our environment, similar to an animal. Or we can choose to act for the value and pleasure within the act itself as a way of showing us to our God-Self.

Consciously going from your old self-image to God as soul-self allows your actions to have a superior value. You eliminate dependency on external gratification. If external reward or gratification happens, that is fine; and if it does not, that is fine too. An example might be cooking a meal for someone. If you did it solely to please the other, or because of duty, your actions are subject to external satisfaction. Your potential for joy would depend on the way the other responded to your act of love through cooking. If you cooked for someone because you wanted to expose and be conscious of the love within you, that is all the gratification you need; anything more than that is an added blessing.

Practising *Purposeful Being* means that you no longer base your choices solely on external benefits, but on their relationship to your God-like image of self. Having *pre-selected* who you are, you go beyond the need for external control.

Accountability and Responsibility

As humans, we are always accountable and responsible to someone or something. Usually accountability and responsibility occur in these three areas:

1. External control—real and imagined.
2. Thoughts and feelings that are not connected with a *pre-selected* way of life.
3. Internal control—the *authentic self* and its *pre-selected* way of life.

Pre-choosing a way such as *Purposeful Being* gives us internal control. It becomes the vehicle that transports us safely through the hills and valleys of our lives. At this point, we begin feeling our own internal power and strength of being accountable and responsible to no one, but to our *pre-selected* God-like way of being.

We then do not have to be accountable or responsible for or to something externally. Our focus is to act responsibly and be accountable to our *P.B.* way of life. Being accountable to our *P.B.* way of life is our way of acting responsible to our highest concept of Godliness.

Muddy Choices

You are driving to work and are wishing you could stay at home. So, you set up a conflict. Your thoughts reflect the following:

1. "Gosh, I wish I did not *have to* go to work today, I'd rather stay home and be lazy."
2. "It is getting close to dinner time. I guess *I'll have* to cook dinner again."
3. "I wish I could get out more. Why do I always *have to* stay inside?"

These three examples show how we are driven by imaginary external control factors, and how we do not feel responsible for the choices we make. It is as if someone else is making us do it.

Ray Woollam has written a delightful book, *On Choosing,* that shows us to our muddy choices and how we divide ourselves internally by doing one thing while wishing we could do something else.

If you have caught yourself thinking the same *have to*'s as are in the above three sentences, then a lot of time you must feel that you cannot have what you want in life. It is like you are a victim to some unknown cause. What you are doing is responding to some imaginary controlling force.

Ray calls doing one thing and wishing you were doing something else "schizophrenic thinking."

In the first sentence, must you be at work? You might answer, "Yes, I must support my family," or "I must eat, and pay my way." Are these *must*'s true? Listen, you never *must* or *have* to do anything you do not want to. There are always other choices. You could choose, at any time, to run out on your family, or you could choose to be a bum; lots of people have. You see, thinking that you would like to be somewhere else belittles the value of your original choice. You chose to be at work for valid reasons.

In the second statement, if you are married and have decided that cooking is your way of contributing to your family, you dishonor your own ability to choose by wishing you did not *have to.* Again, there is an imaginary external controller influencing you, and you are dividing yourself by doing one thing and wishing you could do something else.

The third example of wanting to go out more has all of the by now familiar elements: external control, wanting to be two places at the same time, and playing down your own ability to choose. Who says you cannot be out more? "Well," you might say, "my husband works all hours and I never can go anywhere." Again you are making someone else responsible for the choices you made. You could be out doing a number of things from visiting friends and relatives to volunteering while he is at work. The choice to stay home is yours.

If you are complaining in all of the above three instances, the only person you can complain to, or blame, is you, because it is your choice. Would it not be better to compliment yourself for making worthwhile choices in the first place and get on with your life, instead of trying to be in two different places, such as working at a job you chose and then wishing you were somewhere else?

For example, a friend of mine who suffers from anxiety on occasion was having difficulty adjusting to a new job. I asked him what he was thinking while he was feeling all his anxiety. He said, "I'd like to be anywhere else; I wish I were home."

"How does the wishing and wanting to escape make it any better?"

"I guess it doesn't, except that when I was at home I didn't have the anxiety."

"Have you experienced anxiety before when starting something new?"

"Yes, it always seems to happen this way."

"Did wishing you were somewhere else make it go away?"

"No, but what else am I to think?"

"What made it go away before?"

"Time, it seemed to be less and less as time went on."

"So, time alone was responsible, and nothing else?"

"Well, I guess, as I got more used to the job and the people, it became less fearful."

"So, it's not anxiety you are facing, but fear, and that builds your anxiety, and as you face your fear your anxiety becomes less and less. If this were true, is there another option you could use beside wishing you were somewhere else?"

"Well, I guess I could say to myself, 'As I face my fear, over time my anxiety becomes less and less.'"

"That certainly sounds like a better choice, but your words are still talking of fear and anxiety. What about the choice you made when you decided to take this job? Did you make it for a good reason?"

"I thought so. It offers a great potential to update my skills in my areas of interest, and the work is what I like doing. There is also a potential to not only make more money, but grow with the firm. Furthermore, I cannot sit at home forever. It was getting me down."

"What if you could boil all of the above down to a single sentence or affirmation, and use it every time you felt anxious or fearful? Even if you have to repeat it a thousand times a day, using the unwanted feelings of anxiety as your cue to remember your affirmation? Could you do that?"

"I guess so. It might be better than telling myself how anxious I am and wishing I were somewhere else all the time."

He came up with the following affirmation: "At this new job, I am enjoying the process of updating my skills and expanding my interests, as well as an opportunity to increase my income and expand with this firm, I am enjoying more and more self-confidence and strength as time goes on."

With the above information, my friend created an affirmation and used it effectively. His anxiety did not go away immediately. However, through constant repetition, he reduced his anxiety much faster than he ever had done previously. By using his feelings of anxiety as the inspiration to repeat his affirmation, he was able to transform the thinking patterns that had been creating the anxiety.

He had been caught up in the duality of trying to be two places at once, and not honoring his original choice and the benefits that he would receive as a result of his decision.

There are many situations into which people put themselves, thinking that someone else is forcing them to do that which they do not want to do. This means that they are blinded to their own rational self-serving reasons for choosing it in the first place. If the results of that choice were not what they wanted, they can always make another choice. You are the sum of your choices. You have always chosen what you wanted to be, do and have. If you did not like the outcome, it still does not mean you did not make the choices that got you there.

What you do not have is due to the fact that, for some reason, you have not yet chosen it. Therefore, everything you are today is because you chose it. Often people will say, "I did not choose to have abusive parents, or an abusive relationship, or this illness or accident."

Did We Choose Our Parents?

Many people who have had past life experiences believe we choose the parents we have, in order to work out some purpose in this lifetime. Reincarnationists have a theory which in some ways seems more empowering. They believe that we came to finish that which has been left unfinished from previous lifetimes. They also believe that we choose our families, our economic conditions, even the health challenges and illnesses we come into this life with. If we have been given free will, they then feel that it stands to reason that we should have a say about the families into which we are being born.

When we look at life this way, we go beyond blame and the thought that we are victims of unknown forces. In this case, even our physical and mental handicaps can be seen as the constructs that we chose to push us into our ultimate direction.

When I was a child, my mother wanted me to go on the stage. This was fine with me as I had a lot of illness, and was not able to participate in general sports. I was quite good at acting and won several awards. At this young age, I was being pushed by my physical circumstances into being trained as a communicator. Before I got my degrees in psychology, I had been in sales. Later, I read that the metaphysical meaning of my name 'Philip' stands for power in the voice. Therefore, it seems I *pre-chose* parents and a life where communication would be part of my *soul's purpose*.

Because of my personal experiences and those of my clients, I am convinced that we are here to fulfill a purpose that we chose before conception.

Also, there are those who believe accidents are no accident, in that we create the outcomes in our lives, even our accidents. I overheard a father talking to his son. It seems his son had had three stereos stolen from his car. The dad asked his son, "How come you've had three stereos stolen and I haven't ever had anything stolen from my car?" The father continued, "It's because you park your car down town at some pub where all the street people hang out till three in the morning. At night my car is home in the garage." I believe the father made a good point. The son's lifestyle was creating his vulnerability to being the victim of thieves.

However, even if we do not believe in the theory of reincarnation, or the law of attraction, we still make choices about the way we react to our parents. Therefore, if they were abusive, and even though they may be dead, we are still choosing to act like victims when we choose feelings of self-pity, blame, anger, powerlessness, helplessness, and so on.

Most people have never thought much about the way in which they make choices in life, due to their having never learned a practical method for decision making. In addition, many people today have never been taught a value system.

As adults, each of us needs to reassess his/her own values from time to time. By using the choice empowerment skill methods outlined in this chapter, you can now choose only the values that you feel would give you everlasting satisfaction. *Purposeful Being* neither rejects nor recommends a value or moral system for you to follow. What it does is give you the framework whereby you may now create the values you desire for your own *P.B.* way of life. In addition, looking at the ethical and moral principles found in traditional religions can provide a good base for the values you may wish to employ through practising *P.B.*

Intuition and Choice Making

What is intuition? Webster's Dictionary defines intuition as, "a direct perception of truth, fact, etc. independent of any reasoning process; providing immediate apprehension." In other words, intuition contains information from outside our rational mind. This involves insights that are conducive to helping us be and live the life of our dreams. We access this material through spiritual practices such as prayer, meditation, dreams, visions, visualization and acts of love.

While discussing this chapter on choice, I have left the subject of intuition until now, so that you could acquire a choice-making process for putting your spiritual and intuitive insights into action through *Purposeful Being*. There are two issues regarding choice making. The first concerns the choices you make in the routine of daily living; the second, the choices you make to receive and carry out your intuitive and spiritual insights. *Purposeful Being* provides the framework for both of these. Through consciously realizing your true self through meditation and other prescribed exercises, choosing your values, and expressing your *soul's purpose,* you not only open yourself to spiritual and intuitive insights, but to a way of integrating them and putting them into practice.

Many spiritual and intuitive people have not had a way for making their insights workable. By pre-choosing bicycle riding and focusing on fulfilling their *soul's purpose,* however, they quickly find their lives become more grounded and fulfilling. For others who have felt that spiritual and intuitive insights have not been a common place occurrence, *Purposefully Being* their God-Self and doing their *soul's purpose* begins to bring these insights forth.

By now, you have seen some of the difficulty involved in making choices. Would it not be a relief to have a sure-fire method of making your own choices that would work for you in all situations? Just think of the energy you would save in no more lying awake at night, going over and over the same old problems, or situations. Would it not be meaningful to know that all your choices are the appropriate ones for each and every situation?

In this chapter, we have discussed the folly of total reliance on reason, feelings and external control that has been at the expense of intuition and spirituality. If we are to direct our lives with the confidence we have in operating our cars, then we need to *pre-learn* skills that set us up to make the best choice possible in all situations.

The following list of choice skills is a compilation of the best that I have encountered in order to take us out of our normal way of making choices and into a greater, more advanced method of living from our highest sense of self.

There are five Choice Empowerment Skills which, when applied through the art of *Purposeful Being,* will put you in the driver's seat of decisiveness. Each can be used with similar effectiveness. Choose one, or any combination most suitable for you.

Choice Empowerment Skill #1
Is it fitting with **Purposeful Being?**

As a person who practises *Purposeful Being,* the first question you need to ask is "Does what I am choosing to do fit with my *Purposeful Being* pre-selected way of life?" You now have an idea of who you are (your God-Self), and what you want to do in the way of your *soul's purpose.* Therefore, all your choices and decisions should only concern these two principles, *being* and *doing.* Any choice that does not fit with *being* and *doing (Purposeful Being),* you discard. This helps you limit your choices, as you only want to make choices that are in harmony with who you have chosen to be.

Choice Empowerment Skill #2
Choices which last forever

What if your ultimate realization of *unity-with-the-all* came about by choosing to live with only those qualities of life that are ever lasting?

In his book *Forever Living,* Roger Cotting uses the idea of *forever* as the basis for choice making. For example, suppose your choice fits with *Purposeful Being,* but is only one of many options. Then, in this situation, you could always ask, "Which of these options are ones that I would choose to do *forever*?" He feels *forever* takes you above the realm of reason and feelings to an eternal view. Stretching out a problem for eternity lets you see clearer the consequences of your decisions. When seen from this direction, a shift changes in your relationship to the situation that you are facing. For example, you are upset because someone has smashed up your car. By asking yourself, "Do I want to be emotionally upset about this accident *forever*?" puts you into a position to select another option.

Your next question could be "Other than being emotionally upset, what would I do next that would be all right if it was done *forever*?"

The importance of *forever choices* is better understood when looked at through the framework of previous choices regarding beliefs and attitudes. According to Cotting, any belief or attitude you have now is because at some time in your life you chose it, and you chose it to serve yourself in some way. Therefore, you will have these beliefs and attitudes *forever* unless you make a new choice.

To even define your *forever choices* a little more ask, "Would I want someone to do this to me, in this way, *forever*?"

Addressing 'the way' means that you are concerned with sensitivity, tone of voice, behaviors, caring, as well as the time and place where you choose to resolve an issue.

Making *forever choices* is a way of constantly building self-value. The more *forever choices* you make, the more long lasting joy you bring into your life.

Choice Empowerment Skill #3
Will it serve my highest and greatest good?

This is discussed by author Neale Walsch in *Conversations With God*. With this skill you only make choices that you feel will serve your '*highest and greatest good*,' since every choice you make is to serve yourself in some way (as discussed in our chapter on love).

Many people's first reaction is "To always be serving my *highest and greatest good* would be too selfish." What if your *highest and greatest good* were love, kindness, forgiveness, compassion, creativity, artistry, and doing all the things on your God list? Always making a choice to serve your *highest and greatest good* would keep you on target with *Purposeful Being*.

An example might be to ask yourself, "Would it be to my *highest and greatest good* to stay angry at my spouse? Or would it serve my *highest and greatest good* for me to resolve what has happened and get on with loving this person?" Asking these kinds of questions provides you with the tools to permanently enhance your direction, performance, relationships, character, and self-awareness.

Choice Empowerment Skill #4
Is this a loving thing to do?

The next option for making choices that you might want to consider is to ask the question "Is this a loving thing to do, or would I feel this was a loving act if someone did it to me?" Then, when you have the answer, you can ask, as with all of these questions, "Does it fit with my new awareness of self? Is it me?"

Choice Empowerment Skill #5
Is this a Christ-like (Buddha-like, Mohammed-like, God-like . . .) way of doing it?

This one is related to God-consciousness. By using one of the above God-like person's names, you would ask, "Is doing this, in this way, a Christ-like way of doing it?"

These questions are ways in which you can put your life into perspective through the power of choice. A well thought out choice is the fast track to freedom. Each of these methods takes you from external control and feelings to your highest spiritual standard for making choices. You can use all of these question skills for making a decision, or only the ones that seem more to your liking.

The Five Choice Empowerment Skills Abbreviated

1. Always start with *Purposeful Being,* that is knowing whether or not what you are choosing is in harmony with who you are *Purposefully Being* (God-Self), and what you want to do (*soul's purpose*).

2. Make each choice on the basis of, "Would I want to do this thing in this way and in this manner *forever*?" or, "Would I appreciate having someone do this thing in this way and in this manner to me *forever more*?"

3. You ask, "Is this a loving thing to do, and is it in line with my *P.B.* way of life? Is it me?"

4. Also, "Is this the way I would like to serve my *highest and greatest good*?"

5. *Finally* you ask, "Is doing this, in this way, a *Christ-like, or Buddha-like way* of doing things?"

Then, you might want to combine all of the above into one final tool.

Combining Your Choice Empowerment Skills

If we put them all together, using the combination of all five at the same time, we produce a very powerful choice empowerment tool, such as the following:

"As a person practising *Purposeful Being,* is this the *loving Christ-like way* in which I would like to serve my *highest and greatest good forever?*"

Throughout this chapter, I have focused on the problems of judgment from imaginary external forces as well as the relationship of judgment to good and evil. Through my own spiritual insights and those of others, I have come to believe that God is not into condemnation, but caring, concern, compassion and love.

I was once told a story of a woman, laden with guilt, who had a vision of God. In it she begged for his forgiveness and mercy. His answer was, "Not only do I forgive you this time, but I will forgive you if you do it again."

From my own experience I have come to the conclusion that I cannot afford the luxury of carrying the heavy load of hate, denial, rejection and separation that lack of forgiveness creates for myself and those around me.

For humans, forgiveness is *soul food* that brings us back to our God-Self. It is for this reason that I have included the following poem.

The Ballad of Judas Iscariot

Rev. Morton T. Kelsey discusses this ballad of Robert Buchanan which depicts a view of a God who does not accept good or evil, a God without condemnation.

"This old ballad tells the story of when Judas committed suicide and his soul wandered through the universe bearing his body and seeking a place for it to rest. Hell would not take it in; the earth would not receive it; the sun refused to shine on it. Judas could find no resting place in all creation.

"At last, in a nameless region of darkness ice and snow the soul of Judas saw a lighted hall and the shadows of people moving about within. He laid his body in the snow and ran back and forth outside the windows. Although Judas did not know it, inside Jesus sat at a table with His guests, ready to receive the fleeing soul and relieve Judas of the burden of that body lying in the snow."

> 'Twas the Bridegroom sat at the table head,
>   And the lights burned bright and clear—
> "Oh, who is that?" the Bridegroom said,
>   "Whose weary feet I hear?"
>
> 'Twas one looked from the lighted hall,
>   And answered soft and slow,
> "It is a wolf runs up and down
>   With a black track in the snow."
>
> The Bridegroom in his robe of white
>   Sat at the table-head—
> "Oh, who is that who moans without?"
>   The blessed Bridegroom said.
>
> 'Twas one looked from the lighted hall,
>   And answered fierce and low,
> "Tis the soul of Judas Iscariot
>   Gliding to and fro."
>
> 'Twas the soul of Judas Iscariot
>   Did hush itself and stand,
> And saw the Bridegroom at the door
>   With a light in his hand.
>
> 'Twas the Bridegroom stood at the open door,
>   And beckoned, smiling sweet;
> 'Twas the soul of Judas Iscariot
>   Stole in, and fell at his feet.
>
> "The Holy Supper is spread within,
>   And the many candles shine,
> And I have waited long for thee
>   Before I poured the wine!" (Kelsey 278)

CHAPTER 9 QUESTIONS

1. Do you feel you are the result of all your choices? If not, who else has been making them for you?

2. What is the connection between *pre-choosing* and *feelings* and *emotions*?

3. How has making dualistic choices impacted your life, such as *good and evil*?

4. Do you think God is concerned about judgment? If not what is God concerned about?

5. How would your life be different if you no longer thought in terms of judgment and condemnation?

6. Of the five methods for making a decision, how many can you remember?

7. Give an example of how practising *Purposeful Being* would affect your choice.

8. Give a personal example of how using *'forever'* would help you make a *choice.*

9. Give an example of making a *choice* that would serve your *highest good.*

10. How has real or imaginary external control affected your life?

11. Think of a situation where you would ask, "Is this something Jesus (Buddha, Mohammed . . .) would do?"

12. Are there things in your life you feel you *must* do, or do you always have a *choice*?

13. Give an example of using all five self-empowering skills in one *choice-making* question.

CHAPTER 10

Careers and Purposeful Being

The essential condition
of everything you do must be
choice, love and passion.

—*Nadia Boulanger*

Many people choose careers without giving them the insight and thought they deserve. This is born out by those who spend their lives complaining about their work.

Yet there may be other reasons why their job or career may seem unsatisfactory. Let us begin with the idea that whatever you are doing is because you chose it, and at the time you chose it, you did so for what you felt were valid reasons.

Next, as someone who is practising *Purposeful Being,* no matter how unsatisfactory your job is at the moment, practising *P.B.* by doing your '*soul's purpose*' will bring you a lot of peace, even on the job you have now. After practising this way of life, many people have found that the job they previously could not stand has now become a work of love. *Purposeful Being* helps them be consistent with who they are, regardless of their activities.

What we create, what we demonstrate and the manner in which we do things show us to the kind of person we are being. When goals and outcomes become our main focus, we get caught up in the emotional roller coaster ride of our successes and failures. Life is to be lived, not a goal to be achieved. By concentrating on *Purposefully Being* your *pre-chosen* God-like self, you are being fulfilled, regardless of your goals or circumstances. Happiness, then, is experienced continuously and is not postponed until some future goal, or achievement, is realized.

A nurse, who began practising *Purposeful Being,* was stressed on her job. She complained bitterly about the cutbacks, the supervisors, the doctors and sometimes the patients. However, once she began practising *Purposeful Being,* her attitude towards her job began to change drastically. She came into one of our sessions and said, "Now it is so good going to work, it is like a rest compared to my private life."

Her work environment never changed; she did. She got lots of worthwhile feedback from the staff and patients on how wonderful it was to have her there.

As we noted before, it is not what you *do,* or the kind of work you *do,* that is so important. Rather, it is who you are *being* in the things you *do* and the *way* in which you *do* them that makes the difference. First, love and honor the person you are *being,* and then the way in which you are expressing yourself, and you may find you are in the right place after all.

However, if you practise *Purposeful Being* and still find you are not satisfied, in spite of making the personal changes we have recommended, then a career, or job change may be appropriate.

Finding Your Mission

In the last chapter, I suggested that you go outside of a situation to find the answer. When feeling dissatisfied in your present job or career, it may mean a totally different endeavor or mission is awaiting your acceptance.

The word 'mission' implies fulfilling a purpose in this life. This suggests that there is both a sender and a returning back to the sender after your mission has been completed. However, as discussed previously, because of free will, it would have been a mission of mutual agreement that was made prior to conception.

In his best-selling job-hunting book *What Color is Your Parachute?* Richard N. Bolles feels that we all have amnesia, and have difficulty remembering who we are and why we are here. He also feels it is our task to begin recalling our relationship with God, and to awaken to our *pre-chosen* purpose or mission (354-370).

- The first stage is realizing your true identity as your God-Self.
- The second stage is defining your *soul's purpose* that corresponds with your highest views of God.
- The third stage is awakening to your mission or life's ultimate activity that for you best enshrines your *soul's purpose.*

Some people look at 'mission' as if it were God's responsibility to find it for them. They might ask, "Well, what is it that God wants me to do? I am sure God has a plan for my life." This will get you nowhere. You must understand that you and God are one and that your desires are God's desires. Therefore, being as God means that you have the gift of 'free will.' What will make you happy is when you are consciously *being* and *doing* that which you feel will fulfill your highest and greatest good in relationship to being your God-Self. If there was a God who told you what you had to do, then every time something went amiss, you would be blaming and resenting God's control.

A problem that can occur with the idea of *mission* is what I call the Achilles syndrome. In Homer's *Iliad,* Achilles was a heroic commander in the battle against Troy. He had a belief that his life's mission was to do one great and glorious heroic deed. He had spent his life weighing opportunities against his concept of a heroic deed. In the meantime, he had become a dishonorable character as he lived a life that was less than heroic. In his final battle, he performs his heroic deed; but, mortally wounded, he regrets the way he had wasted his life for this single cause.[19]

'*Make your life your mission.*' Live to your full potential and risk going after your dreams. Express your *soul's purpose* heroically every day. Show to yourself the kind of God-like person you are being, by what you demonstrate and bring forth. Begin by doing this in your relationships, family and workplace. By being faithful in these, you are preparing yourself for greater opportunities of experiencing your God-Self, every step of the way.

The process of finding a new career, job, purpose or mission takes time and energy.

When your passion becomes ignited over a social or environmental concern and you feel that you can make a difference through some specific and personal activity, bring forth all your talent and ability and you will realize you are at one with the nature of God.

Jesus, Buddha, Gandhi, Lincoln, Martin Luther King Jr.—each of these was fulfilled through having a great vision for one of the world's great needs, even though he never lived to see it fully completed in his lifetime.

The Key to Motivation

This takes us back to the first steps in bicycle riding, which were *desire, beliefs and imagination.* Our parents' desire provided the seed for our birth. Everything we have attained came about through the energy of passion and desire. Working with intuition means our going to the place of passion and desire. The first step in discovering your new career or mission is to be aware of what excites you regardless of how impractical it may first appear. Therefore, things with which we are familiar and that we regard as practical, are set aside for now.

When talking about your life's work, it is best to go beyond fame, power and fortune. These may be a consequence of your desire, but should not be the object.

You need to *believe* that there is more to life than you have experienced till now, that there is something for you to do that will always be satisfying and fulfilling.

You create desire through *imagining* and fantasizing about the most exciting and fulfilling career and mission of which you can possibly dream. Begin by asking: "Who are my greatest heroes? What have these figures done that made the world a different place? What are my greatest concerns regarding our planet, my town, city or nation? What would Jesus, Buddha, or Mohammed do if they were here?" Remember the question the miracle worker asked the four truckers in the first chapter: "Are the three trucks all you want?" Wouldn't you want more than that? Imagine that she is asking you these questions. Be aware of any feelings that may arise as you explore your greatest fantasies and desires concerning your career. What in life gives you the most satisfaction? Imagine your work setting, is it in the country or the city? Would it be in a setting where there are lots of friendly people? Or would you be alone? Would you be doing something with your hands, with your intellect, your voice?

I invite you to make a list of all the things you do that you find meaningful and satisfying. This can range from being a volunteer to a skydiver. Take several days to reflect on this question. Do not rush—the rest of your life is at stake. Imagine this as being the time when you have an opportunity to begin your life anew by awakening to the activities and interests with which you would like to be connected for the rest of your life. Compile all your ideas into a list. Commit to the thought that, "Nothing is impossible." Therefore, nothing should be ruled out.

Today, they say a person should be prepared to change careers at least three times in our fast-paced, high-tech world. However, if Jesus, Buddha, Gandhi, or Martin Luther King Jr. were here today, they would not have any difficulty finding a career that would relate to their vision. Neither would they have difficulty staying with it for the rest of their lives. When you find a vision that is bigger than you are, its fulfillment will inspire all of your creative, intuitive and intellectual skills.

Also, within any profession or trade, you could set a higher purpose or principle to which you would passionately commit yourself. Bakers could think in terms of health products, and provide healthier alternatives to their standard baking line. Lawyers could fight for the various injustices they see in society and in the laws of the land.

All of us could choose life-guiding principles which we could stand up for in our individual careers, and be influential in the way our companies and places of employment live up to these principles.

Some may choose to make their life's work out of our *soul's purpose,* as I have. Others will take their *one thing* into whatever type of work they do. For example, I know of one person who went about teaching her *soul's purpose*. Her name is Edith R. Stauffer and her *soul's purpose* is reflected in the title of her book *Unconditional Love and Forgiveness*.

What if Nothing Excites Me?

Barbara Sher, author of an exciting book called *I Could Do Anything If Only I Knew What It Was,* has an exercise which she calls 'The Job From Hell.' She claims that participants quickly get excited and inspired when they are asked to look at the negative aspects of a job which they feel they would hate. It seems that they reveal the negative aspects of every job they ever had. Then Sher has them switch to the opposite aspects of that job from Hell. For example, if one participant said, "My job from Hell would be working in a high-rise in the middle of a city with hundreds of people around," her switching to the opposite might mean that she would enjoy a more rural setting where she could operate more independently. I encourage you to try this exercise, as it is fun and rewarding.

Once you have listed all your clues, prioritize them on a scale from one to ten. The closer to ten, the more desirable is your choice.

At this point you can go back to the chapter on choices, and use your choice skills on the career activities on which you decided. Supposing you chose a career activity like writing, you could ask, "Does it fit with my *soul's purpose and P.B.* way of life? Is writing something I would like to do *forever*? What is it that I would like to write about forever more? Is it a loving thing to do? Does it serve my highest good? Is this a God or Christ-like (Buddha, Mohammed) way in which I would like to spend my life?"

By now, several different types of activities should be standing out for you.

Another way of approaching this is to see what combinations of these ideas could come together. A friend of mine who had a degree in psychology was torn between going further in this discipline or studying that of horticulture, which she really loved. I asked her if they could be combined. She said that she had not thought about it, but then a light seemed to go on as she recalled that there is a new field opening up called horticultural psychology. She has since graduated from this field of studies.

There are still several elements to be considered before settling on your final choice.

Freedom in Structure

When deciding on a career, one should be clear about the role that structure plays in your choices. An overly used and misunderstood reason for change today is heard in the statement, "I want to be free to do my own thing." Often, this is intended to mean, "I wish I could be free of the oppressive structures in which I find myself."

What comes to mind when I think of freedom without structure is a dream that a lady had had of herself. Firstly she saw herself participating in a very structured English tea party, and secondly as a Native American, standing alone on a hill with her arms extended towards the sunset. In the first part of the dream, people, friends, conversations, common interests and so on surrounded her. In the second, she was alone and had no one. Although she was free, she felt very isolated, and realized how lonely freedom could be.

It seems that we constantly tease ourselves about being in either place. Too much structure we interpret as a lack of freedom. We react against this by dreaming of escape to our island in the sun, or to some remote area in the wilderness. But with too little structure, we run the risk of becoming isolated and alone. What are we to do?

Freedom without some form of structure is practically impossible. Being upset about a structure is like barking at shadows. I am not saying that we should sit back and do nothing about the injustices within a structure. However, to make a structure responsible for the dissatisfactions in our life is to put ourselves into another form of victimhood.

What has this got to do with your career or workplace? Too often, people rail against the structure in the work place and project all kinds of dissatisfaction on its systems and policies, rather than seeing it as part of life.

A supervisor of a mental health agency came to me just after she had taken over management of her department. Within a month she was crying about her boss's insensitivity towards her. She wanted to quit and be free of the craziness of her institutional environment.

She strongly believed that the system was out to put her down by its interfering with her ideas, and promoting its own agendas.

We worked on her *reactions* and *expectations* and what she would be like in the same situation minus these emotional responses. At the same time, she became inspired by the awareness of her *soul's purpose*.

She has been there for about five years and now gets along superbly with all members of the management team, her own staff and her clients. She is excited about being a team player and going with the flow. I have not heard her talk about quitting for years. What she did was find a way to be free within the structure she found herself in.

One of the best stories I have heard about finding freedom in structure was that of a prisoner in a Japanese prisoner of war camp in Burma during the Second World War. This prisoner was dying and thought that this was his last night on earth until he heard a voice telling him he would recover. The following day, he began to improve and gradually returned to the level of health to which he had become accustomed in the prison.

Then a strange thing happened. Every day or so, he would hear an inner voice saying that a certain prisoner would die. Sure enough, the prisoner would soon pass away. This happened so often that he finally cried out, "Why are you telling me such terrible news? I don't want to hear it, please stop." Then the voice asked, *"Do you know what is killing them?"* "No," he replied, "but I guess it is to do with their being prisoners." Again the voice spoke, *"It is not the prison that is killing them, it is not the oppressive guards, it is not the prison food, or their surroundings."* "Then what is it?" the amazed prisoner asked. This time the voice replied, *"It is the workings of their own minds."*

After that, the prisoner devoted his attention to his thoughts and attitudes, and began working with the thoughts and beliefs of the prisoners around him. As the prisoners began to address their thinking processes, so did the deaths occur less and less.

I tell this story in order to emphasize how much of the stress that we feel through structures in institutions and organizations is due to our beliefs and attitudes. Some could come out of a Japanese prisoner of war camp more mentally fit than when they went in. Practising *Purposeful Being* by doing your *soul's purpose* allows you to find freedom in whatever work-structure or situation you find yourself.

Freedom could be defined in this way: You can choose whatever you want, but you should realize that you also choose the structure that goes along with it. Therefore, once your choice is made, do not complain about the structure, otherwise you become its victim. Instead, find your freedom within it.

Do Previous Abilities Influence Choosing a New Career?

Actually your past abilities should not be used as the deciding factors when choosing a new career. You could limit yourself by comparing a new opportunity with your previous abilities. You have no way of knowing whether you have the ability or not until you try it.

This would be like asking a five-year old, "What are you going to do when you grow up?" Let us imagine that a child replies, "I am going to be a doctor." Imagine a parent then saying, "You cannot be a doctor, because you do not have the ability."

The child will not know whether it has the ability or not until he/she tries it. The child has nothing in its ability kit that would indicate anything of value about doctoring until it grows up, takes the bull by the horns and tries being a doctor. All it has is the dream. Why do children grow up to become doctors? They dare go after their dreams, and they do not judge their chances of succeeding according to their previous abilities and experiences.

Separating the Spiritual From the Physical

A trap a lot of people fall into occurs when they try to separate the physical world from the spiritual world. Is there any part of the physical world where God is not? If God is in all things and everywhere, then all things must be spiritual. Many people feel that their going to church, working in a charity, volunteering, or creative artistic expressions are spiritual, yet their working with machines, sciences, sales, business are not.

What this sets up is akin to being schizophrenic and creating a split view of life. Did you know that you could not be non-spiritual?

You are as God, therefore, some of your expressions may seem unsatisfactory. But this does not change your identity. You are as God, in everything you do. God always experiences you as Him/Herself, and is concerned about your lack of self-recognition.

As a *P.B.* practitioner, you are conscious of the spiritual content that permeates all things. This eliminates the division between what is spiritual and what is material.

The old Biblical saying is that "You cannot serve two masters." If you believe that the world is dualistic and divided into the material and spiritual, you will be constantly in conflict between the two.

Money and Intent

If you are doing something you do not enjoy, such as a certain type of work because you need the money for school, your family, or whatever, and find yourself complaining and feeling hard done by, then you are enduring a life of conflict. You either have to change your thinking or your job. When you choose to do something for a certain benefit such as money, complaining while you are doing it is, of course, a waste of energy and time and is self-destructive.

Why not stay focused on your intent for being in that position in the first place? For example, I might say, "By writing this book, I am enjoying the experience of being an author and publishing a book that helps others to know their authentic selves." Or, "I am enjoying good health through doing this two-mile run."

Bring all your intentions into the moment and make them present in your daily work, school or life experience. This eliminates the need to complain, gripe and be upset. Instead, you act as if the goal is in the present, and is being achieved now by your current activities.

God and Money

There is no conflict with having money through *Purposeful Being*. This is another trap some fall into by making money bad and God good. As long as this conflict is there, you will always be divided within yourself. If you begin to make money, you will feel guilty, and eventually abort your success, because success does not match your inner belief that money is the 'root of all evil.' Money by itself is simply paper with a monetary value that you and society have attached to it. It can be used for constructive or destructive purposes—it is your choice.

As you practise *Purposeful Being,* money can be used to support all your *P.B.* ideals and aspirations. Suppose you are a successful businessman practising *P.B.,* you would now choose to use your money in a way that compliments your *P.B.* way of life. You could be asking yourself, "What is the way, and manner, I would like to use my money and success? Wouldn't it be through some form of service that would serve my highest good forever more?" As you work with this question, the way for you will become clear, and it has nothing to do with money being good or bad.

Let us say your goal is to get rich. If you did not know about *Purposeful Being,* you would be putting yourself in a conflicting situation. As long as you are trying to *get* rich, there is no happiness in *being* rich; there is only the effort of *getting* rich. What you are focusing on is lack. Second, if you ever become rich, you would fear the possibility of losing what you have, and that would also be unsatisfying. Furthermore, if you should lose what you gained, you would have to start all over by putting your happiness off until a time when you might be rich again. People who practise *Purposeful Being* are imbued with the richness of God-consciousness through expressing their *soul's purpose* all the time. Having financial riches would be just another occurrence around which *Purposeful Being* is practised.

Choosing—'The Essence'

Our approach to career finding is to look at the ESSENCE of what it is that you want to do, and make a choice which is in harmony with your *Purposeful Being* way of life.

Here is an example of what I mean: It cost some of the major railroad companies of their day just about every thing they had, because they never looked at the essence of what it was that they were doing.

Around the turn of the century, cars and trucks were invented. Trucks began to compete with railroads. The railroad companies just laughed and continued to belittle the idea of trucking companies ever competing with their huge corporations. Why? Because they thought they were in the railroad business and nothing could compete with the railroad business.

Pretty soon, the trucking firms were eating into the railroad companies' profits; and the harder the railroad companies fought, the more they lost. Finally, some of them began to invest in trucking themselves, while for others it was too late.

Railroad firms thought they were in the *railroad business.* They had not looked at the *essence* of what they were doing, which was *transportation.* All along they were in the transportation business and never realized this until it was too late.

Our process is about looking at the *essence* of what it is that you are doing and not at the practice, or the skill involved, until the *essence* has been acknowledged.

A client called Alan was concerned about what he should do for a career. Alan had a dysfunctional past, and had been very depressed over his divorce. I asked Al, "If money, or education were not a problem and you could wave a magic wand and do anything you wanted, what above all else would you want to do?" He thought a moment, and then said, "I would like to make guitars."

"For what purpose?" I replied. He said, "For musicians to make music with, of course." "Why?" I responded. He thought a moment and said, "I would like to make guitars for the five top rock bands in North America." "Let us say you have now done that, now what do you do next?" Not waiting this time for an answer, I asked, "Al, what is the bottom-line purpose for making guitars that would turn you on forever and ever?" "Boy this is hard work," he replied. "Come on, Al. What is it you like about guitars?" I said digging deeper. "That they make music." "Okay, what do you like about music?" I asked. Again it took him a while to respond. Finally he said, "You know Phil, I find music healing. I can be all tied up in knots, but if I sit down and jam out on my guitar, I feel centered, kind of like I have been healed of something." This time I felt we hit pay dirt. "What if you made guitars so that they could make the kind of music that heals people. Would you like to be a part of making healing music *forever* and *ever*?" What happened next was the closest I have ever seen Al to shedding a tear. "Yes, that is something I would really like to do *forever* and *ever,*" he replied.

A year later, I received a phone call from Al. He asked me over to his house, as he had something he wanted to show me. When I got there, he took me into his living room and then showed me a brand new guitar.

"What's so important about this guitar?" I asked, puzzled. "I made it," he replied. "Wow, this is fantastic." We sat down and, over a coffee, I reminded him of the talk we had a year ago. "You know Phil, a year ago I had no money, I had never even heard of a guitar school, yet since then, I have been to two guitar schools. All of the money has been paid, and now I have made my first guitar."

This gives you some idea of the digging you must do to get at the *essence* of what you are doing, or what you want to do.

Remember the mental health supervisor I mentioned earlier? On one occasion I asked her what she felt was the essence of her position. She thought about it and came up with answers like, supervising the staff, overseeing the programs, hiring the right people and so on.

I told her that that was not what I asked her. What I asked was "What is the *essence* of your position?" When she still could not answer, I asked her what was the purpose of her mental health agency. This time she twigged to what I was asking and said, "To help people improve their emotional and mental health." I asked her one more time, "So what is the essence of your position?" "Oh," she said, "now I understand. My position is to help people improve their emotional and mental health, which is why I got into this profession in the first place, to help people."

"Yes," I replied, "and if you only see yourself as some kind of manager, controller and supervisor you will miss the purpose for why you and everyone else are there, and your goal will be for efficiency and functionality instead of the welfare of your staff and clients. You will then miss the opportunity of healing that has been given to you, healing that you could give to others. She left, excited about finding the *essence* of what she was about.

You need to look at what is the *essence* of the thing you are doing, or which you want to do, in order to find your ultimate fulfillment in your work or career.

A surgeon in his late fifties came to see me. He was depressed and bored with life. I asked him what was the *essence* of being a surgeon. He talked about skills, knowledge and his abilities that were necessary for his practice. Finally, I asked him, "What does a doctor do?" "He helps people to get better," he replied. "Is that any thing like healing?" I asked. "Yes," he said. "Then is not the *essence* of what you want to do and be that of a healer? And does this limit you to just surgical procedures?"

"You know," he said emotionally, "that is why I went to medical school, to be a healer, that was my dream. I have not felt like that for years. When I go into an operating room, everything is prepared in advance. I do my work, and then I leave. I do not even want to see my patients."

This is a problem for a lot of people. They have lost the *essence* of their reason for their work or careers. After a while, what they are doing becomes boring and dissatisfying, and they suffer from stress or burn out.

Look at what you are doing, or what you would like to do, and see if you can find the *essence* of why you are there. If the *essence* involves helping others, you are probably on the right track. By looking at the *essence* of every job opportunity, you will soon find your niche or activity which fulfills you, providing that the *essence* of your job opportunity is in harmony with your new sense of God-Self, and can accommodate your *soul's purpose.*

What is Job Fulfillment?

A general statement one could ask is, "What kind of work is the most fulfilling?" The answer can be found by looking at history and the lives of the people who have seemed most fulfilled. Invariably, it comes down to helping others. Years ago, I remember a TV commercial for recruiting women as nuns. The picture showed a nun in a run-down village, holding a half-naked child and trying to feed it. The commentator said, "I would not do what you are doing if you paid me a million dollars." And the nun answered, "Neither would I." She received her reward by loving and helping others.

I have found in my practice over and over again that those people whose purpose, mission or career have a philosophy for helping others are more likely to be happy and fulfilled than those who are only after some external material or financial goal. There is nothing wrong with material or financial gain, but if it is your only focus, your life may not have the fulfillment you desire.

I was in business for over twenty years prior to going to University and getting my degrees. I looked back at one time and tried to remember how much money I had made in any one year. What amazed me was that I could not remember my total income for a single year. What I did remember was all the people who were in my life at the time, and the fun and excitement we had shared working together. I will never forget those people, but I wish now that I had been more concerned about those relationships than about the financial bottom line. In the end, it was the relationships and the memories that were really important.

The point of your dissatisfaction may not be that you cannot have what you want, but that what you want is unclear. Look at the *essence* of what it is that you want, and then find it out by asking the questions:

- Does this fulfill my *Purposeful Being* ideals and *soul's purpose*?
- Is this something that would fulfill me *forever* and ever?
- Would this be something that I, as my God-Self, would like to give my life to, and would doing this always serve my *highest good*?

You can soon see how asking these questions will allow you to decide quickly whether or not the vision, career or work you are choosing would suit you personally.

What you have now is due to the fact that at one time you set your mind to it and accomplished it. What you do not have is due to the fact that you have not set your mind to it. You are your source for all you manifest in your life.

I want you to know that the only roadblocks to having the joyful life you want are of your own creation.

At fifty-four, I was without funds, and all I had was a dream. For years, I had been involved in church-related counseling activities. I wanted to be a professional counselor. My vision was for more than a traditional degree in psychology. I wanted degrees that focused on spiritual psychology. So I spent two years at the University of Victoria, then went to Gonzaga in Spokane, WA. There, I achieved a double major degree—in psychology and religious studies.

At that time, it cost eighteen thousand dollars a year to go to school in the United States. I still had no money, having gone through the first two years on student loans which were not applicable in the U.S. I was at Gonzaga for two months, trying everything I could to get enough money to stay. Nothing was working.

Then I remembered an old friend with whom I had been in business many years earlier. Since then, he had become very successful in the windmill power generating business in California. I phoned him and told him of my predicament and how much I needed to get through university. He agreed, and supplied my financial needs for the rest of my schooling in the U.S. for which I am eternally grateful.

After getting my B.A. degree, I went to Holy Names College in Oakland, California where I got my Masters Degree with a focus in spiritual psychology. I had decided to go for what I wanted until there were no more doors that I could go through. As long as there was an open door, I went through it.

I could have held back and said, "I have no money. I am too old. I don't have enough education to enter university. I am not smart enough." But then I would never have known what my potential was. Also, when I started, if I had tried to figure it out by making my decision based on my financial situation, I would never have pulled it together. I had to go for it, not knowing where the money would come from.

When I was at university, I was amazed at the determination of some students in getting their degrees. There were people who were physically and emotionally handicapped, single parents with two or three children to support, as well as elderly people much older than myself. Yet they were following their dreams and would not have it any other way.

I come from a line of late bloomers. My mother got her first degree when she was in her mid-seventies, also in a university in Spokane. At the time, she took along my father whose left side of his body had been paralyzed by a stroke. My Uncle Tom, who also lives in Spokane, WA., got his first degree in teaching in his early fifties, and later his law degree by the time he was sixty. So I come by it honestly. You are never too old.

Summing Up

We talked about *Purposeful Being* as a way of changing who you are being while you are working at a job with which you may be dissatisfied. The idea is to change the way of *being* in your work and profession, including your attitudes and beliefs. This helps you to be happy with your life regardless of what you are doing.

How to have the work you want? You begin by asking the question, "If money, education (and any other excuse) were not a problem, *what is it I would like to do above all else?*" Then fantasize! Let your mind soar to its highest possible desire.

Also, you need to know that your free will is what God wants you to express. Therefore, do not ask what God wants you to do, as God's happiness is in knowing that you are doing what you want, especially when it is serving your greatest good.

We also looked at *finding freedom in structure, prior investment, materialism and spirituality,* and *money and spirituality* all through *Purposeful Being.* Then we talked about finding the *essence* in the things you are doing, and related this also to *Purposeful Being.*

Finally, we talked about fulfillment and how many have found that it comes from helping others. Loving others seems to be a fast track to increasing your appreciation of The God-like person you are. The following is a quote from *What Color is Your Parachute?*

> There are different kinds of voices calling you to all different kinds of work, and the problem is to find out which is the voice of God rather than that of society, say, or the superego or self interest. By and large a good rule for finding out is this: The kind of work God calls you to is the kind of work (a) that you need most to do

and (b) the world needs to have done. If you really get a kick out of your work, you've presumably met requirement (a), but if your work is writing TV deodorant commercials, the chances are you've missed requirement (b). On the other hand, if your work is being a doctor in a leper colony then you have probably met (b), but if most of the time you are bored and depressed by it, the chances are you have not only bypassed (a) but probably aren't helping your patients much either. Neither the hair shirt nor the soft birth will do. *The place God calls you to is the place where your deep gladness and the world's deep hunger meet.* [20]

CHAPTER 10 QUESTIONS

1. Is your way of being in your present occupation in harmony with your *Purposeful Being* principles? If not, what changes can you make?

2. What do 'structure versus freedom,' 'prior investment,' 'money versus spirituality' mean to you?

3. Is God in control of your life and the things that happen to you?

4. What have people who made a difference with their lives had in common?

5. *Purposeful Being* looks at the essence behind your career or occupation? Define the essence of your present employment or profession?

6. Suppose you had a choice to make around your current occupation, or you are thinking of applying for a job you are interested in. Apply the five 'power of choice' skills you learned in the last chapter, which are as follows . . .

7. Would making the following choice be in harmony with *Purposeful Being*?

8. Would it serve your greatest good?

9. Would you want to do it forever and ever?

10. Is this a loving thing to do?

11. Would doing this be in harmony with your personal God-like image as Jesus, Buddha . . . ?

Remember that if the job is unsatisfactory, but helps you appreciate your greatest good, such as working your way through college for a degree, then you can say, "In doing this I am being that which the degree represents."

CHAPTER 11

Towards a Spiritual Psychology

Is spirituality the missing ingredient in traditional and institutional psychology? Can there be lasting and valuable change by keeping spirituality and psychology apart?

The first question in its literal form is redundant, as the word 'psyche' means soul. Psychology should be about the study of the soul meaning your God-Self. As your God-Self, there is no spirit/mind/ body separation, as God is all things. Therefore, all your parts and expressions are God operating in unity. Your arm may seem to be an added appendage, yet it is very much a part of your wholeness. If God is all things, God is all of you including your beliefs, attitudes and behaviors. Until now, you may have expressed them while in denial, but that does not change the reality. When you speak, breathe or touch, you are expressing God, either in consciousness, or in denial. Therefore, there should be no separation between spirituality and psychology. Good psychology makes for good spirituality and good spirituality makes for good psychology.

Psychology, in its clinical and institutional applications, has until recently denied any form of spiritual involvement. This seems to be changing, as hard science is constantly being asked questions relating to the spiritual realm. Examples of this are often encountered when doctors, psychologists, and counseling professionals have clients who talk of seemingly non-rational occurrences. These include, out of body and past life experiences, visions, dreams, revelations, miraculous healing, visitations and directions from beyond the rational mind.

This becomes even more confounding when psychologists find these experiences are pivotal points that inspire people to turn their lives in a whole new direction. Most counseling professionals, having had no training or background in this area, are at a loss when it comes to helping their clients integrate these spiritual experiences.

Today, more and more professionals and institutions are beginning to address the problem of soul-work and its psychological implications. Work is now being done in several universities here in North America and around the world. Princeton, Harvard and Stanford in the United States are but a few of the many universities working in the realm of Spiritual Psychology and the Paranormal.

The great advantage of *Purposeful Being* is that it combines both spirituality and psychology. *Purposeful Being* shows how the two come together through conscious self-awareness. The truth is that all things are spiritual and part of *God*. The problems occur when our greater God-like reality is denied, and is not being realized in consciousness. It is then that we are denying our greatest resource.

Spiritual and psychological unity are found when a counseling professional keeps the path of *Purposeful Being* in mind. In this case the counselor's strategy is to use traditional therapy in issues which may be preventing clients from forging ahead with their *Purposeful Being* goals. The therapist can also introduce *Purposeful Being* at any stage as the ultimate direction for the client's life.

While in university, I read a story about a client who had inappropriate feelings toward his babysitter. His psychiatrist suggested that he take up a hobby to take his mind off her. So, he began building a table in his basement. This may have offered him a temporary solution, but I doubt if it solved anything in the long run.

If the psychiatrist had steered his client towards P.B., there would have been an opportunity for regenerating his life towards a more fulfilling lifestyle, which would have made secondary attractions less meaningful.

Purposeful Being does not see itself as anti-religious or as a specific religion. Rather, it uses all truths that it sees as valuable and supportive of *Purposeful Being.* All religions have some truth to offer a person practising a *P.B.* way of life.

The main difference is that *P.B.* participants have the ability to:

- know their real identity with God;
- choose expression of their *soul's purpose,* which is always a direct expression of their *God consciousness;*
- include spiritual truths and values, from either Christian, or other sources, as part of their individual expression of *Purposeful Being.*

By now you are probably aware that my upbringing is Christian, and that I am more at home with concepts that relate to my Judeo-Christian heritage. It is with these Biblical truths that I often align my *P.B.* process. I do not exclude insights from other spiritual disciplines or religions, but I am not as familiar with their written works and rituals as I am with Christian ones.

Certainly, Buddhists, Hindus, Moslems and people of all religions can adapt their religious beliefs and truths into the way they practise *Purposeful Being.*

As you can see from the following excerpts, this idea of being as God is not a new concept.

God and I Are One

If you dig deep enough, most major religions believe in the *oneness* with God theory, as expressed in the following list:

- ### *Christian*
In Christian terms, the Bible puts it this way. Jesus says, "Has it not been written in your Law, I said you are Gods," (John 10:34 NASB) and that, "You are the Temple of the living God" (2 Corinthians: 6:16 NASB).

- ### *Jewish*
I said, "You are Gods, and all of you are sons of the most High" (Psa 82:6 NASB).

- **Sufi**

  "He who is absent far away from God—His heart can only say: 'God is' somewhere. He who has found the Loved one in himself—for him God is not He, nor Thou, but I" Sufi writings (Das 103).

- **Islam**

  I am in your own souls! Why see ye not? In every breath of yours am I (Das 104).
  "La ilaha illa," ("There is no God other than I my Self") (Das 117).

- **Buddhist**

  "This very mind is the Buddha" (Mumonokan 30, Wilson, World Scripture 74). "Every being has the Buddha Nature, this is the self" (Mahparinirvana Sutra 214) (Wilson, World Scripture 147).

- **Zen Buddhist**

  "Why not seek in one's mind the sudden realization of the original nature of true Thusness? . . . If we understand our minds and see our nature, we shall achieve Buddhahood ourselves" (Platform Scripture 30).

- **Shinto**

  "The human mind, partaking of divinity, is in abode of the Deity, which is the spiritual essence. There exists no highest Deity outside the human mind" (Shintu-Dinju) (Das 159).

- **Taoist**

  "Find the Tao in yourself and you know everything else" (Kwan-Yin-Tse) (Das147).

- **Sikh**

  "Why do you go in the forest in search of God? He lives in all and is yet ever distinct; He abides with you, too. As fragrance dwells in a flower, and reflection in a mirror, so does God dwell inside everything; seek Him, therefore, in your heart" (Adi Garanth, Dahansari, M.9) (Wilson 73).

- ***Hindu***
  I, O Gudakesha, am the Self, seated in the heart of all beings, I am the beginning, the middle and the end of all beings" (Bhagavad Gita 10:20).
  "I am the True, the Real, Brahma. That thou art also. The heart of man is the abode of God" *"Aham Brahma, Tat tvam asi, Esha ma Atma antar-hryaye, Hrdi ayam tasmad hrdayam,"* (Sanskrit) and *"An-al-Haq-tu-I, Qalab-ul-insan bait ur-Rahman"* (Arabic) Upanishads (Hindu) and a well-known Arabic maxim (Sufi) (Das107).

The source for much of this list came from *Divine Revelation* by Susan G. Shumsky.[21]

What of People Who Are Not Religious?

As alluded to earlier, institutional religion is a compilation of ideas, behaviors and rituals created by a group of dedicated believers after a significant spiritual event. It is their intent to keep the insights, experiences and memories of this event alive, and under their guidance lead us to a direct relationship with God.

Spirituality is about an awareness of the active presence of God in humanity regardless of one's religious beliefs or practices. It covers all experiences that are not considered rational, such as psychic phenomena, intuition, visions, and so on. Therefore, some people may be religious without recognizing they are spiritual, and others may recognize they are spiritual without being religious.

There are those who feel neither spiritual nor religious. This may make it difficult to find principles to live by outside religious and spiritual traditions. If there is no God, then there is no sense of accountability.

Without spiritual or religious figures, who would be their role models? Religions have teachers, masters, saints and mystics who, throughout history, have exemplified the highest order of principles, values and virtues to which humans can aspire. Who would they choose as role models or teachers to replace these people? Would they not be sports, rock, movie and TV stars? Unfortunate, but true.

Historically, religions have established moral and ethical guidelines for not only individuals, but also communities and nations. If people had no spiritual or religious beliefs, their principles and values would have to be based on those of the society in which they live, which more often than not is not that impressive. Also, without a common ethical code, interactions between people become difficult. For example, if I do not know your code of ethics, how can I begin to trust you?

It does not take much investigation to see the disorder, violence and destructive effects that the lack of ethical values is having on our society. In North America, we have advanced in science and technology at an alarming rate, yet it seems that we are going backwards when it comes to building character that produces principle, integrity and honor.

It is a sad indictment of our times that many of our political leaders are not good examples of human values. Our young people need leaders of good character for inspirational role models. Instead, we are confronted with those who lie, cheat and have affairs.

Each religion has bibles, scriptures or writings that deal with the ethical lives of individuals and communities. Whether people live by these values or not is another issue. I believe it was G.K. Chesterton who said, "The only thing wrong with Christianity is that nobody has tried it."

For those of you who wish to practise *Purposeful Being,* but have not believed in God or followed a particular religion, you may want to consider what values you would like to incorporate into this new direction for your life. To begin, you may want to research some of the ethical standards usually found in some older religious traditions. For example, you could begin by exploring the ten principles found in the Ten Commandments and then integrate those into your *P.B.* way of life.

In what way is *Purposeful Being* compatible with Christianity and other religions? On the experiential level, *P.B.* offers an experience of God similar to that enjoyed not only by Christians but all religions. Each religious tradition has its means for creating an experience of Union with God. Again I refer to this as *divine fusion.* It happens in those moments when a person experiences no conscious separation between his/her illusionary self and the *authentic self.* While we are always in divine union with God, we have not always lived, believed or acted as if this were so. For those practising *Purposeful Being,* they are always knowingly experiencing *fusion* through the conscious practice of living their *P.B.* way of life.

It has been my experience that *P.B.* participants are able to arrive at, and maintain, these elevated levels of ecstatic *fusion* longer than most average church members. Why? Because, on a daily level *P.B.* practitioners are always expressing their God-like awareness consciously and purposefully in all that they do.

Many people are often overwhelmed when first experiencing an awakening or *divine fusion.* This includes inner and outer spiritual manifestations, which are often felt through all of the body's senses. Again, at times there may be a period of disorientation as they adjust to new beliefs about themselves and their world. However, with the experience of *fusion* they begin developing an internal reference point for being loveable and worthy regardless of the environment in which they live.

This *fusion* experience through *P.B.* gives people an awareness of a higher or deeper level of feelings, which takes them beyond loneliness and isolation. Even though in the beginning, these moments of bliss may seem sporadic and random, they are now aware that they are united with a source that is pure love and joy. These experiences can act as a magnet enticing them to stay committed to their new *P.B.* way of life.

Purposeful Being and the *fusion* experiences it brings can be a turn around for people's lives. Many alcoholics and substance abusers move away from their addictions. Relationships change for the better. Job satisfaction may improve. Acts of caring and compassion become more frequent.

Not all churches and ministers are trained to handle people who have had these kinds of spiritual awakenings. I remember a meeting that I attended years ago where a bishop was present. Someone suggested that if people needed spiritual assistance they should go to their local priest. The bishop replied, "That is the last place I would send them. I don't have a single priest who is equipped to address his parishioners' spiritual experiences." Being a wise bishop, he created and trained a lay group of people to handle these kind of spiritual issues.

At a visit to the previously mentioned Benedictine monastery in Pecos, New Mexico, Abbot David Geraets was giving a talk on spiritual growth. He said something that I have never forgotten: "Spirituality by itself can be demonic, as psychology by itself can also be demonic. But when you put them both together, you have wholeness."

People who have spiritual experiences without proper guidance risk getting involved with immature church groups and leaders. Or, if it happens outside of a church setting, there is the possibility of being psychologically and spiritually traumatized by New Age gurus who are not psychologically and spiritually grounded.

North America has had its share of gurus who have abused their followers by their obsession for power and spiritual dominance. These so-called spiritual giants have inflicted hardships of a horrendous nature, sexually, physically and psychologically on their unlucky recruits.

Without a psychologically and spiritually sound path for directing peoples' lives, they can easily be led astray. Examples in this past century abound when we look at the mass suicides that took place in Jonestown in Guyana, Waco in Texas, and Heaven's Gate in San Diego. These people may have had a lot of spiritual experiences, but they lacked solid guidance, both psychologically and spiritually. *Purposeful Being* is psychologically and spiritually sound all the time. By personally choosing your own activities and expressions that harmonize with your image of God, you are always fulfilling your *authentic self* (Neimark 55).

Through *Purposeful Being,* many of the above concerns are eliminated. *P.B.* is a model through which people can integrate their experiences all along the way. For example, people who practise *Purposeful Being* avoid the dualistic problems religions face on the question of good and evil. *P.B.* practitioners only ask, "Does what I intend to do fit with my *Purposeful Being* philosophy?" My personal choices, judgments or criticism, concerning my actions or beliefs always relate to the way in which I do *P.B.* Choices concerning right or wrong that are not about my *P.B.* way of life are set aside. By consciously being aware of your God-Self and expressing your *soul's purpose,* in the way you would like to forevermore, creates a simple way out of this duality dilemma. With it you are always serving only one master, [22] your *P.B.* way of life.

A goal for any religious or spiritual discipline should be avoidance of dependency. Once a person takes responsibility for developing their own personal 'way,' the training is over and the need for a spiritual teacher, guru, or church has less of an attraction. However, this does not mean that a person would not obtain further insights and reinforcement by having the above remain in his/her life. At a certain age, we no longer have the need for parents to the degree that we did as children, yet there is often much to be gained by continuing our association with them. We usually find that as adults we are more equal in our interactions and friendships with them.

As you are developing expertise in your *P.B.* way of life, one of the best methods of learning something is through sharing it with others. All the values, truths and insights, which you learned in the past, and felt would continue to serve your God-like awareness through the practice of *P.B.,* you may now find useful in the helping of others. And in the process of helping others, you are continually re-educating yourself.

Creativity and Manifestation

Why throughout history do people pray or meditate? Usually they do it to experience peace, and to influence God on their behalf.

First, let us talk about prayer. Praying to *get* something translates as a prayer of lack. If you ask for something, you are saying that you do not have it. In a sense, this is an insult to God. He says in so many ways, "All that I have is yours." How can you ask for something that you already have?[23]

On the radio the other day, I heard a Jewish talk-show host say, "The greatest Jewish prayer is one of thanksgiving." If you already have all that God has, then all you have to do is be thankful for it, even though it is unseen in the moment. Is this not what we call faith?

Now, if you thank God for it, and immediately afterward think doubtful thoughts, then you are erasing your previous prayer with one of doubt and lack.

If you add energy to your thought (energy = feelings and emotions), you have a higher chance of experiencing your desire. '*Thought plus energy produces outcomes.*'

When you express in prayer or meditation a thought with passion and conviction, as if you already had received it, then there is more likelihood of your receiving the desired result.

Think about the things you wanted and how you got them. Again, you used the *bicycle process* to achieve your aims (chapter 5). The more you *desired* and *imagined* having and enjoying it the more likely you were to receive it. In other words, you invested mental energy into that which you *desired.*

Meditation

I would caution you about meditation. It can be a great way to experience God's peace. But often people use it as an escape, like a client who, when feeling angry and upset, would go into her bedroom and meditate until she felt good again.

"What's wrong with that?" you might ask. The problem is that the event to which she chose to react is never dealt with. Every time the same event happens in the future, she will have to go running back to her bedroom. What she could do is work out the situation that triggered her reaction, before she starts to meditate. Then her meditation would be richer and deeper. And the next time the event takes place, she will have no reaction. (see chapter 6 on feelings and emotions and how to deal with them)

On the other hand, there are various types of meditation. Some forms are used to go to the source of the problem, so that it can be dealt with internally, thereby preventing it from triggering a similar reaction in the future.

Using meditation as an escape from the reality of this world can be a cop out; but using it as a means to assist you in manifesting what you desire makes it more realistic. However, meditation that does not help you realize your identity with God and support your life purpose other than for stress release is of little lasting value.

Through the practice of *Purposeful Being,* meditation, prayer, contemplation and reflection benefits are two-fold: First, it is used as a way of understanding the ecstatic experience of being one with God. Second, it is used to manifest all you desire that is in harmony with your *soul's purpose.*

Misusing the Ability to Manifest Our Desires

When I first became aware of my spiritual potential, there was a period when manifesting everything I desired became rather normal. As time went on, it began to dawn on me that something was wrong. Regardless of what I was receiving, it seemed that I was not any happier than before. Gradually, these things became a burden as I worried about their safety, their maintenance and the time and energy involved in being responsible for them. I began to feel that they were controlling me, rather than the other way around.

So I entered a different phase of prayer. My next prayer was: "Please give me only that which truly makes me happy, regardless of what I think makes me happy."

Looking back, this began the rocky journey that followed. Being stubborn and wanting to hang on to old beliefs, values and familiar comforts, I went kicking and screaming towards the happiness I have since found through *Purposeful Being.*

Your God-Self knows what true happiness is. The ego's self-image is insecure and lives in the world of rational and predictable thinking. The ego wants to save itself and the status quo, no matter how miserable life seems. The ego's self-image is also attached to tribal consciousness. It concerns itself with others' opinions, traditions and standards. It lives in fear of losing its relationship with what it has and knows. The ego's self-image becomes the template from which we direct our lives. Your God-Self does not need these external trappings to give it meaning. It has a larger, more open, template, that is God, from which it directs itself. It is already complete and is in love with the source, which is its own completeness. Self-esteem is a non-issue, as your God-Self is always in esteem of its self and others.

I have attempted to demonstrate that being overly focused on getting from the environment is a form of mental dependency on external conditions. However, the same is true with spiritual manifestation. "Same game, different name." Trying to get from God material things such as success, wealth and fame puts you back doing the same things you did when you wanted the environment to give it to you. All you have done is swapped the environment for God and are still enslaved to getting. Manifesting this way can be a form of 'spiritual materialism.'

The answer to this is to manifest and express all that is in harmony with your God-Self and your *soul's purpose;* then you keep adding to your sense of fulfillment and joy.

To put *Purposeful Being* into some perspective that everyone can relate to, let us look at two people who died recently, Princess Diana and Mother Theresa.

Princess Diana was a wonderful, kind, and loving person. Yet, until the time of her death, she suffered from a great deal of personal insecurity. Externally, she had all that life could offer, yet in spite of all this, it seemed that she could not reconcile her feelings and emotions with her surroundings. Her insecurity, bulimia, and lack of self-confidence were well publicized by the press. Princess Diana was insecure about her self-image and her ultimate direction for her life.

Mother Theresa, on the other hand, enjoyed who she was being and what she was doing. It appears that there were no internal conflicts between who she thought she was and what she was doing. In spite of the poverty, disease ridden, war torn places that she lived and worked in, she died at a reasonable age. She was internally happy. Yet she was also famous and powerful. When she spoke, kings, queens, and heads of state all listened. She acquired millions of dollars worth of property to be used for her purpose in life—giving to the needy. She usually got whatever she wanted. Yet everything she wanted was in harmony with the person she was being and with what she was doing.

There have been many people like Mother Theresa in this past century, such as Nelson Mandella, Gandhi and Martin Luther King Jr. These are people to whom we can relate on a worldwide basis, but if you look around your own community, you will constantly come across similar people everywhere.

Let us fantasize for a moment. Imagine you are totally fulfilled by consciously being as *God.* Through doing your *soul's purpose* you are constantly fulfilling your God-Self. You experience no doubts, nor do you question your worthiness. Self-confidence is not an issue as you radiate self-esteem constantly. You are always happy being you, doing you and expressing you. You are aware of your wondrous potential for experiencing joy. You are in love and at peace with yourself, life and all that you do, regardless of your circumstances.

For some, the above may sound a little Pollyannaish, especially if they were raised to believe that self was always attached to self-ish*ness.* Author Caroline Myss explains in *Anatomy of the Spirit* how, through personal growth, we have created words like self-esteem and self-worth, which, up until thirty years ago, were not that big a part of our culture. More recently, we have dropped esteem and worth as the main focus and are now concentrating on the self. The evolution of consciousness has been preparing us to understand the essence of what *self* means.[24]

Psychology is still, for the most part, working with the ego, which process inhibits the amount of change that one can expect within these limits. Our God-Self is about *soul-work,* getting to the essence of who we are, then discovering ways to express this reality satisfactorily. I believe that this type of psycho-spiritual development will be the new wave of growth for the new millenium.

Many have now come to realize that the essence of life involves understanding who we are as God. What has been missing is focusing on our *soul's purpose,* which allows us to expresses and experience our God-Self in whatever way we choose.

It is my belief that we are here to awaken to our true identity, then to purposefully express the meanings we relate to this new identity in all that we do. Of course, this is a choice that we all must decide for ourselves.

Spirituality and Transformation

Transformation does not necessarily come about through divine fusion alone, as reported earlier by people who had had 'after death experiences' in which intense fusion with the Divine was experienced. These people still had to work through a number of beliefs and behaviors, before living more consistently in an elevated *fused* state of being. What did change was the way they wanted to live their lives. Many lost their fear of death, became more spiritual, and were not as attached to material things. Most wanted to serve others in some meaningful way.

Fusion and elevated levels of feelings increase as we consciously identify ourselves *with the All.* They also decrease the more we invest in separation from the *All.* Furthermore, when we accept our true identity, our needs also lessen their hold on us, and as the experience of unity becomes more satisfying, many of our needs just fade into the background.

You might wonder if, by practising *P.B.,* you could lose your identity completely. The answer is, no. However, you will definitely go beyond any unwanted attitudes and behaviors, so that only the joyful, worthwhile things will have any appeal. You will just enjoy being you more and feeling more fully alive.

In Christian circles, *oneness* is often referred to as "being one in Christ." Christ means "the Anointed One, the Messiah." This suggests that a person is God experiencing Him/Herself in human flesh.

"So, whoever is in Christ is a new creation; the old things have passed away." What is referred to here is a new identity, a consciousness of being a Christ, a God Human, a new creation. The old faulty self-image is gone; there is no more false identity. Like Jesus, we now accept ourselves as God Incarnate, as is all creation. As Jesus was the Christ, so are you; this is what is being asked of you.[25]

Unfortunately, most churches and religions have not emphasized this aspect of *fusion* and *unity* with God. This omission tends to leave many people with either a fear of God or an irresponsibly dependent relationship. They tend to see God as judgmental on the one hand, or as Santa Claus on the other. In either case, this type of belief in duality and separation often fosters low self-esteem and low self-worth. Only with a full understanding of *unity with the All* can we be fully content and empowered within ourselves.

Could Life Become Boring?

It's funny, but the opposite seems to take place. As you become more joyful and happy about life, new opportunities seem to open for newer and more exciting ways of experiencing being and doing. I keep hearing *P.B.* practitioners exclaiming how exciting their life is in comparison to their past.

The Problem With Seeking Spiritual Powers

Since the sixties, we have had a cross-cultural stream of collective human consciousness happening simultaneously. Nowhere has this been more visible than in North America. One such stream involves our interest with psychology, which includes all types of personal growth and personal development pursuits. These have grown remarkably and are now a standard item in our society. We also have New Age spirituality, which has focused on the attributes of spiritual powers and insights. It, too, has been growing by leaps and bounds. During this same period, many traditional churches have been exploring spiritual experiences through what has been termed the 'Charismatic Renewal and Fundamental Pentecostalism.' Science has also entered the picture. As mentioned earlier, science is now studying spiritual phenomenon in the lab.

From the above, it would seem that we are entering a new frontier in human consciousness, the like of which has never been seen before on such a grand scale of collective human endeavor. I have personally been a part of this evolution and have participated in each of the above mentioned endeavors. However, I know that there are some dangers that still need to be addressed if we are to go forward with this new stream of consciousness.

It seems that many people today feel that as long as something is labeled 'spiritual,' it must be all right. As I noted earlier, there seems to be a great desire by some people to experience all kinds of spiritual powers before they have the maturity to handle it. This is not only rampant in New Age circles, but also within churches involved in experiential spirituality.

There is also reason to be concerned with science and some of the experiments that scientists are working on, such as using psychic and spiritual powers as a weapon for war.

One time in Berkeley, California, I came across a New Age magazine that advertised workshops that trained people to channel through to the spiritual world. What amazed me was that on the back cover were smaller advertisements on workshops to help people de-channel and rid themselves of their oppressive spiritual entities.

At the time, I believed people were getting in over their heads, but I had never seen it spelled out so literally.

Why are people opening themselves to such risks? Often it is because they feel powerless in their lives and think that by obtaining some form of spiritual power, they will get the recognition and self-empowerment they lack.

There are many who have obtained some spiritual giftedness and then created a following, which practice has often led to tragedy. In our recent past, extremists of this nature have been, Marshall Applewhite, head of the Heaven's Gate Suicide cult, and Jim Jones in Guyana who directed his nine hundred followers to drink Kool Aid laced with cyanide. These calamities usually occur when the immature believe that leaders with spiritual powers are more God-like than themselves (Neimark 55).

Spiritual gifts and powers are everyone's heritage, as everyone is *one with God* and all God has. The problem is that most people do not believe it. Therefore, they do not develop their own spiritual powers, but follow and worship those who do, regardless of their leaders' spiritual and psychological maturity.

How do we obtain spiritual maturity? To begin with, never see yourself or any one else as being special because of enhanced spiritual powers or gifts. Realize that you or they are expressing what is available to us all. Second, always focus on the source of all powers, the Divine All, which is your true identity. Third, adopt ways and standards that help you live in conscious *unity* and *fusion* with your informed understanding of the All, such as *Purposeful Being*.

At some point, one must accept one's self as a unique God-like person with a corresponding purpose in whom it is worth investing time, money and energy, regardless of what is happening in his/her environment.

Each individual creates a self-chosen way of life. Spirituality is not an issue until a person awakens to it personally. It cannot be taught. Teaching is only a guide to a person's individual awakening. Once this awakening takes place, one needs to generate a psychological and spiritually sound path of his/her own choosing.

Purposeful Being provides you with a vehicle that allows you to go forth, knowing you have the tools to bring about the joy and happiness you desire. This means that as you practise it, you are placing a value on your psychological and spiritual development.

CHAPTER 11 QUESTIONS

1. Give examples of when you went after something that you discovered later offered short-term gain and long-term pain.

2. As a practitioner of *Purposeful Being,* how would you judge if something you wanted is good or bad? Explain.

3. What is the difference between praying to get something and a prayer of gratitude? Explain.

4. When is meditation counter-productive? Explain.

5. Is investing time, energy and money in yourself okay or is it selfish? Explain.

6. Who do you know in your life who is aware of who they are and who are constantly doing things which complement their conscious identity?

7. Do you have spiritual powers? If not, why not? Explain.

8. Can spiritual powers be destructive and counter productive?

9. How would you expect to obtain spiritual and psychological maturity? Explain.

STAR DESIGN

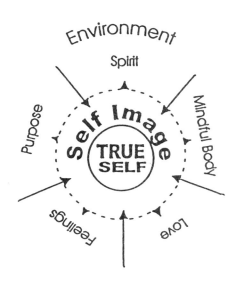

Figure 1

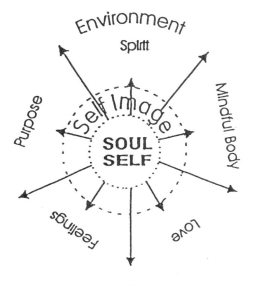

Figure 2

CHAPTER 12

Beyond Healing

In our final chapter, I wish to explore the mind/body/spirit aspects of life and relate them to *Purposeful Being*. I began this work with a diagram (see opposite page). It includes career, spirit, mind/body, feelings and emotions, and love. These five functions are the avenues through which we express our God-Self and interact with life.

In the center of the first circle (Fig.1) is the spiritual essence of who we are, then surrounding this circle is the ego's definition of who we are—our self-image. The ego's self-image has, in this stage of development, a solid line between it and its spiritual source. In other words, it does not recognize that its spiritual center is even there. This spiritual blindness to one's true *authentic-self* forces one to look for an identity elsewhere; hence the creation of a false self-image and the dual personality that goes with it.

The line of the outer circle is open, indicating the belief that all happiness and fulfillment must come from the outer area beyond the perforated circle. Therefore, by denying its central God-Self identity (soul-self, Christ-self, Buddha-self, and so on), a person living in the above belief system will always look to others and the environment not only for an identity, but also for happiness, security and self-worth.

In the first drawing (Fig.1), the ego's self-image is kept out of the inner circle of the true or hidden God-Self. To the ego's self-image this appears to be the way life is. In reality, there is no self–image; there is only you as your God-Self operating in denial of your true identity. As much as we like to compartmentalize and separate mind/body/spirit, the conscious and the unconscious, true self and false self, we deceive ourselves into maintaining our denial of the one true self. There is only you as your God-Self manifesting both the happy and unhappy conditions and experiences of your life.

While at times I may use terms like ego, self-image, or false self to better explain the process, you should be aware that these are just tools to explain different aspects of your God-Self.

If you were color blind, you could believe all you liked that your skin was a certain color, but this does not change the reality of the true color of your skin. Therefore, we can call you Phil, George, Mary, or Edina, yet none of this changes who you are as God, regardless of what you are called.

In our first diagram (F.1), there is a solid line around the God-Self circle which forms a self-made barrier that keeps us separated from our soul or God-Self, thereby limiting the amount of joy we can experience in this life-time.

In the second diagram (Fig.2), nothing is closed. God is radiating outward, all lines are open, and all Godly expressions are flowing out through all five sections at once, thereby expressing and experiencing a continuous flow of God's love all the time. The ego ignores the old self-image and now realizes that it is its God-Self and that this realization and its God-like expressions are now the source of its happiness. The ego no longer looks to *get* from its environment, but is more concerned about what it expresses and gives to its environment.

This concept is important to keep in mind as you are reading this chapter about healing.

Does Ill Health Happen Randomly, Beyond Our Control?

The following is an example of the way 'illness' is manifested.

- When we have depressing thoughts and are feeling down, there is a corresponding physical affect as well. The body slows down and is less inclined to be active.
- When thinking exciting happy thoughts, our bodies seem lighter and freer.
- When we are expressing anger, many physiological changes take place. Breathing becomes more restricted and confined to the upper chest or neck and shoulders become tighter, and our eyes are usually focused directly at the object of our frustration. Facial muscles become stiff and tense. Generally our whole body is tense and on alert.
- If we are suffering from grief and loss, again it seems that we are also suffering physically. We do not eat as much and we sleep more. We generally withdraw and close ourselves off physically and emotionally.
- When experiencing stress at work, we notice things like headaches and body stiffness. Aches and pains become more obvious, and we also feel more fatigued.

These are all examples of how we do things in wholeness. What is done mentally is experienced physically. What we do psychologically is experienced biologically.

Until now, most of us have had beliefs, attitudes and expectations about the way the environment and others should behave, and when our expectations were unfulfilled, we reacted emotionally. Therefore, our beliefs, attitudes and expectations generated our physical and emotional condition. When we have reacted physically and emotionally, we have felt uncomfortable and experienced a sense of '*dis-ease.*' It would be reasonable to assume that if these uncomfortable reactions continued over a long enough period of time, we might go from a feeling of *dis-ease* to producing a real sickness or *disease* from constantly having to carry this stress.

If an illness or *disease* were allowed to carry on indefinitely, it could prove fatal and, in fact, we would become *deceased.* Now if this was so, and I assure you it is, we have a picture of how illness comes into being.

What if illness can tell you the way you are living your life? If this were so, illness is offering you an opportunity to consider whether or not you want to keep on living in the same old way. This, then, is the great gift and challenge which illness can offer. By entertaining the possibilities of this concept, you can begin to search out answers for your life that may have previously been denied.

Illness is not something that happens randomly; it is an expression of the way you think, believe and act. Often, when you change attitudes, beliefs and behaviors, the tension in your body disappears and there is a return to a happier state of being.

Here are a couple of examples. A friend phoned me the other day and said that he was hurting all over; his whole body was in real physical pain. I asked him what it felt like, and his answer was that he felt 'tight,' as if he was being bound up by something. So I asked him how well he was doing at working with his reactions. He said that he had not been angry for some time. So then I asked if there was a chance that he was repressing all his feelings and imploding. I suggested that he go back and work with chapter 6 which explains how to handle reactions. A few days later, he called back in high spirits and happily told me how all the pain had left. He said that he had done what I suggested and had worked with the chapter on emotions and feelings and had felt a whole lot better.

Another client told me how her arthritis was acting up and was the worse it had been in a long time. I asked her what was going on in her life. At first, she said everything was as usual, but after a little digging she mentioned that, for the last two weeks, she had had painters decorating the inside of her home. I asked if they left a mess, if there was an odor, dust in the air, workers coming and going, and if it affected her routine, to all of which she gave a resounding, "Yes!" I then asked her if she felt frustrated, angry and out of control in her own home. Again I received an affirmative, "Yes!" We then addressed her feelings and expectations, and came up with other ways she could have dealt with the problem. A few days later, she was back to normal, and the pain and swelling had disappeared. It is interesting because Arthritis is often explained as inflammation of the joints, which would mean that her inflamed frustrated emotions showed up biologically by inflaming her joints.

Illness, then, is not considered good or bad. It is just you living your life in a way you find uncomfortable. Furthermore, if you look at illness in regards to its message, it could be seen as a profound information center, informing you about the way in which you are living. It offers you a wake-up call for changing your life.

While the idea that illness is good for you because it holds information about you may seem a little radical at first, it nevertheless is ground worth exploring. You have more control over your state of health than you have yet realized. Putting yourself in conflict with illness and wellness keeps up an internal war between good and bad. And while you focus on destroying the illness, you miss the opportunity of insight that it holds for your good. If your way of life and your reactions produced what is termed as illness, living a new way of life without those reactions would mean that your unwanted symptoms and illness would eventually disappear.

The idea of illness becoming a natural outpouring of how we are living our lives has been getting a fair amount of attention lately, both within and outside the medical profession.

Some years ago, I worked with Dr. Michael Greenwood, a best-selling author of two books on the subject of healing, and the Medical Director of the Victoria Pain Clinic, in Victoria B.C. In his latest book, *Braving the Void,* he states that he works with clients

> . . . who have abandoned superficial symptoms and fruitless searches for a specific "cause" and a "quick fix," and have, instead, actively engaged in exploring the symptoms they intensely fear, throuh the heightened attention of the void. They have chosen to turn and confront themselves, owning their dis ease as a part of that self. (23, 30)

Anyone working with Michael and his wife and co-worker, Cherie Greenwood, soon begins to understand that disease and pain contain the very answers for which the client has been searching. For Michael and Cherie, going into the *void* usually meant fearlessly going into the pain or symptom. As long as doctors and patients conspire to obliterate all traces of illness without paying any attention to the message of hope they contain, we shall keep on developing ever-increasing dependencies on external methods of healing and sabotage their message for personal change.

Thorwald Dethlefsen, a noted psychologist, and Rudiger Dahlke, a medical doctor, have also written an international best-seller, *The Healing Power of Illness: The Meaning of Symptoms and How to Interpret Them.*

In their opening remarks, the authors courageously state:

> We propose to show that the patient is not the innocent victim of some quirk of nature, but actually the author of his or her own sickness. Thus we shall not be addressing ourselves to environmental pollution, the ills of civilization, unhealthy living or similar familiar scapegoats; instead we propose to bring the metaphysical aspects to the fore. From this viewpoint symptoms are seen to be bodily expressions of psychological conflicts,

able through their symbolism to reveal the patients current conflicts (91).

They further state that, "Illness prevents us from straying from the road that leads to oneness. For that reason ILLNESS IS A PATH TO PERFECTION."

These are very strong challenging statements that confront our previously held beliefs surrounding healing and medicine.

I would like to relate a story concerning this topic, which may help put it all into perspective.

The Unhappy Healer

Many years ago in a city in China, there lived a well-known doctor. He was always in demand, with many people waiting in line every day to partake of his healing skills. Oh! he did have skills, the result of a lifetime of learning and practising on everyone who came to him for help. Because of this, he was well known as a great healer in his city.

Yet Lee Yang felt somewhat discouraged. He realized that, although he had learned much and practised what he had learned with good results, still something was missing. The worst part was that he did not know what. This feeling that something was missing bothered Lee for many years. He often noticed that his patients seemed to get well for a time with his healing arts and remedies, but they would always come back. Sometimes it was for treatments of the same malady all over again, while at other times, it was for something totally different and often worse than what they had come with the first time. He kept pondering about the reason why they could not stay well indefinitely. Finally, he decided to take a leave of absence and look for answers. Deep within himself, he knew there must be an answer somewhere; so he began his journey.

You must understand that Lee was hardly a young man when he began his journey. In fact, his friends chided him and suggested that he retire in comfort and rest on the laurels he had already obtained in his profession. But Lee would have none of it. No, he believed that he must search for an answer and find that 'special something' that was still missing.

His travels began in search of a new process, a greater skill, or perhaps a more powerful medicine than anything he had yet experienced, something that would cure his patients so that they would never have need of healing again. He began visiting the leading clinics and calling upon the renowned healers in every city and town through which he traveled. And each time, he would compare what he learned with what he already knew. Sometimes the skill may have had some merit, but it was never great enough nor profound enough when compared with his own expertise. He continued travelling and searching, yet became more and more discouraged along the way.

Finally, exhausted and tired from all his searching and constant inquiring, he decided that he needed a rest. There happened to be an old monastery near the town he was visiting. A wise old abbot looked after the monastery, as he had done for many years. So, Lee applied and was accepted as a resident for as long as he would care to stay.

He spent his days in prayer and meditation, which he found peaceful and relaxing. But, the Tao (God) seemed far away as no answers or divine revelations came to show Lee the way. One day, the old abbot agreed to meet with Lee in his study. The old abbot asked him why he was there. Lee explained that, in spite of his successes, he felt despair over not finding that special something that could make a difference in his healing practice. He needed the one skill or medication that would help people overcome their need for healing, once and for all.

They talked late into the night. Finally, the old abbot asked him to come back again in a couple of days when they would talk again.

Two days later, Lee returned to the old abbot's study. After making some minor inquiries, he asked Lee if he would take on an assignment that might give him the answer for which he was searching. Lee agreed to undertake anything that would solve his dilemma.

"Well," said the old monk, "there happens to be a village not too far from here that has been plagued with a mild disease that no one has been able to cure. Would you be willing to go and see what you could offer them in the way of healing?" Lee agreed, sensing that there was more to the question.

"There is just one thing that I will ask of you. If you accept this assignment, you must not use any previous skill that you have learned in the past, or any that you have yet to learn." "But what will I do? How will I help them? What could I possibly offer them without my skills?" moaned Lee. "Well this is your assignment; it will be up to you to discover the answer to that, and in doing so, I am certain you will find your answer. Do you still agree to take on this assignment?" asked the old abbot, staring intensely at Lee who winced under his steady gaze. Lee's head was reeling with doubts and uncertainties. Finally, Lee said, "Well, what have I to lose? I have tried everything else. I agree."

That evening, Lee packed his belongings, and the next morning, he bid the old abbot and the monastery goodbye and set off on his journey.

After several days, he arrived at the village infected with the incurable illness. He acquired some rooms and began acquainting himself with the layout of the town.

Lee was used to making friends, and had no trouble getting acquainted with the town's people. When asked why he was there, he would just say that he was a scholar and was studying the history of the area for future publication of some papers he was writing. He hoped that he would be forgiven for this small lie, but what else could he say? He could not tell them that he was a doctor who had no skills, now could he? At least that was his reasoning.

He began to question those who were sick, asking them traditional questions that a doctor might have asked, like,

"When did it start? Did you ever experience this before? What were you doing prior to your being ill?" But this line of questioning availed little. He realized that he had to go beyond the idea of cause and affect if he was to ever to do any good. Gradually, he began to look at the illness as a means for telling him something about the way the person was living. To his amazement, the way the person was living his or her life was reflected in his/her illness. He also discovered a significance in the location of the illness in the person's body.

As he showed them what it was that they were doing, or reacting to in life, they seemed more empowered. He began to see that all of them, no matter how humble their existence, had desires and dreams that could take them way beyond their present limitations. Usually these desires and dreams went beyond the need for immediate security and personal welfare. Each of them became aware that they were greater than they had allowed themselves to believe. Lee discovered that as they realized their Taoist self (God-Self, Christ-self) and as they could stay with this awareness in even the most humble of ways, then their life began to change and illness dropped away. Even more amazing was the fact that all illnesses began to fade, including those that were not related to the plague.

As people became aware of the Tao in and all about them, they became stronger. Furthermore, they seemed to grow in ever more healthy and powerful ways when, as he suggested, they offered from themselves a gift of life to others, some *'single Taoist-like thing,'* which action seemed to empower both the giver and receiver. It was as if they had at last become aware of their ultimate purpose and destiny. It was usually some single insight that, as they offered it continually to others, both the giver and the receiver became more and more transformed. Sometimes, it could be quite simple, like offering others understanding, or showing them how free they were within the structures in which they lived, whether they involved a marriage, a job, or a place. Yet another would show others to their power and freedom of choice, as still another helped people see the magic within and all about them. Whatever it was, as they gave of this single expression and practised it themselves, both the giver and receiver grew in health, joy, and happiness.

Often Lee would say, "Dear one, let us meditate and be one in silence with the All, and allow any images, thoughts, or pictures to reveal for us the insights that this sickness, ache, or pain, has to offer. And yes, be aware of your dreams, as they, too, provide the secrets to living your life." Many had their health restored on the spot. They also found greater purpose and fulfillment as they discovered their authentic selves. People changed in the ways they interacted with one another. There was so much happiness all about that strangers came from miles around to experience these joyous, wonderful people. And many would stay to learn what the townspeople could teach them about their Taoist God-like selves and what their purpose was all about.

The town began to recognize Lee as a teacher of how to purposefully live a healthy and fulfilling life. And at last, Lee began to understand what the old abbot had wanted him to find. There was no special technique. All along, it was about his being himself and showing others how they could be themselves, their real Taoist selves. He, at last, discovered that the 'special something' missing was none other than 'Himself.' There never was a great skill to get, or to have. He had always had it; he was 'the special something' and so was everyone else. "Oh, why did I take so long to discover this simple truth?" he wondered, as he thought about the years he had spent trying to get skills and techniques for healing. He recalled how he had acquired a new skill, only to drop it for the next one that came along. But, as he pondered all this, he realized that everything he had ever done was necessary to get him to where he was now. Nothing was wasted or lost.

Yes, Lee did return to his home city, but he could no longer continue just as a doctor. Now he could teach people how to live their lives with purpose so that healing, as it was formerly understood, was no longer necessary. He became more fulfilled than anything he could ever have imagined. His city gained more and more fame and popularity as a friendly healing center that could regenerate people's lives. But what continually thrilled Lee the most was just teaching people about their natural ability to help others go beyond their need for healing. He was amazed that they could do this merely by showing others, as well as themselves, to their true Taoist-selves. Through the giving of some simple thing to others, both the giver and the receiver would be empowered and enriched. By practising this, they soon turned their lives and the lives of others into a continuing experience of joy, happiness and fulfillment.[26]

The Meaning of Lee's Healing Journey

What did Lee Yang learn about healing? He learned a very important lesson that healing the disease was not as important as showing people to their God-Self and to their *soul's purpose*. He found that when they lived their lives through knowing their true identity and purpose, they went beyond their need for constant healing. Furthermore, he discovered that the illness provided them with the information they needed about how they were living, and that this information enabled them to make new choices for their lives.

How Was the Term 'Great Healer' Limiting Lee?

Having a self-image as a *great healer* was the very thing that was wearing Lee out. As long as he was stuck with the self-image of a healer, he took away the responsibility of healing from his patients. It was up to him, his medicines and skills to fix his patients again and again. They were forever dependent on him for healing, and were victims of their own illnesses. Also, because Lee carried the label 'great healer,' he personally carried the burden of responsibility for their healing needs. If they continued to need healing, he would blame himself for not having the right skill or medication. He felt that he was to blame for their continuing ill health. Carrying the title of 'great healer' also kept Lee's focus on himself, his fame, his reputation and his healing skills, all of which prevented him from teaching his patients how to live in a way that would take them beyond their own healing needs.

Furthermore, Lee had to learn that insights from the illness were not enough. His patients still needed to realize their true Taoist God-like self and their *soul's purpose* in order to have the kind of fulfilling life that would eliminate healing once and for all.

When Lee considered himself a healer, he was supporting the theory that illness was an activity separate from the patient, operating with a life of its own. This theory suggests the illness is intent on doing evil to the patient. It also supports the dualistic idea of illness being bad and wellness being good. Furthermore, it implies that the patient has no involvement in the life of the illness and is, therefore, its victim. With this model, the illness is outside of the patient and needs to be eliminated by some external means, such as drugs or therapy. Therefore, the patient has no responsibility for his or her own wellness.

Through practising *Purposeful Being* we see that illness is expressing itself for the patient's good; that we create illness in ourselves to benefit ourselves in some way. As mentioned earlier, we always do things to serve ourselves, even if we may not like the outcome. Therefore, the great crime that may be committed in the name of healing would be to fix or heal the patient by external means, while missing the opportunity for change that the illness is offering. This is also true with many of the symptoms around mental disturbances, such as depression, anxiety and stress. By taking medication like Prozac, a patient is masking the life-changing message held in the symptom which, if understood and integrated, could move him or her beyond the need for medication.

Healing is not only a matter of fixing or correcting something, but making new choices about your life that is being acted out and portrayed through the way you have been living. The use of the word healing is diminished, as the emphasis is on making life changes, as through *Purposeful Being*. Many people who have had a terminal illness and recovered look back at their illness as a gift which influenced the important life-changes they made.

In truth, the only person that can ever heal you is yourself. This is true even with the traditional medical model. The problem with the word healer is that it presumes there is something a doctor can do that 'cures' the illness, irrespective of the patient's participation. This concept is false, as the only person that can actually heal you is yourself. If you have a cut finger, in spite of the medication involved, it is your biological system that rushes to close off the blood supply and bring about the new cell structure that heals the wound. You in mind/body/spirit decide to co-operate with the medication until you are physically healed. This is true of any type of healing, even that which is called a miracle. The Self must, in mind/body/spirit, wholly decide to co-operate with the healing process.

The same miracle cure that works for one may not work for another. Why? Because openness by an individual to be healed must agree with his/her totality involving body/mind/spirit. We have all heard of people who have 'lost the will to live.' No matter what help is offered, they still die. In the end, it is the person who decides whether healing occurs or not.

Irrespective of all kinds of cures, even miracle cures, illness reoccurs if no life-changes have been made. Examples are found with those who have more than one heart attack, repeated cancer outbreaks, or multiple strokes, just to name a few.

Neither healing nor insight may provide a permanent cure or prevent its return if there are no changes made in one's life. A lasting change takes place when a person makes conscious life-changes that are in harmony with his/her concept of being as God, from which flows a fulfilling purpose and direction. Again the term 'cure' is out of place, as nothing was wrong or bad. The disease was just doing what nature does when a person lives a life that is *ill* conceived. A person has a perfect right to carry on doing his or her life in illness. The numerous people who smoke while knowing the risks are an example of this; yet they still continue smoking.

Do we do *Purposeful Being* to heal ourselves? No, we do it because it is the most joyous, fulfilling way we can live our lives. The fact that illness may disappear along the way is a secondary benefit.

Scientifically, the proof that the practice of *Purposeful Being* is good for your health is offered in chapter 5. You might recall two studies: "Mommy and I Are One" and "The Mother Theresa Affect." In the first trial, scientists gave students subliminal messages saying *Mommy and I are one* and their grade scores improved. Since then, this method has been used to help people both physically and mentally. In "The Mother Theresa Affect," the students watched a movie clip of Mother Theresa helping the poor, in other words doing acts of love. In these instances, the students' immune systems improved.

Both principles, *oneness* and *love,* are embodied in *Purposeful Being. Being* means being '*one*' *with God,* and God is love. By *purposefully* doing your *soul's purpose* and offering it to others, you are *purposefully* and *consciously being as God.*

Should You Stop Seeing Your Doctor or Taking Your Medication?

The symptom-reading process may require time to research and understand the message within the illness. It may also take time to put into effect the kind of changes one chooses to make. Even once the changes are made, the physical body may require time to adjust to these changes. So what do you do about the illness? Medically, you carry on in the traditional manner, particularly if the illness is life threatening. By no means do I advocate giving up on your current treatment or medication until such time as you and your doctor agree that you no longer need it. In the meantime, you are working with the symptom's symbolism and mythology in order to fathom the story behind your illness and realign your life accordingly.

Making a change for the sake of change can have you risk creating something worse than you had before. This is where changing to the *Purposeful Being* way of life comes in. By living your life in a way that expresses your soul's purpose and concept of being as God means that you are making the most desirable change you can imagine. With your *P.B.* healthy way of living your life to the full, the need for healing becomes less and less.

Does Practising Purposeful Being *Improve Your Health?*

Again we do not do *P.B.* to improve our health; we do it to have a fulfilling life. However, if you wish to check out some of the benefits people experience while practising *P.B.,* I refer you to the section in the book following the introduction, which reports the changes people experience through *P.B.*

Practising *Purposeful Being* over time creates and generates spiritual, physical and mental health simultaneously, because the above three functions are one. I again refer you to Circle Number Two (Fig. 2), at the beginning of this chapter. As you can see, by practising *Purposeful Being* you are radiating your God-Self outward into all areas of your life.

Did God Answer Lee's Prayers?

Lee wanted something that would heal people forever. He wanted to be the person to find it, so that he could maintain his self-image as that of a great healer. Yet it was this image and role that was making him so miserable. We could say that Lee's search for truth and his willingness to put all he knew about healing on hold provided him with an opportunity to try something new. Lee, as his God-Self, found the answer. Therefore, Lee's prayers were answered, albeit differently than Lee expected, yet more perfectly than he imagined. Lee had to move out of his professional self-image in order to find the answer. It is interesting that it was through his spiritual function represented by the monastery and the Abbot that Lee finally obtained his direction.

Was the answer always there? Yes, through all the years that he practised healing, the answer was right in front of him. But it had taken a crisis, an internal conflict over his patients not being permanently healed that finally provided the motivation for him to search for a solution. This is similar to the way a lot of us are motivated? We lose our jobs, have an accident, or get sick, then realize we cannot continue living our lives the way they were before; yet we are afraid to change. What was it that Lee was afraid of the most? Was it just giving up his skills and knowledge of healing, or was he also afraid that he might have to change his old *self-image* as a *great healer*? What if you could no longer do the things that gave you your present-day identity? What would be harder to give up, the things you do, or the self-image you gained from doing them?

When in my fifties, I went to University, I had an identity crisis. I no longer knew who I was. Before going to school, my main identity had been that of a businessman. If I was not that, then who was I? After graduation, I took on the image of a professional counselor and therapist, and thought

of myself as a healer. As with Lee, I thought I was responsible for clients' mental and emotional wellness. This became troublesome and motivated me to look for answers—hence the trip to Hawaii, which led to the creation of
Purposeful Being. Through the work of *Purposeful Being,* I
became aware of my true identity and self-image, my God-
Self, and have become increasingly free from the need for an
external self-image ever since.

Notice the resistance Lee had to the abbot's solution to
his problem. This is often the case when we are faced with a
choice from our God-Self rather than our ego's self-image.
In the past, we often wanted God to fix things according to
the wants and desires of our old self-image, rather than from
the way of our souls. Lee's God-Self was leading him to his
next level of greatness. It was up to him to accept it.

What Meaning Can be Derived From a Plague That Affects a Whole Village?

Earlier on, we talked about social conditioning and the
taking on of a tribal self-image. In a tribe, most of the members have to conform to the will of the tribe. Therefore,
when the tribe is operating in a self-destructive way, it may
be reasonable to assume that tension could show up in the
form of ailments affecting a large part of the tribe's population.

Again Caroline Myss refers to the attitude and beliefs of
people during the Great Depression. She cites the polio epi-
demic of the 1930s and 1940s, saying that in 1929, after the
American economy crashed, the popular way of describing
that state of affairs was that of *"learning to live with a crippled economy"* (105-106).

Polio is a physically crippling disease representing, in
symbolic form, the crippled spirit of the nation. Children,
being susceptible to the prevailing thinking, picked up the
disease as easily as adults did. The American people were so
infected with the symbolic nature of being crippled by the
economy that they elected Franklin D. Roosevelt as presi-

dent, who was also crippled with polio. Caroline Myss further states:

> He was a living symbol of both physical weakness and of indomitable resilience. It took a physical tribal event and the experience of physical strength through World War II to heal the American tribal spirit (106).

By the end of the war, the United States was again a world leader due to its dominant role in nuclear armament and its great ability to have responded so powerfully to the call to arms both at home and abroad. Again Caroline states:

> Once again, this recovery was reflected in the language of the tribal spokespeople who described their newly healed culture as economically 'on its feet again.' With the end of the American tribal consciousness around a crippled economy, a relationship to polio was no longer necessary, hence Jonas Salk discovered the vaccine for polio in the early 1950's (107).

Another example of tribal or social illnesses since the war is the change in social values regarding sex. There has been an explosion of sexually transmitted diseases, some of which, such as HIV, were previously unheard of.

It would be interesting for a historian to revisit the social attitudes of people during and before the great plagues. Perhaps we would discover the correlation between the type of illness and the affected physical location of the body, and then to see how this might relate to the tribal and social consciousness of the times.

Social conditioning presents us with a tribal self-image of which it is hard to break free. It tells us how to dress, how thin we should be, how to think politically, what material standards we should live by, and so on. If we do not meet these social and tribal images and expectations, we react with guilt and shame. Take thinness for example. Centuries ago, plump was the fashion, and being thin by today's standards was out. There are few of us today who are not affected by the social commandment that states, "thou must be thin."

To do, or believe something different, you must be prepared to face the wrath of the tribe. Changing religions is not as hard to do in North America today as it was a century ago. Yet, even today, if you come from a strong Christian family and entertain the idea of becoming a Buddhist, you would face a lot of criticism. Perhaps some would still face social and family banishment for daring to go outside of the time-honored beliefs of their tribe.

We are not told what the villagers' collective beliefs and attitudes were that might have brought forth the plague. This is also an interesting point—does one have to know what is involved within every physical ailment to produce a healthier life? The truth is, that just like in the story, as you learn and practise *Purposeful Being,* many ailments begin dropping away automatically, because practising *P.B.* realigns your life so that all conflict within mind/body/spirit is eliminated. The more the *authentic self* is generated, the less need there is for physical ailments that express your disharmonic way of living.

Another element in the story worth noting is the way that the villagers grew stronger by loving others. This was done through offering the gift of their *souls' purpose,* such as showing others to the magic within and all about them. The villagers were suffering from a plague that was experienced as anything but magical, but as they showed themselves and others to the magic all about them, the plague dropped away. What was experienced was a change in focus: instead of the illness, they now focused on something entirely different—their *soul's purpose.* Through offering its magic to others, they began to realize that it must have been within them, or they could not have given it away. Through the daily practice of giving it away, they experienced joy and elation and went beyond the need for healing.

Finally, Lee suggested that they meditate and await the intuitive answers that might help them find meaning in their illness. By taking your questions into a deep meditation you may often receive answers in different ways. Answers may appear in picture form, in words and in the events of your waking life. Meditation now becomes a useful means for fulfilling your life. Answers may also come in dreams. Every night, dreams reveal the way that you are living your life, offering you the opportunity to make new choices.

Lee's going back to his home base is symbolic of returning to one's *authentic self.* Lee would never again be the same, yet everything he had learned on his journey was there for him to have seen all the time. Lee had to get away from the surroundings that related to his old self-image in order for change to happen. Where he was living, he was too deeply immersed in his professional image to make the necessary changes. For many of us, this is often the case, yet it does not have to be this way. As Lee was able to bring back what he learned, this book is able to give you that same information, and without your having to go through what Lee did. Lee learned through trial and error. Going through the questions in this book and rereading the chapters will bring about the changes you desire in your life, if you are willing to commit.

This is your opportunity to go beyond your need for healing, your fears of loneliness, insecurity and depression to your *authentic self* which is always united with all that is. Through *Purposeful Being,* you now have the 'way' in which to live a joyous, happy and fulfilling life. What will you decide, choose and bring forth into your life now?

> And I have given them the glory you gave me, so that they may be one, as we are one, I in them and you in me, that they may be brought to perfection as one.[27]

In the appendix you will find meditations and information for putting this book into practice. The endnotes list the books and quotations that relate to each individual chapter. The bibliography lists all works cited in this book.

CHAPTER 12 QUESTIONS

		Agree	Disagree
1.	If sickness happens, it is never my fault.	[ ]	[ ]
2.	My environment has a lot to do with my getting ill.	[ ]	[ ]
3.	When I get sick I am responsible.	[ ]	[ ]
4.	Sickness can tell me about the way that I live my life.	[ ]	[ ]
5.	All illnesses are bad.	[ ]	[ ]
6.	I always need to be searching for the right cure.	[ ]	[ ]
7.	A miracle cure is a permanent healing.	[ ]	[ ]
8.	Only a doctor or health professional can heal me.	[ ]	[ ]
9.	My genes are responsible for my health.	[ ]	[ ]
10.	Whether I get sick or not is a matter of luck.	[ ]	[ ]
11.	How I live my life does not matter, I will still get sick.	[ ]	[ ]
12.	If I meditate enough I wont get sick.	[ ]	[ ]
13.	People do *Purposeful Being* to stay healthy.	[ ]	[ ]
14.	Consciously loving yourself and others is a healthy way to live.	[ ]	[ ]
15.	I have no control over whether I live or die.	[ ]	[ ]
16.	I should never see a doctor.	[ ]	[ ]

Purposeful Being practitioners agree with 3, 4 and 14 only.

APPENDIX

WARNING: *Meditation and visualization are best prac-tised with the aid of someone who has had considerable training. If you are new at reflective inner work, you may be well advised to work with an accredited meditation trainer. Many traditional and new-thought churches, such as Unity and Science of the Mind, offer meditation classes. Medita-tion is also integral to Buddhist, Taoist and yoga disciplines.*

Three-part Exercise Relating to Chapter 3

Exercise #1

Some of you may be scared off by my next request. I am inviting you to draw a tree. You might complain, saying, "But, I can't draw." In the professional sense, neither can I. However, this is not about artistic talent, in fact, if you are an artist we suggest you use your opposite hand, so that you will not get carried away with your artis-tic expertise, allowing it to misdirect you away from this assignment. It is for your eyes only. However, by doing it, you will be well re-warded with new insight and self-realizations for your effort.

On a full-sized sheet of paper, draw a tree that you feel repre-sents the way you have been until now. This part of the exercise is about who you are in your life now, not who you may want to be.

You will need your journal or a scribbler, not only for this exer-cise, but also for any notes, ideas, inspirations, art or future assign-ments that you may care to do.

In your journal, or on a full-sized sheet of paper, draw your tree. Later, on the page beside it, you will be drawing another tree. Then, because they will be side by side, you can compare the two. You may color them if you wish.

From this exercise you will have a single symbol representing your present self-image. This will give you something to which you may compare your future changes.

Now complete the drawing of a tree.

Looking at your finished drawing, make some notes on the same page or on the back concerning your feelings about your tree. Is it well rooted, too straight, too bent, top heavy, or with too little foliage? Are there enough branches or limbs, does it look flexible? Is your tree in bloom? In what season does your tree seem to be? Does it bear fruit? What surrounds your tree? Is there a sun, or are there clouds in the sky? Does it have other plant life like shrubs or grass around it? Are there animals, birds, or anything else around your tree?

Now use what you wrote about your tree drawing to describe yourself. If you wrote that the tree did not have many limbs, your reflections may be something like this: "Like the tree, I do not have enough branches to feel the sunlight and reach out to others. I keep much inside, including my gifts and abilities."

Next, in the privacy of your home, stand up, give yourself some room to move around, and imagine you are your tree. Spend at least five minutes doing this part of the exercise. Take your time. Take a few deep breaths, letting yourself relax before you start. Make an effort to experience your tree. Use your imagination. Move if you wish to the wind and weather. Try going through the seasons.

Again, write down all of the above insights and words that describe your experience of acting as your tree. What is the mood of your tree? What is it lacking? How open were your leaves and limbs to receive the sun and weather? Was the tree protective, fearful, and barren or was it open and flexible?

Finish with this: What did you learn, feel, or experience by drawing and acting as your tree?

Please complete this part of the exercise before reading further, otherwise you may influence your next assignment.

Exercise #2

Now, on another sheet of paper, draw a tree of God. If God were a tree, what would He/She look like? Again color it if you wish.

For now, list all the traits you feel God has, such as all knowing, love, compassion, forgiveness, creativity, power, and so on.

Even if you are an unbeliever, imagine for a moment that there is a God. What traits or characteristics might your imaginary God have? It is important that you go along with this exercise, even as a non-believer. It is not how you feel about God. Rather, it is about your imaginary view of God's attributes and personality traits.

You can now compare your God-Tree to your first tree. How are the two pictures different? Which do you like the best? Which seems stronger? Does your God-Tree have features that your first tree does not? Again, you can note the differences on your paper or in your journal.

Towards the end of chapter 3, you will complete the last part of this exercise. Please go back and finish reading chapter 3.

Exercise #3

This process is about working with your imaginative and intuitive abilities in order to bring about deeper experiences and awareness of self.

To make it even more effective, we encourage you to put this exercise on tape, then relax and go with it. (We also have tapes of this and the other exercises available upon request.)

Begin by finding a safe, comfortable, quiet spot. Do not do this exercise if you are in a hurry, or emotionally upset about someone or something. The exercise time will vary; it can be anywhere from twenty minutes to half an hour, or more, depending on each individual's process.

Start by spending some time with all the characteristics and traits of God that you have on your God list. Then refocus on your God-Tree drawing. Breathe deeply as you stare at it, and let in the image.

If you wish to make any changes to your God-Tree, do so now.

When you feel ready, begin taking ten deep breaths into your stomach. Tell yourself to relax with each breath, in the following manner:

1. "While being aware of any sensations in my feet, I am relaxing all tissues and muscles."

2. "I am aware of relaxing my ankles, calves and thighs, and am noticing all sensations in my legs."
3. "I am aware of relaxing my groin, buttocks, hips and stomach, as well as any feelings I have in these areas."
4. "I am aware of a deep relaxation in my chest and lungs."
5. "Starting at the base of my spine, I am experiencing each vertebra relax all the way to the base of my neck."
6. "My neck, shoulders, arms, elbows, wrists and hands are all relaxing as I am aware of all sensations in these parts of my body."
7. "I am aware of all skin and muscle sensations in my scalp and face as each part relaxes more and more."
8. "As I relax, I am aware of the temperature on my skin."
9. "Relaxation is happening as I am aware of any sounds around me."
10. "I have come to a place within, of deep relaxation and peace."

Now, and for the remainder of this exercise, I invite you to find a place in the room where you can stand, extend your arms and move slightly without disturbing anything.

Go now in your imagination to a place in nature where you feel safe, relaxed and at peace. If you do not have such a place, create one in your mind.

Begin to notice the colors of the foliage, sky and water (if any). Imagine red, orange, yellow, blue and green colors in the foliage and scenery.

Be aware of the sounds, birds, breeze, insects and rustling of leaves.

Notice the temperature, brightness and mood of the place.

The next thing you notice is a trail that you have never seen before, which goes off to the left, or right.

Once you have located it, and just before you enter the trail, you notice a full-sized mirror. Look into this mirror and evaluate yourself. What do you see? (If you do not see yourself, then just sense that you are there.)

Not everyone sees an image, but usually people get a sense of what is happening.

Next, begin walking along the trail, noticing the colors and details of your surroundings, until you come to a huge hill.

You climb a winding trail to the top of the hill. At the top, it levels off, and below you is a beautiful mist-covered valley. For some reason, you feel strangely excited, not just because of the beauty of your surroundings, but also because you sense that you are about to witness something wondrous and special.

Gradually the mist begins to clear, and what you see next is an experience of splendor, which goes beyond the beauty of the surroundings to the overpowering image that is in the center of all this beauty.

As the fog lifts, what is left is a tree so wondrous, majestic and glorious that your heart begins to pound, and your legs feel weak at the overall power of this image.

You feel a heady and fulfilling intense love-like force emanating from this tree. And, as if in a daze, you move toward it. The difficulty is that as you go closer, the deep golden-like rays of compassionate energy that assault your senses are almost too much to endure without your collapsing in a meltdown of golden sunshine.

Soon, you are standing before this glorious illuminating image, and you feel that this overpowering force understands and knows everything there is to know about you.

You feel that you can ask it anything, and it will give you an answer.

You might ask "Who am I?" or "What was the reason for coming into this life time?" or anything else to which you have ever wanted an answer.

When all of your questions have been answered to your satisfaction, something even stranger happens. You feel drawn ever closer to the tree, until you and your God-Tree are one.

Allow yourself to enjoy this experience of unity, love, power, ecstasy and bliss. Know that you have come to your core and that you are home at last. Stay with this for as long as you like.

When you are ready, you may return along the path on which you came, until you are back in front of your mirror. Then, take another look at yourself—observe what is different—and return to your normal state, telling yourself that you are bringing all the wonder, joy and ecstasy with you.

Back in the room, write out all that you can remember from this experience. You may wish to keep this for future reference.

Participants in our seminars have had some pretty amazing experiences with this exercise. Some of their comments have been:

- "I felt total love and understanding."
- "Anytime I am having difficulty, I go to my God-Tree and . . . it all works out."
- "I felt so much energy go through me. It was . . . overpowering."

The reason why you created a neutral symbol for a God-Tree and not one relating to some specific religious belief was so that you would be free of all biases.

Had I used a religious figure rather than the neutral symbol of a tree, some may have felt discomfort. If they had beliefs of unworthiness, this could have hindered the experience of intimacy with their God-Self, which this exercise offered them. However, for others, this may be just one more experience to add to an expanding awareness of their spiritual wakening.

If you have not done the exercise, I suggest you do it now.

The exercise can be repeated as often as you wish. However, for the sake of convenience and maximum effectiveness, it is recommended that you put it on tape, or order one from us.

Strategies for Practising **Purposeful Being**

To take the concept of *Purposeful Being* into the reality of your daily life requires a continuing conscious effort until it all becomes automatic.

Each day, time should be spent focusing on *Purposefully Being* your God-Self through the following awareness exercises:

1. Meditation
2. Manifestation
3. Affirmation
4. Bicycle riding process
5. Activating your *soul's sole purpose*
6. Focusing
7. Star Design

1. Meditation

The object of this form of meditation is not to escape, but to help you focus on being your God-Self. This should be done without any thought of trying to get something through your efforts, but to be in constant *union with God.*

The following is a simple daily meditation to help you maintain a conscious experience of being one with God. The object is to practise this exercise until every cell in your body recognizes and experiences its God-Self. With constant practice, you are more easily able to identify the times when you are being as your God-Self or have gone back to a false self-image

Whenever you feel threatened, defensive, or rejected, you will be able to see the folly in these reactions as you realize through your meditations that, irrespective of the external circumstances or events, by being your God-Self you are always worthwhile.

To make it even more effective, we again encourage you to put this exercise on tape, (or order one through us) then relax and go with it. Begin by finding a safe, comfortable, quiet spot. Do not do this exercise if your are in a hurry, or emotionally upset about someone or something. If you are not used to meditation, start with fifteen to twenty minutes a day and gradually work up to an hour. To avoid falling asleep, do this in a sitting position. When you feel ready, begin by taking ten deep breaths into your stomach. Tell yourself to relax between each breath (just as you did for the tree meditation). Next begin your meditation by saying the following:

1. "While being aware of any sensations in my feet, I am relaxing all tissues and muscles."
2. "I am aware of relaxing my ankles, calves and thighs, and am noticing all sensations in my legs."
3. "I am aware of relaxing my groin, buttocks, hips and stomach, and I am aware of all feelings I may have in these areas."
4. "I am aware of a deep relaxation in my chest and lungs."
5. "Starting at the base of my spine, I am experiencing each vertebra relaxing all the way to the base of my neck."
6. "My neck, shoulders, arms, elbows, wrists and hands are all relaxing as I am aware of all sensations in these parts of my body."
7. "I am aware of all skin and muscle sensations in my scalp and face as each part relaxes more and more."
8. "As I relax, I am aware of the temperature on my skin."
9. "Relaxation is occurring as I am aware of any sounds around me."
10. "I have come to a place within, of deep relaxation and peace."

Now, in your imagination, go to a place in nature where you feel safe, relaxed and at peace. If you do not have such a place, create one in your mind.

Begin to notice the colors of the foliage, sky and water (if any). Imagine reds, oranges, yellows, blues and greens in the foliage and scenery.

Be aware of sounds, of birds, insects, the breeze, and rustling of leaves.

Notice the temperature, brightness and mood of the place.

Find a suitable bench or log on which to sit, and slowly repeat the following affirmations over and over:

- "God and I are one."
- "I am the temple of God."
- "I am the image of God."
- "I am God, present in human form."

Now stay in this place for as long as you want in order to enjoy and prolong the peace and tranquility. Each day, see if you can stay longer in this place of *oneness*.

2. *Manifestation*

The next stage is to manifest all that you want and desire that is in harmony with you as your God-Self and your *P.B.* way of life. This is done through doing the first stage of meditation for a while until you become accustomed to what your God-Self feels like. Then, introduce manifesting by taking an issue that is blocking your *P.B.* journey and visualize its resolution. Do this at the end of your meditation when you have reached that place of peace. Then, bring in what it is that you want, as if you already have it. You may visualize its successful resolution, or you can just inwardly affirm its resolution.

The three steps are:

1. Go into meditation.
2. Go to your place of peace.
3. Bring into your meditation—in either picture form, affirmations, or both—what you want, as if you already have it.

Always feel gratitude for what you desire, as if it was already yours.

3. *Affirmation: Affirming the* **Purposeful Being** *Way of Life*

The following affirmation embodies the philosophy and meaning of *P.B.* and is worth going over from time to time to remind yourself of the reason behind your efforts:

Through the *Art of Purposeful Being,* I am purposefully and consciously aware of being my God-Self and of bringing this reality into the doing of my life. My life becomes predictably fulfilling because of who I recognize myself to be. This means that I consciously pre-choose soul-like values, expressions, actions, attitudes and responses that are always allowing me to express and experience God consciousness. This is experienced through consciously doing my soul's purpose, regardless of the events or situations in which I may find myself. Furthermore, this is a most joyful task, as I am experiencing the ecstasy of being my true God-Self through my conscious being and doing of it.

This affirmation that constantly acknowledges the truth *you and God are one* will ultimately be realized in every cell in your body.

4. Bicycle Riding Process

Use the *bicycle riding process* whenever you want to make a change and are considering something new. Also, when having to go outside of your comfort zone to acquire something that is in line with your *P.B.* way of life, use the four elements of bicycle riding to get you there:

- *Desire:* believing, thinking, imagining.
- *Choice:* attending, focusing, learning.
- *Risk:* acting, experiencing.
- *Commitment:* to being and doing it over time.

5. Activating Your Soul's Sole Purpose

Use the power of choice in regard to the way you:

- think;
- act;
- relate to others;
- do your *soul's purpose.*

In each case, use all or some part of the choice-making question:

As a person who is practising *Purposeful Being,* is this the God-like way in which I would like to serve my highest and greatest good, by giving my life to doing this thing, in this way, forevermore?

Use this same choice-making technique when choosing an activity, be it a career or otherwise, always keeping in mind that you are looking for the activities that give you the greatest opportunity for expressing your *soul's purpose:*

- Share what you are learning as a way of teaching yourself and others at the same time.
- Look at illness as an opportunity for feedback on the way you are living your life.

6. *Focusing*

Practice focusing on your soul's sole purpose and its meaning for your life by recognizing your God-like traits and potential for happiness and reviewing your God list.

7. *Star Design*

Use the Star Design with the five sections (career, spirituality, mindful/body, feelings and emotions, love/social) as a way of determining where you are stuck, and as a means for living your life through *Purposeful Being* (p. 232).

Example: Looking at the five sections of the Star Design, you could ask yourself in which sections are you feeling the weakest, or the least fulfilled at the moment. Then, address the issues involved that require your attention to get yourself back on track. Suppose it is the love section. You could assess what it is that you are doing in the relationship that may be generating the outcome you are experiencing. It may be that you need to work on the way you handle your feelings, so you would review the section on beliefs, feelings and emotions. You might also review how your needs are getting in the way of love. In addition, you could look at the things you are doing that may be influencing your partner to react in a certain way. By also going to the book's chapter on choices, you could begin asking yourself the appropriate choice-making questions that are discussed in that chapter.

Furthermore, at the center of the circle in the Star Design is your God-Self—*soul-self* and around it is your *self-image.* You can often bring clarity into a situation by asking yourself if you are trying to satisfy your *soul-self* or your *self-image.*

STAR DESIGN

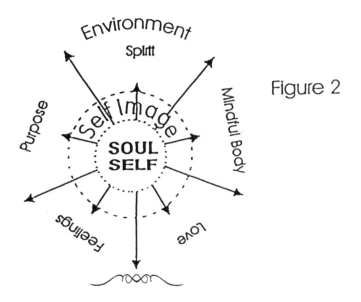

Figure 2

By now, you realize that *The Art of Purposeful Being* not only gives you practical steps for working with various situations, but by doing it, situations and problems seem to diminish and your level of joy and excitement for living continues to increase. As you apply these steps, you begin to feel the power you have to direct and control your life.

If you wish to order meditation tapes or inquire about other tapes, books and seminars, see page 246.

ENDNOTES

CHAPTER 1

[1] Ferrucci, 16.

[2] Eknath Easwaran, Gandhi's anger as a youth, 6-7; his accomplishments and the joy he maintained while in jail, 71-73.

[3] John 17:13, New American Bible.

[4] This story was inspired by the Parable of the Talents, Matt. 25:14-28, NAB and the many conversations Roger Cotting and I shared.

CHAPTER 3

[5] 2 Cor. 2:16, NAB.

[6] 1 Cor. 1:9, NAB.

CHAPTER 4

[7] Price, 35.

[8] Matt. 8:23-27, NAB.

[9] Ring's study represents quite an exhaustive survey of the various experiences reported by people with near-death experiences.

[10] Jovanovic, 48-50. First told to Jovanovic by Kenneth Ring. Later it appeared in the *Journal of Near Death Studies,* 10.1 (1991): 11-29.

[11] Ibid.

CHAPTER 5

[12] Hack, 84; Alchity, 66, 139; Copleston, vol. 2: 70-71, 363; vol. 4: 259, 260.

[13] Dr. Dossey refers to a number of studies that deal specifically with prayer and meditation: "Nonlocal healing" 41; "Mind over machine" 112-114, 120-121; "Sub-atomic particles" 119-120; "Pears Random Event Generator" 111-113; and "The Mother Theresa Affect" 109-110.

[14] "The Manitoba Longitudinal Study on Aging," as reported in J.M. Mossey and E. Shapiro in "Self-Rated Health: a Predictor of Mortality among the Elderly," *American Journal of Public Health* 72 (1982): 800-807. The Alameda County Study was reported in G.A. Kaplan and T. Camacho, "Perceived Health and Mortality: a Nine Year Follow-up of the Human Population Laboratory Cohort," *American Journal of Epidemiology* 117 (1983): 292-304. Both studies quoted in Ornstein and Sobel, 250.

CHAPTER 6

[15] Luke 12:24-31, NAB. How God feeds the ravens and the birds of the fields. How much more important are we than these.

CHAPTER 7

[16] As documented by Mantak Chia and Michael Winn, and also by Ashley Thirleby

[17] Neale Walsch's books are a real treat and are quite profound in the wisdom revealed during his conversations with God.

CHAPTER 9

[18] Gal. 2:20; 2 Cor.3:18, NAB.

CHAPTER 10

[19] This work relates to the heroic tradition of the Iliad and Achilles's misadventure and life purpose.

[20] Excerpt from Buechner's *Wishful Thinking: A Theological ABC*, quoted in Bolles, 370.

CHAPTER 11

[21] This impressive survey of religions was formulated by Susan G. Shumsky, 50-52.

[22] Matt. 5:24, NAB.

[23] John 14-12, NAB.

[24] For more information concerning the evolution of consciousness in North America, see Carolyne Myss, 230.

[25] Cor. 5-17, NAB.

CHAPTER 12

[26] This story was my own. However, I did receive insights for its interpretation from Roger Cotting in Hawaii and the other authors mentioned in this chapter.

[27] John 15:22-23, NAB.

BIBLIOGRAPHY

Achterburg, Jeaneanne and Mark S. Rider. 1989. "Effect of Music-Associated Imagery on Neutrophils and Lymphocytes." *Biofeedback and Self-Regulation* 14.3: 247-57.

Alchity, Kenneth, Ron Hogart and Doug Price. 1987. *Critical Essays on Homer.* Boston: GK.Hall & Co.

Bolles, Richard Nelson. 1993. *What Color is Your Parachute?: A Practical Manual for Job Hunters.* Berkeley: Ten Speed Press.

Buchanan, Robert. 1932. "The Ballad of Judas Iscariot." *The Standard Book of British and American Verse.* Garden City, N.Y: Garden City Publishing Company.

Buechner, Frederick. 1975. *Wishful Thinking: A Theological ABC.* New York: Harper Collins.

Burlingame Michael. 1994. *The Inner World of Abraham Lincoln.* Chicago: University of Illinois Press.

Burns, David D. 1989. *The Feeling Good Handbook.* New York: William Morrow and Company.

Chardin, Pierre Teilhard de. N.d. "The Future of Chastity." Unpublished.

Chia, Mantak and Michael Winn. 1984. *Taoist Secrets of Love.* Santa Fe: Aurora Press.

Chopra Deepak. 1995. *The Way of the Wizard: Twenty Spiritual Lessons for Creating the Life You Want.* New York: Harmony Books.

Copleston, Frederic S.J. 1958. *A History of Philosphy.* Vols. 2 & 4. London: Search Press. 4 vols.

Cotting, Roger, B. and Dr. Diane E. Mistler. 1994. *Forever Living.* Kailua-Kona, HI: Natura Music and Production Company.

Covey, Stephen R., A. Roger Merril and Rebecca R. Merril. 1995. *First Things First.* New York: Fireside Books.

Dethlefsen, Thorwald and Rudiger Dahlke. 1997. *The Healing Power of Illness: The Meaning of Symptoms and How to Interpret Them.* Rockport, MA: Element Books Inc.

Dossey, Larry. 1993. *Healing Words.* New York: Harper Collins.

Easwaran, Eknath. 1983. *Gandhi the Man.* Petaluma CA: Nilgiri Press.

Ferrucci, P. 1982. *What We May Be.* Los Angeles: Tarcher.

Frankl, Victor E. 1973. *The Doctor and the Soul.* New York: Vintage Books.

Glasser, William. 1998. *Choice Theory.* New York: Harper Collins.

Goldstein, D. 1993. "Special Report." *Prevention* April: 57-60.

Greenwood, Michael. 1997 *Braving the Void: Journeys into Healing.* Victoria, B.C: Paradox Publishing.

Hack, Roy Kennth. 1970. *God in Greek Philosophy to the Time of Socrates.* New York: Burt Franklin.

Hampsch, John H. N.d. *Healing of Memories.* Audiotape. Word of the Spirit Tape Ministry. Markham, Ontario. Ser. 26.

Houston, Jean, and Mary Kathryn Bateson. 1997. *A Mythic Life: Learning to Live our Greater Story.* San Francisco: Harper Press.

Janov, Arthur. *Primal Scream.* 1970. New York: Dell Publishing Co.

Journal of Near Death Studies. 1991. 10.1. New York: The Language of Science Plenum Publishing Corporation.

Jovanovic, Pierre. 1995. *An Inquiry into the Existence of Angels.* New York: M. Evans and Company.

Kaplan, G.A., and T. Camacho. 1983. "Perceived Health and Mortality: A Nine-year Follow-up of the Human Population Laboratory Cohort." *American Journal of Epidemiology* 117: 292-304.

Kelsey, Morton T., Rev. 1976. *The Other Side of Silence.* Toronto: Paulist Press.

Kermis, D. Marguerite. 1984. *The Psychology of Human Aging.* Newton MA: Allyn and Bacon, Inc.

Martin, Steve, actor. 1992. *Leap of Faith.* Dir. Richard Pearce. With Debra Winger, et al. Paramount.

Moody, Raymond A. 1995. *Life After Life: The Investiagation of a Phenomenon—Survival of Bodily Death.* Atlanta: Mockingbird Books.

Moore, Thomas. 1992. *Care of the Soul.* New York: Harper Collins.

Mossey, J.M., and E. Shapiro. 1982. "Self Rated Health: A Predictor of Mortality Among the Elderly." *American Journal of Public Health.* 72: 800-807.

Myss, Caroline. 1996. *Anatomy of the Spirit.* New York: Three Rivers Press.

Neimark, Jill. 1998. "Crimes of the Soul." *Psychology Today* March-April: 55-60.

New American Bible. 1992. St. Joseph Edition. New York: Catholic Publishing Co.

Ornstein, Robert and David Sobel. 1987. *The Healing Brain.* New York: Simon & Schuster.

Ostrander, Sheila, Lynn Schroeder, and Nancy Ostrander. 1994. *Super Learning 2000.* New York: Bantam Double Day.

Pransky, George S. 1990. *Divorce is Not the Answer.* Blue Ridge Summit: Tab Books Inc.

Price, John Randolph. 1997. *A Spiritual Philosophy for a New World.* Carlsbad, CA: Hay House Inc.

Ring, Kenneth. 1985. *Heading Toward Omega.* New York: William Morrow Inc.

Schlessinger, Laura. 1997. *Ten Stupid Things Men do to Mess up Their Lives.* New York: Harper Collins.

Sher, Barbara, and Barbara Smith. 1994. *I Could Do Anything If Only I Knew What it Was.* New York: Delcorte Press.

Shumsky, Susan G. 1996. *Divine Revelation.* New York: Fireside Press.

Stanilsav Grof. 1988. *The Adventure of Self Discovery.* Albany: New York State UP.

Stauffer, Edith R. 1987. *Unconditional Love and Forgiveness.* Diamond Springs CA: Triangle Publishers.

Thirleby, Ashley. 1978. *Tantra the Key to Sexual Power and Pleasure.* New York: Dell Publishing Company.

Tyrell, Bernard J. 1975. *Christotherapy.* New Jersey: Paulist Press.

Walsch, Neale Donald. 1997. *Conversations with God.* Vol 2. Charlottesville: Hampton Roads Publishing Co.

Willard, R.D. 1977. "Breast Enlargement Though Visual Imagery and Hypnoses." *The American Journal of Clinical Hypnoses* 19: 195-200.

Woollam, Ray H. 1989. *On Choosing.* Duncan, B.C: Unica Publishing Co.

INDEX

—F—

—G—

—H—

—**Z**—

ORDERING INFORMATION

Philip A. Winkelmans, MA
Self-Directional Services
(Home of *The Art of Purposeful Being*)
PO Box 496
Lantzville, BC V0R 2H0
Canada

*Visit our interactive web site for a free newsletter, seminar
and product information, latest offerings, free offers:*

www.purposefulbeing.com

*To order books and tapes, to obtain seminar
information, and to contact the author:*

Phone: (250) 390-4696
Toll free: 1-888-887-1872
E-mail: phil@purposefulbeing.com
Web site: www.purposefulbeing.com